ROUTLEDGE LIBRARY EDITIONS: ADULT EDUCATION

Volume 25

UNIVERSITY ADULT EDUCATION IN ENGLAND AND THE USA

UNIVERSITY ADULT EDUCATION IN ENGLAND AND THE USA
A Reappraisal of the Liberal Tradition

RICHARD TAYLOR, KATHLEEN ROCKHILL
AND ROGER FIELDHOUSE

LONDON AND NEW YORK

First published in 1985 by Croom Helm Ltd

This edition first published in 2019
by Routledge
2 Park Square, Milton Park, Abingdon, Oxon OX14 4RN

and by Routledge
52 Vanderbilt Avenue, New York, NY 10017

Routledge is an imprint of the Taylor & Francis Group, an informa business

© 1985 Richard Taylor, Kathleen Rockhill and Roger Fieldhouse

All rights reserved. No part of this book may be reprinted or reproduced or utilised in any form or by any electronic, mechanical, or other means, now known or hereafter invented, including photocopying and recording, or in any information storage or retrieval system, without permission in writing from the publishers.

Trademark notice: Product or corporate names may be trademarks or registered trademarks, and are used only for identification and explanation without intent to infringe.

British Library Cataloguing in Publication Data
A catalogue record for this book is available from the British Library

ISBN: 978-1-138-32224-0 (Set)
ISBN: 978-0-429-43000-8 (Set) (ebk)
ISBN: 978-1-138-36676-3 (Volume 25) (hbk)
ISBN: 978-1-138-36685-5 (Volume 25) (pbk)
ISBN: 978-0-429-43009-1 (Volume 25) (ebk)

Publisher's Note
The publisher has gone to great lengths to ensure the quality of this reprint but points out that some imperfections in the original copies may be apparent.

Disclaimer
The publisher has made every effort to trace copyright holders and would welcome correspondence from those they have been unable to trace.

University Adult Education in England and the USA

A REAPPRAISAL OF THE LIBERAL TRADITION

Richard Taylor,
Kathleen Rockhill and
Roger Fieldhouse

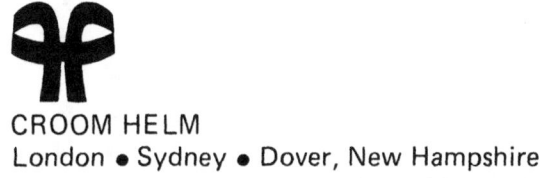

CROOM HELM
London • Sydney • Dover, New Hampshire

© 1985 Richard Taylor, Kathleen Rockhill and Roger Fieldhouse
Croom Helm Ltd, Provident House, Burrell Row,
Beckenham, Kent BR3 1AT
Croom Helm Australia Pty Ltd, Suite 4, 6th Floor,
64-76 Kippax Street, Surry Hills, NSW 2010, Australia

British Library Cataloguing in Publication Data

Taylor, Richard
    University adult education in England and the
    USA : a reappraisal of the liberal tradition.
    1. University extension – Great Britain 2. Adult
    education – Great Britain 3. University
    Extension – United States 4. Adult education –
    United States
    I. Title II. Rockhill, Kathleen
    III. Fieldhouse, Roger
    378'.1554'0941   LC6256.G7

ISBN 0-7099-2431-3

Croom Helm, 51 Washington Street, Dover,
New Hampshire 03820, USA

Library of Congress Cataloging in Publication Data
applied for.

Printed and bound in Great Britain by
Biddles Ltd, Guildford and King's Lynn

CONTENTS

PREFACE
LIST OF ABBREVIATIONS
Chapter 1 Introduction - Richard Taylor,   1
           Kathleen Rockhill, Roger Fieldhouse

Chapter 2 The Liberal Tradition in Adult   15
           Education - Richard Taylor,
           Kathleen Rockhill, Roger Fieldhouse

Chapter 3 The Problems of Objectivity, Social   29
           Purpose and Ideological Commitment
           in English University Adult
           Education - Roger Fieldhouse

Chapter 4 The Ideological Determinants of   52
           University Adult Education in
           England - Richard Taylor

Chapter 5 Radical Developments in University   85
           Adult Education in England:
           Redefining the Liberal Tradition
           - Richard Taylor

Chapter 6 The Liberal Perspective and the   123
           Symbolic Legitimation of Univer-
           sity Adult Education in the USA
           - Kathleen Rockhill

Chapter 7 Ideological Solidification of   175
           Liberalism in University Adult
           Education: Confrontation over
           Workers' Education in the USA
           - Kathleen Rockhill

Chapter 8 The Future of University Adult   221
           Education - Richard Taylor

Index   242

'Our primary mission ..... is to the educationally underprivileged majority ..... who need a humane education both for their personal happiness and to help them mould the society in which they live'.

>R.H. Tawney (in a lecture, 'The WEA and Adult Education', delivered to celebrate the WEA's fiftieth anniversary in 1953).

PREFACE

The idea for this book arose from a suggestion from the series editor, Jo Campling, and we are grateful to her both for this and for her continued support throughout the writing of the book.
    Although the book is very much a collaborative and cooperative enterprise, Richard Taylor has acted as overall editor. All three authors have worked on the text as a whole, but there are differences in interpretation so that each writer takes final responsibility for his or her work. Chapter 3 is the work of Roger Fieldhouse, Chapters 4, 5 and 8 of Richard Taylor, and Chapters 6 and 7 of Kathleen Rockhill: Chapters 1 and 2 were written jointly.
    Richard Taylor is grateful to both the British Academy and the University of Leeds, which made grants to him in 1983 enabling him to visit Kathleen Rockhill in Toronto to discuss and plan the project in detail.
    Roger Fieldhouse is grateful to the Leverhulme Trust Fund for a research grant, and also to the University of Leeds for a year's study leave which enabled him to undertake research into aspects of Adult Education, including the problem of objectivity which constitutes the basis of Chapter 3.
    Numerous colleagues have given valuable comments and advice. Thanks are due in particular to: Keith Forrester, Jill Liddington and Kevin Ward. Richard Taylor also received a large amount of very useful material relating to contemporary policy and provision from colleagues in University Adult Education Departments throughout Britain.
    Kathleen Rockhill is grateful for the support of the secretarial staff of the Department of Adult Education at OISE, to Edmund Sullivan for his comments and support, to her mentors Jack London and Paul Sheats for their inspiration, and to her

family who suffered with her through the upheaval of job changes, immigration and work overload.

Typing the handwritten drafts has been undertaken efficiently and cheerfully by the hard-pressed clerical staff in the Department of Adult and Continuing Education at Leeds, and we are also very grateful to Liz Dawson for producing the camera ready copy.

Finally, as this book covers wide and sometimes controversial issues in University Adult Education, we should emphasise that we accept full responsibility for the opinions expressed here, and for any infelicities or inaccuracies which remain.

LIST OF ABBREVIATIONS

AAAE	American Association for Adult Education
AF of L	American Federation of Labour
ASUET	American Society for the Extension of University Teaching
ATAE	Association of Tutors in Adult Education
CAT	College of Advanced Technology
CDP	Community Development Project
CEU	Continuing Education Unit
CJAC	Central Joint Advisory Committee on Tutorial Classes
CSLEA	Centre for the Study of the Liberal Education of Adults
CQSW	Certificate Qualification in Social Work
DES	Department of Education and Science
EASA	Education Advice Service for Adults
ERA	Equal Rights Amendment
MIND	National Association for Mental Health
NACRO	National Association for the Care and Rehabilitation of Offenders
NCLC	National Council of Labour Colleges
NCB	National Coal Board
NIACE	National Institute of Adult and Continuing Education (formerly NIAE, National Institute of Adult Education)
NUEA	National University Extension Association
NUM	National Union of Mineworkers
OU	Open University
PEVE	Post Experience Vocational Education
RB	Responsible Body
SCAUP	Steering Committee on Adult Unemployed Projects
TU	Trade Union
TUC	Trades Union Congress
U3A	University of the Third Age

UAE	University Adult Education
UCACE	Universities Council for Adult and Continuing Education (formerly UCAE, Universities Council for Adult Education)
UCLA	University of California, Los Angeles
UGC	University Grants Council
UNESCO	United National Educational Scientific and Cultural Organisation
USA	United States of America
WEA	Workers' Educational Association
WEB	Workers' Educational Bureau
WETUC	Workers' Educational Trade Union Committee

Chapter One

INTRODUCTION

This book is a critique and comparison of the nature, structure and provision of University Adult Education (hereafter UAE) in England and the USA. The focus is both contemporary and historical, as the intention is to identify 'from where we have come, where we are now, and where we might be going' during the closing years of the twentieth century. The current structures, and even more important the ideology or ideologies of UAE cannot be understood without detailed reference to earlier events and movements. This study is thus interdisciplinary, involving both social scientific and historical modes of enquiry and analysis.

Similarly, although the focus is upon <u>University</u> Adult Education, this cannot be discussed in a vacuum: both in England and the USA the relationship with other agencies has been of considerable importance and, whilst these are not discussed here in detail, some contextual consideration is necessary. In the USA especially, where UAE is not an autonomous arena of practice, developments are discussed within the broader frameworks of higher and adult education.

This study is not a <u>general</u> comparative analysis of UAE in the two countries. The central concern, as the title makes clear, is the liberal tradition as it has operated, in rather different ways, in both England and the USA. The second chapter opens with a discussion of the nature and importance of this tradition. Here, it need be noted only that it is a central contention of this study that the liberal tradition has been of crucial importance throughout the development of UAE, but that this tradition has been under attack, both explicit and implicit, for some time, and is now considerably weaker than in the past. The reasons for, and nature of, this erosion, and the resultant contemporary structure of UAE, is the major theme of this study.

The specific development of UAE has been part of the response of the tertiary educational system to the wider socio-economic and political pressures of twentieth century society. In order to explain how and why UAE has developed in the ways that it has, this study also considers the relationship between UAE and the wider society.

In general terms, it is argued that, in their very different ways, UAE in England and the USA has been characterised increasingly by provision geared towards the already relatively highly educated, and, to a greater extent in recent years than previously, has fallen outside the liberal tradition in terms of both content and approach. Paradoxically, it is also argued that this transition is the logical consequence of the contradictions inherent within the liberal tradition as manifest in advanced capitalist societies. In England there have been notable exceptions to the general pattern of liberal elitism - particularly working class education, and community adult education - and some more detailed consideration is undertaken of both these areas. In the USA there have also been exceptions, but in general these have been so marginalised as to be beyond the pale of UAE at the present time. In what ways, if at all, the liberal tradition is, or can be made, relevant to working class education and/or education for social transformation, is an important subsidiary theme.

There can be no doubt that UAE in both countries is in a period of profound change, if not crisis. This is in part due to the recession, the ideologically inspired squeeze on public expenditure, and its corollary of encouraging self-financing education. Augmenting these trends, technological and educational expansion exert strong pressure upon UAE to develop a much more post-experience and professional training orientation, at the expense of the wide range of traditional priorities and objectives.

In these circumstances, the future of UAE, with its increasingly disparate provision and objectives, is very much an open question. Whether or not the liberal tradition, in a revitalised form, has anything to offer UAE in this new situation, forms the final focus of attention for this study.

The structure of the book follows these major thematic concerns. In the remainder of this introduction a brief historical and descriptive outline of UAE development in both England and the USA provides the setting within which the specific themes of the study are pursued. The second chapter begins with a discussion and definition of the liberal tradition, and outlines the major cluster of themes to be developed later in the study. Centrally important to the whole discussion are the related questions of objectivity, social purpose and political bias within UAE, and the third chapter is devoted to a detailed analysis of these within the English context. The fourth chapter analyses the contemporary structure of UAE in England and links this to the wider development of tertiary education in the post-war period. The key exception to the predominating pattern of development in English UAE has been the various modes of provision for working class and other 'educationally disadvantaged' groups. This is, of course, of particular importance in the context of this study, given the 'social purpose' orientation of the liberal tradition, and chapter five discusses these various aspects of the provision. Chapters six and seven are devoted to the American experience. In chapter six, the legitimation of UAE in terms of the liberal values of democracy, equality, service and excellence, is outlined, and the consequences for the institutionalisation of a set of ideological practices that define UAE to the present time, are analysed. This includes not only the specifically educational concerns of UAE in the USA, but also a discussion of the wider ideological and socio-economic influences upon the development of UAE. Chapter seven, mirroring the concerns of chapter five, concentrates upon the workers' education movement in the USA and considers the ways in which the values of the liberal tradition were invoked to delegitimise the education of workers as a class in UAE. In the process of the controversy over working class education, it is contended that the ideological premises which define current professional practice in adult education were sealed. In setting up false dichotomies between education and propaganda, education and action, and in delegitimising notions of class, separatism and socialism, UAE was severed from its progressive base in movements for social transformation.

In the final chapter, chapter eight, an attempt is made to draw some conclusions from the general comparative analyses, with particular attention being paid to the future prospects for UAE and the relevance for these prospects of the liberal tradition. Before beginning these analyses, the general historical context within which UAE has developed in both countries is briefly outlined.

UAE IN ENGLAND

From the mid-nineteenth century, 'missionary dons' from Oxford and Cambridge began to travel the country, giving lectures to mechanics' institutes, ladies' educational associations and other organisations as part of the movement to reform the universities by making them less exclusive. After Cambridge formally agreed to organise 'local lectures' in 1873 (followed three years later by London, and by Oxford in 1878), a network of university lecture courses developed throughout the country. In this early phase it was closely associated with the founding of provincial university colleges, both developments being part of the university reform movement. This nineteenth century university extension movement was a mixture of democratic idealism (providing intellectual nourishment for 'the whole nation') and Oxbridge paternalism (tying the new university colleges to the ancient universities). However, as the colleges increased their independence, they gradually cut their ties with the Extension movement. Another problem the movement encountered was financial: the lectures had to be self-financing and this forced student fees up to a level beyond the means of most working class men and women. Far from being university education for 'the whole nation' it became almost exclusively middle class.

These university extension lectures began to decline from their peak in the early 1890s, when there were some 574 extramural centres, but UAE was given a new lease of life by the foundation of the Workers' Educational Association (WEA) in 1903, whose object was to make university scholarship available to the working class in order to equip the workers with the necessary knowledge to help them in the struggle for social change. At first it was hoped to achieve this by promoting university extension lectures, but the problem of high fees led the WEA to press Oxford to support a network of tutorial classes in industrial towns, 'specifically adapted to the needs of workpeople'[1], and to provide machinery for ensuring that a number of working class students progressed to study at the University itself. Oxford acceded to the former request (although not the latter) because powerful university reformers were seeking to extend the ancient universities' cultural influence to the working class as it emerged onto the political scene (with the extension of the franchise, the growth of a mass trade union movement, and the formation of the Labour Party). The famous Report on *Oxford and Working Class Education* stated in 1908: 'It seems to us that it would involve a grave loss both to Oxford and to English political life were the close association which has existed between the University and the world of affairs to be broken or impaired on the accession of new classes to power'.(2)

In recognition of the significance (and political reliability) of the tutorial class movement, the government agreed in 1907 to pay a grant towards the cost of running tutorial classes, thereby enabling the WEA to reduce students' fees to a realistic level. This direct grant was paid to the rapidly growing number of Joint Committees (of WEA and university representatives) which sprang up in imitation of Oxford's example, enabling them to promote a significant programme of liberal, non-vocational adult education, while allowing the government to exercise a degree of control over this provision.

It was the fear of this controlling influence which led to a split in the Adult Education movement. Ruskin College had been founded in 1899 by two Americans, Walter Vrooman and Charles Beard, as a workingmen's college, with the object of equipping the students for more effective service in the working class movement. In 1908 a group of rebel students formed the Plebs League to promote 'independent working class education': that is, independent of establishment control. In the following year, after a students' strike, they abandoned Ruskin and established their own Labour Colleges, to teach workers to identify and then eliminate the economic causes of social injustice. A National Council of Labour Colleges (NCLC) was formed to co-ordinate and extend 'the education of the workers from the working class point of view' with the specific object of 'bringing an end to the system of capitalism and enabling the workers to achieve their social and industrial emancipation'.(3) But the financial support given to the WEA and the Tutorial Class movement by the state and the bulk of the politically cautious trade union movement, gave structural confirmation of the ideological marginality and isolation of the NCLC's Marxist orientation. Meanwhile, the WEA attempted to introduce more orthodox university scholarship to the working class by forging closer links with the trade unions through the Workers' Educational Trade Union Committee (WETUC), formed in 1919. Throughout the interwar years this provided a direct, if sometimes tenuous, means of providing university education for trade union students.

For nearly four decades after the birth of the Tutorial Class movement, which was coordinated and institutionalised by a Central Joint Advisory Committee on Tutorial Classes (CJAC), the WEA remained the major agency through which UAE was organised. But gradually an increasing number of universities and university colleges established their own extramural departments to organise courses quite separately from the WEA and tutorial class network. This process was given further impetus in 1924 when the government relaxed the adult education regulations, not only extending recognition to each of the twenty-one WEA Districts as separate 'responsible bodies' (RBs), each in receipt of its own grant, but at the same time extending the range of university courses qualifying for grant aid. The result was to loosen, although by no means cut, the ties between the universities and the WEA, and to divert some of the energy and limited manpower of the Adult Education movement from its original objective of organising and stimulating a demand for tutorial classes, towards the offering of shorter, less demanding courses which were organised and provided both by the WEA and the universities themselves. These easier alternatives to the rigours of the tutorial classes lacked some of the earlier commitment to university level work. At the same time the Adult Education movement between the wars began to lose some of its social purpose dynamic, becoming more concerned with general provision which satisfied the needs of individual members of society, rather than with a social studies orientation, geared to the objective of providing the working class with the necessary educational means to pursue the struggle for social change.

This trend was magnified after the second world war with the expansion of university extramural departments and non WEA UAE. In 1948 the Universities Council for Adult Education (UCAE) declared that extramural departments should no longer 'regard their services as available exclusively to any one organisation or section of the community'.[4] During the next twenty-five years, although there were some exceptions (e.g. the development of university day release courses for trade unionists), the general drift of English UAE was away from its earlier commitment to the needs and aspirations of the working class. At the same time there was a large expansion of relatively short, undemanding courses in response to the 'popular demand' of a predominantly middle class constituency seeking leisure and relaxation. This further shifted the emphasis of adult education away from social studies subjects to a broader spectrum of subjects studied 'for their own sake'. This quasi-populist phase had little in common with earlier UAE, with its class orientation and social purpose dynamic, except that both could be classified as liberal, non-vocational education. However, even here, in the post-war period, there was a significant dilution of the traditional liberal approach, with the rapid increase in certificated courses which narrowed considerably the gap between vocational and non-vocational adult education. An important milestone along this road was the establishment of the Open University in 1969, offering part-time degrees for adults through a process of distance learning, based mainly on a combination of television, radio and correspondence modular courses.

The 'Russell Report' in 1973 gently hinted that the universities should 'concentrate on work of university quality' and satisfy 'the need for adult education at a high intellectual level'.[5] It was envisaged that this would involve the universities in a continuing provision of liberal studies of the traditional kind, together with liberal, academic education for all levels of industry; research project work; role education for both professional and voluntary groups; 'balancing' studies to complement earlier specialisation in education; and 'pioneer work'. The latter included: refresher and post experience vocational education (PEVE) courses for professional or vocational groups; informal courses with disadvantaged sections of the population; and part-time degrees.[6]

It could be argued that there was a certain lack of coherence or prioritising in the Russell recommendations and that this has been reflected in UAE in the years since the Report's publication. (The recommendations were, of course, never formally implemented). Different aspects have been emphasised by different universities, but generally there has been a downgrading of the traditional liberal studies provision whilst PEVE courses, and the complementing of previous tertiary education, have been given higher priority. These forms of continuing education reflect a growing trend towards elitism, utilitarianism and 'relevance' - that is, provision relevant not to the forces for social change but to the perceived socio-economic needs of the existing society (a tendency that has characterised university priorities in general).

English UAE has moved radically from its early twentieth century commitment to both the educational advancement of the working class and the achievement of social change (however muted and controlled). In the post-war period there has been a growing tendency for UAE to see its primary purpose as the servicing of the needs of 'the economy', as interpreted by government, industry and the professions. As always, however, contradictions and counter tendencies can be identified, and it is to an exploration of these and their significance, in the contemporary context, that this book is in part devoted.

UAE IN THE USA

The idea of university extension in the USA was imported from England. John Vincent, President of Chautauqua Institution, and Herbert Baxter Adams, a professor of history at John Hopkins University, were the most influential early proponents. Reacting to the entertainment orientation and the lack of seriousness in the more popular forms of adult education, they argued that more sequential and systematic opportunities for serious study were needed. With the encouragement of Adams, Vincent unsuccessfully experimented with extension at Chautauqua in 1888. More successfully, Adams participated in the formation of the American Society for the Extension of University Teaching (ASUET) founded in Philadelphia in 1890. Richard G. Moulton, 'the most popular lecturer in England', launched the American experiment as principal lecturer.[7] In 1891, Moulton was lured to the University of Chicago by William Rainey Harper, who had the financial backing of John D. Rockefeller, to establish a great institution of higher learning. Harper's unusual plan included extension as an integral component of the University; largely unrealised, it is exemplary of the attention given to the extension idea in these years.

Extension undertakings, sponsored by a great variety of institutions, chequered the country. It was a period of institution building. As Adams remarked of extension: 'education like government, is expanding its functions'.(8) By the turn of the century most of the initiatives of the 1890s had faltered. The period of decline began to be reversed in 1906 when the University of Wisconsin marched forward with a distinctly American version of extension under the banner of 'service to the people of the State in every practicable manner'. In 1915, the first meeting of the National University Extension Association (NUEA) was convened at Madison, Wisconsin. Representatives were Extension Divison heads from universities across the country, with the state universities eclipsing the private in prominence. The event marked the ascendance of a form of university extension in the USA which is quite distinct from the English plan after which it was initially modelled. In the USA, extension has been supported as part of the general advancement of education: the intended audience has been the general public, not the working class. In keeping with the decentralised approach to education in the USA, extension too was decentralised. But it was brought quickly under the hegemony of individual universities, and thus, through them, it came effectively to service state and business interests. This decentralisation represents a key difference between UAE in the USA and England, and brings with it, in the USA, a relative lack of public funds, a lack of public policy and articulated programme direction, as well as the absence of national statistics.

Extension has always depended on tuition as its primary source of income. The extent of its dependence upon student fees has meant that UAE has been almost entirely the province of the middle class. It has also meant that offerings must be those that the public is willing to pay for, influencing greatly the practical and recreational nature of programme content. Since an important form of indirect support is through employers - either through cosponsorship, tuition reimbursement and/or salary increments - programmes in continuing professional education have long been the mainstay of extension. This is especially true in the present era when competition for student dollars is at its zenith.

As never before, extension must labour under the university mandate of self-support. To a considerable extent this has always been the case, but in the economically lean times of the 1980s, the meaning of self-support has changed drastically. No longer are indirect costs hidden in university budgets; extension has had increasingly to absorb the costs of being housed in the university, paying for everything from staff salary benefits to the rental of space. As more educational and private institutions have competed for the continuing education market, extension has had to develop astute management and marketing techniques to stay alive. In doing this, it has segmented the market, appealing to the most elite sectors, the highly educated public with the money to pay for 'quality' in programme. Today, extension work is framed in terms of service to a clientele, not the education of students, nor the improvement of social conditions.

The funding basis for extension has been critical to its history. Though it has varied between institutions, there has been some support from the states, but the great bulk has come from tuition. Since the Depression years, Federal support has also entered into the picture, although it was indirect (i.e. through legislation for other purposes) until the Higher Education Act of 1965. Since the 1970s, government support has declined drastically, forcing extension to rely increasingly on private funds.

Extension has not been conceived as an end in its own right, but as marginal to the interests of the university. From its earliest days, extension has been caught in the conflict between elite and democratic values that have coexisted in uneasy wedlock in the USA's 'comprehensive' university. This same conflict is inherent in the liberal tradition in the USA. University extension, as the 'popular arm' of the university, represents the democratic impulse of the institution, while graduate education, the advancement of knowledge, and the maintenance of high academic standards represent the elite impulse. These impulses coexist uneasily within the university; more academically conservative university staff struggle to this day with ways to control extension work and ensure that it conforms to academic standards. Hence, the development of extension in the USA is in part a story of conflict - a conflict essential to the contradictory demands placed upon the liberal tradition by the American ideal of democracy and its dependence upon a capitalist economy.

The distinctively American character of university extension, as well as the liberal tradition of which it has been an expression, must be understood in terms of the USA's democratic experiment. In the post Civil War years, the country was alive with the challenge of reform: workers, newly freed slaves, and women, all fought for the expansion of democracy to include their numbers. Populists echoed the cry of Jacksonian Democrats in the pre Civil War era, 'Equal Rights for All, Special Privileges for None',(9) while the Progressives called for reform in the name of morality, human dignity, social responsibility and scientific progress. It was at this time of economic expansion, millionaires made overnight, and vast regions of land and resources as yet unclaimed, that the myth of the USA as the land of opportunity became firmly entrenched.

The USA's economic abundance and democratic opportunity structure have been taken as articles of faith: they are the fundamental assumptions upon which the myth of unlimited opportunity has rested. Challenges to the myth from workers, urban reformers and frontier populists echoed in the 1890s, but so internalised was the myth, and so subtle and decisive the means of political control, that a basic social critique or alternative political movement did not materialise as a major force. The Espionage and Sedition Acts of World War I, McCarthyism after World War II, technologically advanced surveillance procedures in the present era, and more subtle educational means throughout the history of the USA, have all contributed to the silencing or marginalisation of alternative viewpoints.

Liberalism, democracy and education have been closely linked in American thought. The great hope of the democratic experiment has been perceived to be in the access of all - who could benefit from it - to education. Education would function in two ways: as the great equaliser of opportunity, and through the development of the informed citizenry deemed essential to the democratic process of government. The great fear has been that the uneducated person would fall prey to propaganda, dogmatism, and unrest, thereby threatening democratic institutions. Education, throughout American history, has been used as an instrument of social reform; it has been the USA's 'Imperfect Panacea'.(10)

The egalitarian ideals so inherent in the concept of democracy have meant more than access to existing institutions. They also carry the notion of many institutions, each equal in its own right; and even more radically, the idea that all knowledge is of equal value. Although this more extreme conception of egalitarianism has been highly controversial in the history of American education, its consequences are evident in the unprecedented expansion of educational institutions to include even the most practical and popular areas of public interest. The hallmark of the USA's educational system has become its mass, comprehensive, decentralised system of public schooling, eventually stretching from the kindergarten through to college completion, including, in theory, all branches of knowledge and all people. Class distinctions have been largely unacknowledged, the myth being that the USA is a land free of classes - people are of one 'mass'; the 'common man' is the prototype. If there is a class, it is the great middle class to which virtually all belong. Thus, we have mass education, not class education, in the popular conception.

Paradoxically, extension's story can be seen as both a manifestation of this egalitarian spirit and as a reaction to it. Alongside the voices calling for the levelling of culture have been those calling for its preservation. In reaction to the rampant pragmatism and materialism of the age, institutions of higher learning were founded in the twentieth century. The pressure upon these institutions to be pragmatic and democratic is evident in the Morrill Federal Land Grant Act of 1862 which mandated that the universities receiving the funds must serve the educational interests of the farmers and industrial 'classes'. Though there was much controversy as to what this meant, the idea that the university must serve the new political interests upon whose support it depended was clear. In reaction to farmers and mechanics - and later businessmen - who argued that the universities were not serving their interests, lay boards of trustees were formed, practical subjects were included in the curriculum, and outreach activities which were the predecessors of extension were undertaken. When the Hatch Act was passed in 1887, agricultural extension began to develop in a direction separate from general extension, which initially was more closely allied to liberal subjects of study. An important early goal of universities in sponsoring extension was to develop secondary education, the missing link between the recently established common schools and institutions of 'higher' learning.

The history of university extension reflects also an ongoing tension between liberal or human values and the pragmatic requisites of survival. The ideal of 'service' bridges this tension. Service is the peculiarly American approach to social purpose goals, although its egalitarian tinge sets up a conflict with more traditional liberal values. Except for the period of social upheaval in the 1960s, the ideal of social purpose has been seen as quite consistent with government service.

'Americanisation' and vocational training programmes gave adult education a new permanence on the institutional landscape during World War I. The great flowering of the movement took place in the immediate post war years when, with the encouragement of a significant grant from the Carnegie Foundation, the American Association for Adult Education (AAAE) was formed. Messianic in its fervour, the liberal education of adults was eagerly turned to as an alternative to guns in making the world safe for democracy. The cataclysmic threat of communism to democracy was deeply ingrained in the USA's collective psyche. The Depression intensified this concern and brought UAE unquestionably into the service of capitalism in the discouragement of worker organising and the encouragement of skills training for displaced workers. But it was in World War II, with the Engineering Science Management War Training Act that government most directly made the universities - and through them extension - an instrument of national policy. So, too, the GI Bill in the post war period massively extended the universities' involvement in adult education. The 1948 President's Commission Report, <u>Higher Education for Democracy</u>, held that access to higher education should be the right of all with the ability to benefit thereby, approximately half the population. A vastly expanded role for community colleges and university extension was called for; they were asked to recognise adult education as their 'potentially greatest service to democratic society'.(11) As in the years following World War I, this period also saw a resurgence of liberal values, and in 1956 the Ford Foundation established the Fund for Adult Education which spawned the influential Centre for the Study of the Liberal Education of Adults (CSLEA). In the 1960s, social purpose became a major issue and adult education became an instrument of the government's War on Poverty programme. The Higher Education Act of 1965 moved UAE programmes a little more in the direction of providing a 'second chance' for minorities to gain access to higher education. Not surprisingly, in the 1980s, there has been a major reaction to the 'great society' programmes and the liberalism they represented. The survival of all of education has been seen to depend upon more direct service to business and industry as the financial base of support has shifted from the public to the private sector. In the 1980s the emphasis is on continuing professional education and marketing approaches: adult education professionals are sought who have marketing skills, not some 'utopian vision' of a future society.

This historical sketch may have over-emphasised the pragmatic at the expense of the liberal, in part because of the peculiar tie in the USA between liberal values and a particular form of government. Then, too, liberal values are not so often seen, as the march of history eclipses underlying tensions and personal struggles. Despite the weight of evidence in the direction of pragmatism, the liberal tradition continues to prick at the consciences of many educators. In the chapters on the American experience that follow, the conflicts inherent in the liberal tradition and their particular manifestation in UAE are more fully developed.

NOTES

1. The Joint Committee of University and Working Class Representatives, Oxford and Working Class Education, Oxford, 1908, second edition, 1909, p. 55.
2. Ibid, p. 48.
3. J.P.M. Millar, The Labour College Movement, 1979, pp. 34 and 53.
4. UCAE, The Universities in Adult Education: A Statement of Principles, 1948, p. 2.
5. Department of Education and Science, Adult Education: A Plan for Development, 1973, p. 72.
6. Ibid, pp. 72-3.
7. George M. Woytanowitz, University Extension: The Early Years in the United States, 1885-1915, Iowa City: American College Testing Programme, 1974, p. 40.
8. United States Bureau of Education, Report of the Commissioner of Education for the year 1885-1886, Washington: Government Printing Office, 1887, pp. 748-749. Quoted by Woytanowitz, op. cit., p. 24.
9. Richard Hofstadter, The Age of Reform, New York, 1955, p. 63.
10. Henry J. Parkinson, The Imperfect Panacea: American Faith in Education, 1865-1965, New York, 1968.
11. President's Commission on Higher Education. Higher Education for American Democracy, Vol. I, p. 97. Washington: U.S. Government Printing Office, 1947.

Chapter Two

THE LIBERAL TRADITION IN ADULT EDUCATION

The discussions and analyses in this book centre on the various ways in which the liberal tradition has formed the central concept in UAE in both England and the USA, and the diminution in its importance in the face of recent, and quite other, pressures. It is thus essential to define at the outset what is meant by the liberal tradition, and to discuss the different emphases within the tradition that have been evident in the two countries.

In neither the USA nor England is the liberal tradition in UAE to be defined exclusively within the confines of liberalism construed as a general ideological stance. (Still less should it be identified with political Liberalism, in either its nineteenth or twentieth century forms). Nevertheless there are certain important and fundamental characteristics of the liberal tradition in UAE which derive directly from the generalised liberal ideology. Perhaps most basic of all has been the assumption that adult education (and for that matter education per se) is concerned with the individual. Liberalism itself has been characterised as essentially an ideology of possessive individualism, and this assumption has certainly underlain much of the liberal tradition in UAE. However, it should be noted that, as is discussed below, this has been by no means an uncontested position within the liberal tradition in UAE. Those who have espoused a social purpose orientation have had very different emphases. Even here, however, whilst the objectives of the individualist perspective have been assigned a lower priority, they have none the less continued to form a significant part of the overall approach. Thus, for the most part, it has been the educational advancement (variously defined) of the individual, which has been seen as the major, and sometimes the exclusive, purpose of adult education within the liberal tradition. Of what does this individual educational advancement consist? All the perspectives within the liberal tradition emphasise the importance both of introducing individual students to new and different ideas and areas of knowledge, and of evolving a critical analysis. Within these concepts can be found much that is central to the tradition, and it is worth exploring them in some detail.

The liberal tradition maintains centrally that the whole educational project is concerned with opening out and indeed challenging the individual's conception of his or her own environment. The relationship between the individual and the wider society, and the perceived problems and/or interests of the individual, are both seen as being the basis from which different perspectives of reality, and hence differing solutions to problems, can be studied. Thus the individual's social and personal location, and his or her perceptions of that location, are seen as the starting point for the liberal educational approach, which must be analysed from within differing perspectives. Sometimes, as in social science subjects, this may take the form of the exploration of differing schools of thought - Freudian, Jungian and behaviourist psychology, for example. On other occasions it may be more appropriate to broaden out from the individual's particular subject interest - from Renaissance art to that of other periods, for example. The motivation, and the justification in these and other cases, however, is always the same within the liberal tradition: to widen the student's experience and understanding and thereby to increase his or her awareness of alternative conceptions and priorities. Because this increases the individual's knowledge, understanding, and appreciation of the world, this is held to be <u>a priori</u> desirable.

Closely related to this 'broadening' educational function is the notion of developing a critical analysis: that is, that every statement, or position, or interpretation, or ideological system must not only, <u>a priori</u>, be open to question and therefore to doubt, but, further, that the function of adult education is to help students to formulate, or at the very least, to <u>understand</u>, these alternative interpretations. An important part of this process lies in the tutor's knowledge of his or her <u>discipline</u> which, when transmitted to the students, will enable them to construct, with the tools of the subject, their own series of interpretative frameworks. The construction of a critical analysis is thus as much a matter of method and approach as it is of content. Fundamental to this conception, therefore, is the idea that <u>all</u> positions on <u>all</u> subjects must be open to the most rigorous and critical analysis: the agenda for discussion is always potentially all-embracing, and no issues or positions are debarred.

These tenets of the liberal tradition lead on to other central contentions (which may also be held to have a relationship to liberalism <u>per se</u>): the idea that education should be dialectical rather than propagandist, and that there should be total freedom of discussion. Both are logical developments from the earlier positions and perhaps need little elaboration here. In contrast to both the extreme Right and the extreme Left - which in this context at least have in common their authoritarianism - the liberal tradition has drawn a sharp distinction between education and propaganda, even in the problematic arena of social, political and industrial education, and has insisted upon the open approach described above. The propagandist approach, apart from its obvious demerits because of its narrowness and unilinear nature, is also a one way, undynamic teaching <u>method</u>. The dialectical approach, on the other hand, ensures at the very least a developing dialogue among students, and between students and tutor. Moreover, if the whole exercise develops properly, then a <u>group</u> understanding of the issues, problems and perspectives may emerge, and a qualitatively improved educational level will have been reached by all participants.

However, how far in practice the parameters of this liberal tradition have been allowed to extend is a central and complex question which will be considered in detail in later chapters. Nevertheless, at least in principle, the liberal tradition has asserted the absolute necessity of free discusion: again, all questions are open questions and all opinions and interpretations should be considered fully.

All of this has implications for teaching methods and the principle of democratic control of the adult education class. The liberal tradition has stressed the importance of adult education as a two way process: a mutually beneficial co-operation between professional knowledge and expertise on the part of the educator, and life experience in all its variety on the part of the students.(1) The notion is thus one of an educational praxis, with the total experience benefiting from the contributions of both parties. This has been combined with, and been a part of, the commitment to the seminar discussion method of education rather than the formal lecture. The class is seen as a partnership, a mutual exploration: a formal lecture, implying the one way transmission of a body of knowledge from the expert to the ignorant, has been seen, at least in more recent years, as entirely inappropriate.(2) Mansbridge, although perhaps overstating the case, put the point succinctly: 'the students control the class ... it is _the_ class of the students - each student is a teacher, and each teacher is a student; the humblest is not afraid to teach, and the most advanced is willing to learn'.(3)

Thus, although syllabus outlines must be predetermined by the tutor, it has been the general practice within the liberal tradition for the class as a democratic group to decide, as the course progresses, on the detailed content and priorities for study, and on the time to be allocated to particular areas. Linked both to this practice and to the more general tenets of the liberal tradition, has been the opposition to UAE becoming concerned with examinations and qualifications. Individuals must be allowed to proceed at their own pace, and begin from whatever ability and knowledge base they have. To impose entry requirements for courses, or even worse, to insist upon a rigid adherence to a predetermined examination syllabus and a uniform standard of assessment, would destroy the whole basis of the liberal tradition approach.

These pedagogic considerations lead, however, to a more general and, in some senses, more fundamental aspect of the liberal tradition: the insistence that adult education must be seen not as _utilitarian_ in some vocational or material sense, but as either education for intellectual advancement, or as 'education for citizenship'. (This latter is a crucially important distinction and is discussed further below). This rejection of utilitarianism in education has a more general application than adult education. It has been argued, for example, that the pressure for universities to justify their whole provision in terms of utilitarian relevance must be resisted. Universities exist to study, analyse and discuss all areas of knowledge: if this principle is conceded then the whole nature of a university system based upon free inquiry and the furtherance of knowledge would disappear,(4) and, some would say, is indeed in the process of disappearing as 'Thatcherite' and 'Reaganite' policies become the order of the day.

In UAE, many of those, especially in England, who espouse the liberal tradition are thus, at the very least, suspicious of the trends towards role training, qualifications-oriented and professional education which have tended to dominate recent UAE in both England and the USA (as is argued in Chapters 4 and 6). The liberal tradition stands in opposition to the dominance of such trends, and indeed by implication to the values within both the wider educational system and the wider society, which have inspired such developments. The liberal tradition is thus embattled, but not defeated, espousing a series of values and practices which are, in the 1980s, by no means wholly congruent with prevailing orthodoxies.

The matter cannot be left there, however. It is not a simple dichotomy between a liberal tradition espousing educational, humanistic objectives, and increasingly hard-faced utilitarian governmental systems arguing for greater 'relevance' and 'training'. Thus far the liberal tradition has been presented as a unified and cohesive, as well as a coherent, framework of belief and practice within adult education. It has also been implied that it is uniformly applicable to both England and the USA. Both these positions must be explored a little further if we are to arrive at a general but accurate view of the liberal tradition before moving into the main body of analysis.

The liberal tradition has so far been discussed in terms of liberal individualism which, it was asserted at the outset, is a key concept within liberalism as a general ideological stance. But, in UAE, the liberal tradition encompasses far more than this liberal individualism. Indeed, in some ways, the liberal tradition should be seen as a continuum, beginning with liberal individualism but extending to include more collectivist and implicitly socialist perspectives, pre-eminently 'education for citizenship', and having a highly ambivalent relationship with the various forms of 'social purpose' UAE.

In England the continuum is relatively well-defined. The strand of the liberal tradition which has emphasised 'education for citizenship' in fact spans the individualist/collectivist divide. After all, it can be argued that the individual citizen needs a good grounding in education in order to be able to exercise his or her vote, and other democratic functions, in an informed manner. And this was indeed seen as a powerful argument in England in the early years of adult education around the turn of the century, as has been argued in Chapter 1. Similar arguments, emphasising the importance of transmitting the predominant ideological norms, were used to an extent, too, in relation to the collectivity of the working class. But, as in most modern societies, the ruling class was unhappy with collectivist concepts such as 'class', because of the very real political dangers inherent in encouraging large and potentially powerful groups of individuals to think of themselves as a unified (and by implication under-privileged and alienated) group in society.(5) Working class students, and those professional adult educators who shared their ideological outlook, however, were keen to emphasise the collectivist view. Thus, there has always been a strong strand within the liberal tradition in England that has stressed the importance of working class adult education. This has been partly on grounds of social justice (giving educational opportunities to those who have been denied them through no fault of their own), but also because of a deeply-held belief that only through education could the working class become equipped intellectually and politically to play its full role in a democratic society.

It should also be noted, however, that there is a sense in which education generally, and the liberal tradition in adult education in particular, neutralises and ultimately renders innocuous any political commitment. This is the case in two respects. The experience of study can, of itself, become an all-absorbing, almost obsessive, preoccupation. The initial impetus for studying some aspect of historical, economic or political interest may be 'to understand in order better to accomplish change'; but in the process of study the subject area itself becomes of such interest that the original objective is lost. Second, the liberal approach in particular encourages an appreciation of the complexity of all issues, and thus leads to the undermining of originally firmly held opinions by exposing them to other viewpoints. Thus, adult students are liable to fall victim to the perennial academics' disease of 'fence sitting' and indecision, leading to inactivity. This can result in a profound hostility within UAE towards any linkage between education and social action.(6) In this sense, the ability to see all sides of all questions, and to appreciate the other points of view, can be a <u>depoliticising</u> process, and can be an effective means of social control.

Nevertheless, the preponderant effect of UAE, indeed <u>all</u> education, is generally, in the long term, to raise the consciousness of students as they become more aware, in diverse ways, of their environment. Certainly it has been this latter interpretation of the effects of adult education that has motivated those who have espoused the social purpose view of UAE activity. In its more moderate expression this took the form of arguing that the working class needed to 'improve itself' educationally in order to be able to take advantage of the benefits <u>and responsibilities</u> which the newly democratic form of society offered. Thus, only by learning about economics, politics, history and so on, could the working class challenge seriously and responsibly those who would conserve the existing, unequal social structure. The attaining of power via the existing democratic system, and hence the attainment of social justice for the mass of the people, was seen primarily as a matter of argument - of convincing the electorate, and hopefully one's more conservative (and in the British context, Conservative) opponents - of the <u>rightness</u> of the case in both the moral and the intellectual sense. The key to this process was seen as education. This is, of course, a <u>liberal</u> position in the sense that it rejects one of the central notions that underlies Marxian socialism: that politics is essentially about class conflict and that, although ideologies and the mobilisation of political movements are of crucial importance, the issues at stake will be resolved not through rational, consensual <u>discussion</u>, but through <u>conflict</u> in one form or another. This liberal position was central to the whole social democratic reformist politics of late nineteenth and twentieth century Britain, as has been argued at length by many political analysts and historians.(7) In this, and many other ways, social democratic politics has been both collectivist <u>and</u> liberal in its ideological framework - in addition, of course, to significant elements of socialist idealism, Fabianism, and other perspectives, in its overall make-up.(8) The point here, however, is that this variegated, somewhat confused, and certainly integrated and reformist, ideological stance, has been articulated in the UAE (and WEA) context in the conception of 'education for citizenship'.

Further to the Left, but still very much a part of the continuum, has been the concept of adult education for radical social change. This has taken different forms in differing periods - from workers' industrial education to community adult education in the more modern period (both are discussed in the English context in Chapter 5 and in the American context in Chapter 7). But it has always had at its core the contention that radical social change within the wider society is necessary, and that the whole educational process is a part of a grossly unjust and elitist system, favouring the privileged few at the expense of the large majority. It is argued that this system underpins in a variety of ways (not least culturally) the whole exploitative structure of capitalism.

This differs from the preceding paradigm of 'education for citizenship', in part because it is more insistent on the need for radical change, in part because it takes a more fully collectivist view, but primarily because it is not necessarily linked in to a parliamentarist, conformist, integrationist view of the process of achieving that social change. Many of those advocating this radical social change perspective have thus argued from outside the parameters of the social democratic politics previously described, although arguably within the liberal tradition.

Do those within UAE advocating this perspective fall within the liberal tradition? Certainly, there have been some - most notably those in the narrowly Marxist National Council of Labour Colleges (NCLC) - who have viewed adult education in wholly illiberal terms: who have seen working class adult education as being exclusively about the teaching of Marxism from an uncritical perspective (arguably, a thoroughly un-Marxian approach in itself!). Generally, however, in the past those who have been within this perspective have found little difficulty in allying themselves with the liberal tradition. (The fact that radicals in contemporary UAE are far less happy with the liberal tradition is a point of some importance and is discussed further in subsequent chapters).

The point, then, is not necessarily the degree of political commitment to socialism, or for that matter to Marxism, it is rather a question of adherence to certain tenets of educational values and teaching methods, the most important of which have been discussed briefly above. In practice, of course, in both England and the USA, the power

structure and the pervasive ideology of advanced
industrial capitalism have made it exceptionally
difficult for a genuinely liberal, open-ended, educational system to operate. In reality, UAE for the
most part has been deeply imbued with, and integrated into, capitalist and bourgeois values and
assumptions.

Nevertheless, in principle (and sometimes in
practice too) it is the values underlying the
methodological practices of UAE which lie at the
heart of the liberal tradition in both England and
the USA.

But, it may be objected, if socialists see the
primary purpose of UAE as radical social change,
surely this negates the central tenets of the
liberal tradition, and subordinates the educational
to the political? We are now directly into the
complex area of objectivity and commitment. It is
arguable that to be neutral or objective in the
sense of being value free is an impossibility for
an adult educator in his/her role as a tutor.
Everyone is operating from within an ideological
framework, from which values, priorities, disciplinary and methodological procedures and so on, are
culled. If this is an unconscious process so much
the worse, for the tutor is unable to take any
action to counteract this necessary bias, and indeed
thinks of himself/herself as 'objective', and thus
presents educational content as if it were selected
on an objective basis. (More detailed discussion
of this question of objectivity and commitment is
held over until Chapters 3 and 7).

In relation to England, then, the liberal
tradition should be seen in general terms as embody-
ing a continuum of ideological stances, but with the
defining characteristics being essentially pedagogic
in nature. The fact that exponents of the liberal
tradition have often not practised what they
preached (in that Marxian ideas and activists have
generally been discriminated against) is of central
importance in this study, as it places the whole
basis of the tradition in some jeopardy. After all,
if the discussion is open to the extent only of
those ideological stances which are agreed in their
fundamental assumptions, and therefore conform to
the prevailing consensus, the liberal tradition
becomes somewhat empty, and merely rhetorical.
Given the continuance of a broadly similar society
and political culture in England, the question of
whether the liberal tradition can achieve in reality
the educational ideals to which it aspires, is a

question of central importance to be returned to in the final chapter.

In the USA such considerations loom even larger. The liberal tradition in the USA, whilst containing many of the same elements and basic outlook, is far more constrained within establishment parameters. The central, consensual framework of American society permeates adult education, as it does other sectors of American life. Ideological stances are implicit, but none the less strongly held. Liberalism, democracy and pragmatism are fundamental to adult education - not at all as mutually exclusive philosophies, but as unquestioned, often unarticulated, assumptions, which form the basis for action.

This does not mean that there are not differences between the libertarian values of liberals, the egalitarian premises of the social progressives, or the more survival-oriented concerns of the pragmatists, but rather that these values have tended to coexist within the same institution, the same programme, and, on occasion, even the same person. Certainly there are exceptions, but the key point is that in the USA the tendency is to blend and reconcile, to ignore rather than accentuate ideological differences. Rather than attempting to define the liberal tradition in the American context in terms of a coherent and specific set of values, it is more pertinent to see it, in characteristically unsophisticated American fashion, as the imperative 'to do good'. This spirit was captured by Paul Sheats in his 1953 presidential address before the AEA when he remarked, 'Let's face it friends, we are a "do-good" movement'. (9)

A recurring theme in the USA has been that liberalism is in a state of crisis. Key controversies within the liberal tradition in UAE have concerned mass education, standards, social action, propaganda, workers' education, the idea of class, socialism, vocationalism, and the utilitarian emphasis upon service. Ironically, the first threat to liberalism came from the egalitarian pragmatism of the American democratic experiment; to this threat, liberalism responded by becoming more inclusive, allowing for the uneasy coexistence of sometimes mutually competing ideologies within the liberal framework. The consequence is that liberalism has become identified with strengthening the American government and the capitalist economic system, rather than the values of democracy and human welfare. The ideals have given way to the defence of a particular set of institutions, practices and values that have themselves in reality become increasingly inimical to the fundamentals of the liberal tradition.

In the USA, therefore, the liberal tradition in UAE and in adult education generally has become a nebulous, all-embracing concept, committed predominantly in practice to the status quo, and an establishment perspective. In Chapters 6 and 7, which are concerned with the American experience of the liberal tradition in UAE, the ideological solidification of liberalism, first through the paradoxical implications of the American tradition and conception of democracy, and then of socialism, will be considered. The focus is on controversies over standards, service, propaganda, social action, mass education and workers' education.

In this examination of the problems that the liberal tradition has posed for UAE in the USA, it is contended that there are contradictions inherent within the liberal tradition itself, as well as contradictions between liberal ideals and educational practices, which have directly contributed to the decline of liberalism as a visible tradition upon which to base education for social transformation. It is suggested that the 'broadening out' and 'critical analysis' values of liberal education are not only not practical, but philosophically inconsistent within a perspective that is politically rooted in the activities of education for citizenship, individual advancement or economic development, and epistemologically rooted in scientific rationality. In the American context, the tradition, both in terms of its politics and its epistemological premises, remains closed, however much its values may argue the contrary. Thus, it is argued that method, or education, cannot be divorced from ideology; education cannot be sharply distinguished from propaganda - action is integral to education for social transformation.

To a much greater extent in the USA than in England, the traditional liberal position has interpreted education for radical social change as a threat to liberal democracy; the limitation of the perspective is in tying the ideal to the means, that is, to the idea that the vote is the basis for political change. Advocates of radical social change challenge the viability of the vote and governmental intervention, arguing for the importance of organisation and action outside these channels as integral to the lifeblood of democracy. To the extent that their stance has been delegitimised, they have been forced to work outside the mainstream in the USA. Chapter 7 shows the annihilation in the USA of the left progressive perspective within liberal adult education, and with it, the demise of socialism and any semblance of a collectivist orientation. Education for citizenship is equivalent to Americanisation: in the USA, it is a process of indoctrination rather than critical analysis.

In the USA, the notion of a continuum of perspectives within liberalism which includes a socialist strand, is not appropriate. While there have been individuals within UAE who have had a progressive orientation, and who would consider themselves to be liberals, they do not form a cohesive programme or operating base. A related and important difference between UAE in the two countries is the strongly utilitarian aspect of the liberal tradition in the USA which, as is shown in Chapter 6, has been there from the beginning. Moreover, this utilitarian orientation has been legitimized in terms of the liberal values of service and equality of opportunity. Perhaps nothing so fully captures the difference between the USA and England than the idea of service as the American interpretation of social purpose. The consequence is that the liberal tradition in the USA appears to be considerably to the right of its political location in England.

In somewhat different contexts, then, the liberal tradition in UAE in both England and the USA is under threat from two directions. The longstanding problem of attempting to fulfil in practice its radical and libertarian educational ideals have led many radicals to question its overall viability; it has come to be regarded as an ideological smokescreen, obscuring the essentially supportive functions played by UAE (and adult education in general) within the bourgeois capitalist system. Such critics have urged that the liberal tradition be jettisoned, and a new, genuinely radical, approach be adopted.(10) Second, there has been a criticism of the whole liberal tradition, and all it stands for, by powerful forces within and outside adult education, which have advocated an educational approach geared far more to utilitarian and vocational criteria. Such critics have already secured changes in structure and priorities within UAE and seem likely to increase their influence further over the next few years.

In other words, the liberal tradition is under attack from both the Left and the Right, and from both within and outside UAE. Whether or not it remains a viable tradition, and whether it can or should be preserved in some modified form within UAE in both England and the USA, is the central theme of the discussion in the final chapter of this study. Before this, however, attention must be turned to the various aspects of UAE, in theory and practice, in England and the USA, and in particular to the position occupied by the liberal tradition within the structures and practices of the two systems.

NOTES

1. See E.P. Thompson, Education and Experience, Fifth Mansbridge Memorial Lecture, Leeds University Press, 1968.

2. It should be noted, however, that in the early years of the extension movement it was the practice for a formal lecture to a large audience to precede the more intensive 'seminar' discussion with a smaller group. It was this latter practice which became the basis of the tutorial class system in the early years of the twentieth century.

3. Albert Mansbridge, The Kingdom of the Mind, 1944, p. 24.

4. Ralph Miliband, Staff Seminar Paper (unpublished) Department of Adult Education and Extra-mural Studies, University of Leeds, 1973; and subsequently in, A State of Desubordination, British Journal of Sociology, Vol. XXIX, No. 4 (1978), pp. 399-409.

5. This is by no means of historical importance only. As recently as 1983, a UAE department was advised, quite explicitly, by the DES Inspectorate, to remove all references to the 'working class' in a major report to the DES. Some more 'apolitical' term (e.g. the educationally disadvantaged) was suggested as being less likely to raise ministerial and bureaucratic hackles.

6. This important element within the argument is discussed in relation to the USA in Chapter 7, and in the more general context in Chapter 8. For a discussion within the English context, see Roger Fieldhouse, The Workers' Educational Association: Aims and Achievements, 1903-1977, Syracuse University Publications in Continuing Education, (USA), 1978.

7. See, for example, Ralph Miliband, Parliamentary Socialism, second edition, 1983; David Coates, The Labour Party and the Struggle for

Socialism, 1974.
   8. See ibid, for further discussion. See also, Tom Nairn, The Nature of the Labour Party, in (eds) Anderson and Blackburn, Towards Socialism, 1965; David Howell, British Social Democracy, 1976, etc.
   9. Quoted by John B. Schwertman, I Want Many Lodestars. Notes and Essays No. 21, Chicago, CSLEA, 1958, p. 52.
   10. See, for example, ed. Jane Thompson, Adult Education for a Change, 1980.

Chapter Three

THE PROBLEMS OF OBJECTIVITY, SOCIAL PURPOSE AND IDEOLOGICAL COMMITMENT IN ENGLISH UNIVERSITY ADULT EDUCATION

Since the early days of English UAE, objectivity and political neutrality have been widely regarded as an essential element of the liberal tradition. It has long been a central tenet of that tradition that tutors and students pursue their studies together in an atmosphere of open enquiry, free of all prejudice and political propaganda, considering all possible answers to their enquiries before ultimately alighting upon the truth.

Thus it was that Joseph Eames, a Gloucestershire miner, expressed an uninhibited faith in objective truth, and the ability of the universities to attain this state of grace, at a university extension summer meeting in 1892:

> What we want as working men, are teachers who will mount the glorious tower of truth, and soar above the smoke of contending parties, who will tell us the whole truth and nothing but the truth. I think the University teacher is the best able to give us unprejudiced, unadulterated education ..... (1)

Much the same point of view was held by Robert Halstead, the Yorkshire cotton weaver, who was one of the pillars of strength of the Hebden Bridge extension centre and became an even more important influence in the formation of the WEA. At a meeting in Hebden Bridge in 1893 he pleaded for 'access to a knowledge of all truth' untainted by 'political tacticians and extravagent socialists' and sought 'contact with men whose great work is to impart knowledge from sources as uncontaminated as anything that is human can be .....'(2)

Within a few years this laudable objective apparently had been achieved, according to the

'Special Report of H M Inspector Mr. Headlam and Professor L T Hobhouse on certain Tutorial Classes in connection with the Workers' Educational Association'. This famous report assumed 'that University teaching is teaching suited to adults; that it is scientific, detached, and impartial in character' and will train students to distinguish between matters of fact and opinion: 'between the white light and the coloured'.(3)

This white and black absoluteness of objective truth was a crucial part of the ideology of the early twentieth century liberal intellectual elite, of which Hobhouse was a leading member. Some years later, when the liberal certainties looked somewhat less certain, another leading Liberal, J A Hobson, admitted the possibility that some intellectuals might 'sometimes weakly yield to narrower pragmatic or emotional biases'. Nevertheless, he felt assured that 'intellectual craftsmanship, with the personal pride or satisfaction in good work which it evoked, is so alluring and dominating a force in most of its regular practitioners that ... they will normally return to the more disinterested course, helping to get out truths irrespective of their immediate utility or popularity'.(4)

However, this commitment to objectivity and belief in a totally disinterested intellectual craftsmanship posed a number of questions for those engaged in adult education: what is objectivity; what do we mean by political neutrality, and is it compatible with adult education's social purpose dynamic; and, is there an irredeemable conflict between Marxism and the English liberal tradition?

This chapter will attempt to answer these questions in the context of the historical development of English UAE.

THE SHIBBOLETH OF OBJECTIVE TRUTH

In the sense that the term objectivity was loosely used to mean 'the whole truth and nothing but the truth', it came to be seen as a shibboleth. In 1946 the philosopher H A Hodges identified four factors of subjectivity which imposed logical limitations to objective thinking and teaching in this sense.(5) They were: the methodological assumptions which determine the interpretation of data; the selection of the data from the raw material, which is determined by pre-existing ideas of what is worthwhile;(6) the methods and principles of each scholar's particular specialism; and the intellectual horizons of the society and historical epoch in which we live. In addition to these subjective factors, the thinking of both individuals and social classes is partly determined by their psychological bias, and by a whole host of deep-seated hopes and fears, dreams and imaginings which are altogether alien to 'factual truth':

> All of us can detect the mythologies of other people. Our own can appear to us as well grounded convictions, and we are zealous in their defence. To unravel the confusion would require a clarity and persistence in self-examination such as is beyond most of us.(7)

Many adult educationalists have recognised this inevitable subjectivity, as is illustrated by quotations from three people who were prominent in English UAE during the formative years after World War II. In 1949, S G Raybould asked: 'How, in the last restort, can anyone know that ..... the opinion he holds or the actions he recommends are "right"? A feeling of conviction is clearly not sufficient'. He went on to state that 'selection is bound to be affected by the interests of the person concerned, by his judgement of what is important, by the existing limits of his knowledge. Complete objectivity is thus impossible'.(8)

E P Thompson claimed that tutors frequently failed to 'give a fair presentation of views ..... in the fields of Philosophy or International Relations or Economic Theory' because of the impossibility of a tutor being fully responsive to opinions he does not tolerate.(9) The same point was made by Thomas Hodgkin:

> I suspect that a lack of objectivity in teaching is usually the consequence, not of any deliberate desire to convert students rather than to teach them, but of a lack of flexibility of mind on the part of the tutor, which makes it difficult for him to grasp imaginatively theories and beliefs which he does not happen to hold.(10)

Similarly, at a series of staff seminars in the UAE Department at Leeds in the mid 1970s, there was a strong element of agreement that objectivity, in any absolute sense, could not exist ..... It was argued that cognitive frames were biased by external

values ..... making objectivity impossible', and
that the question is not whether to adopt a value
system to operate by, but which value system should
be seen as the most relevant and useful:

> Clearly, as tutors, we cannot achieve objec-
> tivity. Our language, our choice of con-
> ceptual frameworks, our selection of concepts,
> even our choice of sources, all introduce
> bias ..... We see things as we perceive them,
> and different people may see the same thing
> in different ways ..... It is not possible to
> be objective. It is of course possible for
> the teacher to allow for his own <u>conscious</u>
> biases, and so to be <u>less</u> subjective, but he
> cannot allow for biases of which he is unaware
> ..... Given that objectivity is impossible,
> I would argue that a more intellectually
> honest and educationally constructive approach
> is to admit the impossibility of being objec-
> tive, but nevertheless to work as much as
> possible towards it.(11)

This approach can lead to the belief that
education <u>must</u> adopt a value system, that it legit-
imately operates within a certain range of values,
that it cannot be neutral and ought to have a particular leaning, and that objectivity is not only
impossible, but is undesirable.

The logical conclusion is that 'everyone may
think as he likes, and ..... therefore the wise
man will think and teach what is likeliest to
bring him to power',(12) or that, as it rules out
any objective history, history is merely what the
historian makes. 'Since all historical judgements
involve persons and points of view, one is as good
as another and there is no "objective" historical
truth'.(13) It was this prospect of 'the very
concept of objective truth ..... fading out of the
world', to be displaced by an amalgam of propaganda lies, that haunted George Orwell after his
experience in the Spanish Civil War(14) (and which
later became a central theme in <u>Nineteen Eighty
Four</u>). He regretted the abandonment of the belief
that history <u>could</u> be truthfully written and that
'"facts", existed and were more or less discov-
erable'.(15) Now, out of the amalgam of lies and
propaganda:

> ..... <u>Some</u> kind of history will be written,
> and after those who actually remember the war

are dead, it will be universally accepted. So
for all practical purposes the lie will have
become truth ..... The implied objective of
this line of thought is a nightmare world in
which the leader, or some ruling clique, controls not only the future but the past.(16)

Orwell's nightmare becomes a reality if certain attitudes or beliefs are equated with objectivity and regarded as the 'absolute truth'. Some adult educationalists' concept of objective truth has been influenced by an essentially Marxist view of the future, which envisages the destruction of the bourgeois capitalist hegemony, to be replaced by the dictatorship of the proletariat, progressing to a classless, genuinely free and communist society. Far more adult educationists, however, have adopted a liberal view that social ills will be gradually eliminated by teaching people greater tolerance and understanding. Out of this knowledge, social reforms will spring, without the need for any radical structural change. This liberal ideology has been frequently regarded as somehow more objectively 'true' and non-political - ignoring the fact that it embodies certain values (and highly questionable assumptions) and that anyone consciously or unconsciously inculcating these values is, in an Orwellian sense, manufacturing social and political attitudes.

The Final Report of the Adult Education Committee of the Ministry of Reconstruction warned in 1919 of the dangers Orwell perceived some twenty years later. The state should not discriminate against certain types of education 'merely on the grounds that they have a particular "atmosphere"', declared the Report, for this would almost certainly involve the state in 'manufacturing public opinion'.(17) It would involve the state in censorship and require value judgements that inevitably would be derived from subjective attitudes and prejudices. As A D Lindsay said, in a letter to the President of the Board of Education, referring to this passage of the 1919 Report some six years later, 'no-one is absolutely impartial in practice and, what is more important, people's views about what is impartial vary'.(18)

During World War II the Board of Education was understandably concerned about the inflammable nature of certain controversial topics taught in adult education classes. The Board did not wish to invite opprobrium by openly prohibiting such topics, which were matters of the liveliest interest at the time. But it did consider issuing a 'very carefully worded circular stressing the necessity of treating such topics objectively and impartially and of avoiding any ground for complaint that the Board are encouraging an anti-national point of view', (19) thus quite overtly equating objectivity and impartiality with the perceived national interest. In the event, the Board decided that such a circular would be represented by some 'extremists' as a limit to free discussion, so it confined itself to exhorting the adult education bodies to warn their tutors that their 'freedom' was 'limited by scholarship and judiciousness of mind'.(20) Of course, what was considered judicious was itself a value judgement.

In 1950, E P Thompson demonstrated that, in some quarters, adult education was being used to foster a _particular_ attitude, 'variously described as "objective", "tolerant", gentlemanly, calm, equitable, wise, or a combination of these'.(21) It was this prescription of a particular attitude which was equated with objectivity and extended from a tolerance of a person's _right to hold_ certain opinions to a required tolerance of actual opinions, and to certain patterns of behaviour in society. 'The exponents of this theory of "objectivity" were not only agreeing to make available facts about society to their students, but were also claiming to dictate the student's response, and therefore, behaviour in relation to these facts'.(22)

At its blandest, this could mean merely that tutors did not try to define objectivity closely but relied on their 'common sense'. In September 1945, Karl Polanyi, who had taught for the Oxford Delegacy for a while, expounded the need to guard against the infiltration of a specifically capitalist outlook under the guise of this 'common sense' objectivity. He pleaded for adult education:

> ..... free of the underlying assumptions of a capitalist society - such as the natural fitness of a condition in which man is supposed to act in everyday life on the principle of gain; the inevitability of the wage system; the acceptance of a community in which economic activities are removed from the orbit of public life and social morality; the erroneous view that radical change is either impossible or immoral; the evolutionist tenet which holds that all progress is merely a semblance unless it happens spontaneously, 'by itself', through

the imperceptible growth of the social
organism; that planning is the road to serfdom;
that popular rule is the natural enemy of
culture; and that he who even doubts the
unique authority of traditional education puts
himself outside the pale.(23)

But it was precisely these assumptions that
Raybould, the foremost exponent of an objective
attitude, did equate with 'the disinterested pursuit of truth'. He argued that adult education
should help people to understand and want 'unpleasant economic policies, like, for example, wage-freezing or labour redeployment', and that adult
education should secure 'the voluntary acceptance,
by those most affected, of the necessary measures'
to resolve these economic problems. The irony is
that at much the same time Raybould was questioning
whether the adult education movement could tolerate
those people who used it 'to secure support for
their own opinions and policies' and, more specifically, whether members of the Communist Party
should be allowed into the adult education movement.(24) But he could not see that his own Labourist attitude was as much devoid of objectivity in
this sense as any other attitude, and that in trying
to foster it he was attempting to secure support
for his own subjective opinions and policies.

Thompson pointed out that 'there is an element
of truth in this emphasis on "objectivity" and
"tolerance". The mistake lies in confusing desirable by-products of the educational process with
ends'. A tolerant attitude may very well be
appropriate, but only if 'the facts of society are
such as merit toleration'. It is quite possible
that they do not. A student who joins a class 'with
a burning sense of class injustice or an attitude
of compassion to his fellow workers' should be
educated to change his attitude of indignation or
compassion to one of tolerance only if he was mistaken. But he may well not have been mistaken:

> We must ..... bear in mind that, because we
> find a tolerant disposition or attitude on
> the whole desirable, there may be other dispositions or attitudes - compassionate, or
> militant, generous or spontaneous - equally
> desirable (and more appropriate) in certain
> circumstances.(25)

Thus this 'common sense' objectivity could lead

to a politically biased form of teaching, tolerant
and even encouraging of certain attitudes and
beliefs, but restrictive and inhibiting of others.
There is always a danger, especially if it is
publicly funded, that adult education will be required to reflect the majority or predominant orthodox views, as 'common sense' and objectively true.
And that 'national interest', whether determined by
the demands of wartime or economic crisis, will be
regarded as the correct and indeed the only tenable
attitude. In these circumstances tutors are expected to be 'judicious' in their treatment of controversial topics so that the correct or relevant
attitudes are fostered. Thus in the 1980s UAE is
expected to concentrate its provision increasingly
on such professional training or post-experience
up-dating courses that are regarded by government
as relevant to the national economic need, while
broad liberal studies in the humanities and social
sciences are virtually dismissed as irrelevant.
This nurturing of certain beliefs and attitudes
might be justifiable, even desirable - depending
on one's values - but it should never be confused
with an objective educational process.

OBJECTIVE PEDAGOGY

So far, an attempt has been made to demonstrate
that objectivity, defined as teaching the absolute
truth and nothing but the truth, does not exist,
and that equating objectivity with certain values
or attitudes, or regarding it as common sense, is
merely disguising one's own conscious ideological
preferences and unconscious prejudices as objectivity. It is not so much in the content of their
teaching, but in the method by which tutors teach
their students, that objectivity is to be found.
In this sense it is a fundamental part of the
liberal tradition, for it guards against education
becoming the Orwellian nightmare of 'manufactured
truth' and contradicts the 'logical conclusion' that
scepticism about absolute truth must lead down the
nihilistic slope to the tutor merely propagating his
beliefs, or teaching whatever will bring him power.
Lindsay made this point clear in an article in
The Highway in 1925:

> There are people who say that because no one is
> absolutely impartial it is silly to try to be
> impartial, and that we should therefore all be
> as avowedly partial as we can. That is like

saying that because none of us can be perfectly
truthful it is no use trying to tell the truth
at all ..... It is very hard both to feel
passionately and yet not allow our feelings to
pervert the impartiality of our judgement, but
the double lesson is what we have to learn,
if we are to serve our Cause truly. (26)

One characteristic of this objective teaching method is that it should endeavour to develop students' critical faculties:

to enable students to acquire a critical
attitude to all judgements about the objects
studied, including and especially their own
judgements; to distinguish as carefully as
possible between matters of fact and matters
of interpretation; to ensure that all basic
assumptions, both those held by the tutor
and those held by the students, are questioned;
to encourage students to distinguish between
significant questions, which can open up
fruitful lines of investigation, and trivial
questions, to accustom students to understand,
state and criticise theories and points of
view which they do not themselves accept and
so forth. (27)

A recent survey of WEA students' recollections of pre-1950 classes (28) revealed that the development of students' critical faculties was regarded as an important part of the educational experience. Several respondents stressed this point:

(The class) taught me to think clearly and
to use discrimination in arriving at conclusions.

..... for perhaps the first time, many of us
were induced to look at two sides of a
question and critical faculties were brought
into use.

The WEA made me realise the importance of
knowing or discovering the background of a
situation or problem before passing comment.

(It) helped me to develop a humane, liberal
and critical attitude. To seek to be fully
informed; think things through; resist
slogans and myths.

> The greatest advantage I gained from WEA
> classes ..... was (the knowledge) that there
> was no ready or simple answer to any question.
> Further, there should be no ready acceptance
> merely on authority in matters of opinion
> ..... I am always apprehensive of dogma.

The liberal tradition thus encourages a critical approach to authorities and fosters the capacity to distinguish between matters of fact and mere matters of opinion. It rejects any overtly persuasive or manipulative presentation by the tutor, who is expected to present both factual information and various views and interpretations as dispassionately as possible, and to make allowance for his or her own beliefs and take a sufficiently critical attitude to them. (However, paradoxically, the students' task of distinguishing facts from the tutor's opinions is rendered considerably more difficult in the typical adult education seminar situation where the tutor ceases to play the role of authoritarian or polemical teacher, and apparently becomes merely one member of the discussion group, while still retaining the real power to direct and manipulate the discussion).

At one time, concealment of a tutor's views and the adoption of a strictly neutral stance, in order to encourage students to make up their own minds, was advocated. But this approach came to be seen as rather naive and tutors now more often prefer to make their predilections and prejudices quite clear, and open to challenge, discussion and opposition by and from the students. Provided tutors are judicious in stating their position and at the same time attempt to state fairly, and even sympathetically, the alternative views, and also ensure that perspectives not held or shared by either tutor or students are also presented and examined with the maximum degree of sensitivity, then this approach is felt to be more honest than pretending to be a neutral presenter of 'the facts'. Although these high standards of objectivity are not always achieved, it is widely accepted in adult education that provided tutors aim to achieve them to the best of their ability, it is not always necessary, or possible, or even desirable, to appear uncommitted or impartial. This position was well summarised by Tawney:

> In reality ..... the way for an institution
> or movement to achieve impartiality is not to

> attempt to chase all the partialities out; for, being human, we can none of us be other than partial. It is to draw as many as possible of the partialities in, on two conditions. The first is that, if the spirit moves their votaries to propagate a creed, they should do so by the frank exchange of open argument, not by subterranean intrigue. The second is that they shall accord to the opinions of their neighbours, however nauseating or absurd, the same respectful hearing which they claim for their own.(29)

In adult education perhaps more than other forms of education, the liberal approach is essentially dialectical:

> Whether we believe we know the 'right answer' or not, we must strive for objectivity in presentation and for a genuine spirit of discussion in our teaching. If we are convinced we have the truth, and it is important for our students to know it, we should be content to let our case win consent from the students by its intrinsic strength.(30)

Liberal adult education means giving people access to the arguments and helping them to make up their own minds; it is a tentative, provisional and undogmatic approach; it is an openness of mind and readiness to listen attentively to what other people are saying; it is the avoidance of preaching any specific attitudes or beliefs; it is a desire to develop students' powers of independent judgement and a conviction that 'the process of teaching (should not be) confused with the process of winning souls for God, liberalism or the revolution'.(31)

If students emerge more radical or more liberal or more religious from a class, this should be because they have come to that conviction by a dialectical process, not because the course or the tutor aimed to radicalise or liberalise or convert them.

OBJECTIVITY AND SOCIAL PURPOSE

One of the tensions within the liberal tradition has been how to respect this objective approach to teaching and at the same time preserve and foster the social purpose of English adult education. As indicated in Chapter 1, one important strand of the English adult education movement adopted a strong sense of social purpose - to equip its students with the necessary knowledge to bring about such a fundamental change in society as could only be regarded by most of its proponents and opponents as socialist, although what hue or intensity of socialism was much debated. The question this posed was whether such a social purpose dynamic can be compatible with the liberal tenets of objectivity and political neutrality.

In the passage quoted earlier, Tawney made it clear that he did not consider it desirable or possible to chase away all partialities and be politically neutral, but this was not always the establishment view. For example, when, in 1925, the WEA wanted to take the adult education movement into a TUC scheme which frankly aimed to provide 'education for social and industrial emancipation', the Board of Education and local educational authorities opposed the move on the grounds that it contravened the Responsible Bodies' non-political status.(32)

One of the major criteria of success in the early tutorial classes provided by Manchester University was that the students should be detached or disentangled from their previous 'extreme' or passionately held views, 'especially in the case of those who take part in public affairs'.(33) In the turbulent, quasi-revolutionary atmosphere before World War I, this was politically very significant for it could help to create a quiescent and unsocialist leadership for the infant Labour Movement, socialised or persuaded into accepting the ideology of the liberal establishment and rejecting its preconceived notions of socialism. Thus political neutrality was frequently interpreted by the authorities as education which reinforced the status quo by undermining students' attachment to alternative ('alien') ideologies.

Even when the attachment to 'political neutrality' did not so obviously protect the status quo, there was a real danger that in the pursuit of objectivity students would fall victim to the damages of 'fence sitting', and consequent inaction, which were discussed in Chapter 2. A respondent to a survey of student opinion in the mid-1930s highlighted this predicament:

> The material given might have been good and sound, but it was not inspired or inspiring. In the discussions, the tutor never had any

definite points of view, and seemed to restrain those who wanted to go to the left or the right. The student rapidly gained the idea that no problem was capable of solution, that there was so much to be said on all sides of a problem that one should take no action at all. It was only fools who gave adherence to a party, or had plans of action for changing the <u>status quo</u>.(34)

In 1938, Richard Crossman, then Dean of New College and part-time tutor for the Oxford University Extramural Delegacy, warned of the danger of university dons undermining trade union activities by producing educated individualists; and disparaged the concept of 'academic standards' which paralysed students' capacity for action and rendered them politically innocuous.(35) This accusation of reducing the political effectiveness of good working class students was frequently made, and tutors were aware of the problem, but this did not solve it.

Another one-time Oxford staff tutor, Karl Polanyi, suggested that 'traditional' education, designed for the middle class, was not always suitable for the working class student:

> He may in the end have gained more knowledge of facts, and he may have learnt to appreciate all possible opinions, but he will at the same time have become incapable of standing by any conviction of his own. He has only acquired the semblance of an education. The results are disastrous.(36)

A similar warning against sterile neutrality rendering the whole educational system empty and meaningless was expressed by Hodges in his pamphlet on <u>Objectivity and Impartiality</u>:

> If the individual scholar is over-careful to give full expression to all legitimate views within his field, he may fail to give expression to his own view at all; he may even spend so long weighing considerations on one side or another that he never comes to the point of personal decision. There may have been many scholars who deliberately cultivated this conscientious indecision, in whom objectivity came to mean aloofness, and who had a perverse pride in being outside the conflict of doctrines.(37)

Such conscientious indecision could cause students to form 'the impression that there is just as much to be said on one side of a question ..... as on the other, and that the sensible thing to do is to reserve judgement, and take no action, on every issue'.(38) Even if it has some virtues, this incessant balancing of pros and cons induces weariness in the student, and will render some students incapable of making up their own minds. 'There is nothing easier than for an able tutor to pick holes in every opinion on a complex problem advanced by his students, and to leave them feeling that it is quite hopeless for them to come to a decision. Nothing easier; and nothing more mischievous'.(39) The tutor who interprets impartiality in this way does a serious disservice to his students.

This 'putting-both-points-of-view' approach protects the tutor, and the educational bodies, against criticism, but it neutralises the education they provide, so that it seems completely devoid of any opinion.

Of course, it suits the establishment to encourage this approach, which fosters an attitude of docility and obedience. But many adult educationalists have questioned its relevance to a movement which was conceived with a strong sense of social purpose. G D H Cole made his feelings very clear when he declared unequivocally in 1925:

> We have seen too many (WEA) branches wrecked by the well-meaning educationalist, who is so keen on fostering what he calls the 'student mind', that he has no desire, or no power, to attract the militant Trade Unionist who wants to turn his education to definite and practical purpose. Personally, I have seen too much of the 'student mind' to have any love for it, or to want it to dominate our movement. I want to serve the live-wired practical worker, who wants guidance in facing the practical problems of living.(40)

Similarly, Mary Stocks, when a Manchester tutor, recorded gratefully the absence in adult education classes 'of that impersonal objectivity which often characterises the study of economics in our two ancient universities'.(41)

In a statement on the future of adult education produced in 1944, the Association of Tutors in Adult Education warned its members against for ever sitting on the fence and giving the impression that a wise person is one who avoids taking a decision:

> We believe this is a vice and that the tutor in social subjects has the responsibility to be constructive in his teaching, that is, to be aware that in the social subjects we acquire information partly at least in order that our decisions may be wiser - not merely in order to discover reasons why we should never make decisions.(42)

Raybould, who was active in the ATAE (and may have had a hand in drafting the statement cited), certainly agreed that it was the tutor's business to be aware of the danger of sterile neutrality. Adult students, he believed, were not primarily interested in knowledge for its own sake, but for the sake of the guidance it can give to action. Therefore tutors should help their students to come to some conclusion, if only a provisional one. '<u>Some</u> solution' to the many complex social and other problems which concern students 'must be found, whether a final solution is possible or not', and such provisional conclusions 'may, if action is necessary, even serve as the basis for action'.(43)

This adult education for social purpose is 'perfectly compatible ..... with intellectual integrity in the tutor and the student', Raybould claimed,(44) and a wide cross-section of adult educationalists would agree with Hodgkin that 'the greatest teachers have been those who have believed passionately in certain human ends, and that those teachers who regard all ends as equally illusory and worthless have a depressing effect upon the minds of their students and are, to that extent, bad teachers'.(45)

In fact, the social purpose wing of the adult education movement has consistently sought praxis - action based on thinking - in place of sterile neutrality, in order to enable students to shape the world with the assistance of an adequate knowledge and historical understanding of their activity. This social purpose strand of the liberal tradition seeks to deepen students' understanding of class solidarity and to achieve social and industrial emancipation. Those subjects such as economics, history, politics and social theory, which enable the workers to defend themselves against the pressures of the capitalist economic system, are regarded as the most important ones to study.

This social purpose was the main dynamic of the adult education movement for many years, although the rhetoric became more muted and the commitment more tentative after World War II. In recent years the emphasis increasingly has been placed on social and political <u>responsibilities</u> and economic relevance, rather than emancipation or education for social change. A discussion of the nature and implications of this current climate forms a major theme of Chapter 4.

In 1950 Thompson regarded the spread of university 'ivory tower' attitudes as the reason for the erosion of social purpose in adult education:

> To attempt to carry over this fallacy from the university to the tutorial class ..... is to destroy the dynamic of adult education ..... Can it be that the atmosphere of our classes is too 'pure and clear'? Can it be that we ourselves have tried too little to learn about the history and conditions of life and work of those we desire to see in our classes? Can it be that as tutors we have given the impression that we welcome them into our classes only on our own terms, asking them to leave their suspicions outside the classroom door: instead of welcoming them in, suspicions and all, yes, even welcoming the suspicion as a rich ingredient of the class? Can it be that we are (without deliberate intent) allowing the University to stifle the WEA?(46)

More recently, pressures for education to reflect more closely the 'relevant' needs of the economy have further eroded this social purpose aspect of the liberal tradition. Workers' and community adult education, with its rationale still firmly based on praxis, is regarded generally as less acceptable or valuable than either a blander education for individual personal fulfilment, or the new modes of continuing education intended to retrain and refit people for their economic function in a post industrial society. But however much it has been eroded, this social purpose is a fundamental part of the liberal tradition of English UAE. And provided it is accompanied by a genuinely objective approach to teaching (as described earlier), it is a perfectly valid part of the tradition which scorns the notion that adult education is concerned only with aesthetic discrimination and personal development, and has nothing to do with social change.(47)

MARXISM AND THE LIBERAL TRADITION

Finally, there is the question whether a Marxist perspective to the social purpose dimension of adult education is compatible with its liberal tradition. It has been mentioned already that, at certain periods, cold war attitudes have led to doubts about whether communists should be permitted to teach UAE classes, and to the belief that Marxists per se are less capable of objective teaching than others. In a vigorous debate in the pages of The Highway during the early months of 1951, it was argued that Marxists were demonstrably less likely to be objective because Marxism denies both the possibility and desirability of objectivity. In the same issue, it was also claimed that Marxists, who have a 'passionate belief in dialectical materialism, the class struggle, and the theory of ideology', and who question the concept of objectivity, are necessarily less likely to be objective than those 'in the liberal tradition (who) admit the difficulty (which does not mean impossibility) of achieving objectivity ..... (and who) affirm that there is a moral obligation to seek it and realise it in practice as fully as possible'.(48)

In reply, Henry Collins pointed out that the antagonists had apparently confused objectivity and objectivism, which had caused them wrongly to assume that Marxism denies the existence of objective truth. (What it does contend is that man's approximation to this objective, absolute truth, is limited by his historical experience).(49)

The fallacy on which the anti-Marxist argument was based (and it was shared by many others in adult education) was that a belief in the possibility of achieving that state of grace of absolute objectivity referred to at the beginning of this chapter, somehow made the believer more likely to achieve that objective (or objectivity), than those who argued that it exists ideally, but humanity's approximation to it is limited by factors of subjectivity and psychology and by historical materialism. It is false logic. Faith in God does not prove his existence. Faith in objectivity does not make a tutor objective. It could as well be argued that a rational scepticism helps the tutor to guard against covert subjectivity. As Hodgkin said in closing The Highway debate, 'to say that one approves of objectivity ..... does mean that -

whatever problem one may be examining – one regards the use of reason as preferable to the use of magic and incantation'.(50) Hodgkin has more recently explained that part of the point of <u>The Highway</u> debate was to show that Marxism is a <u>valid and rational</u> theory just as much as liberalism or social democracy, and that Marxists are just as capable of objectivity, and objectivity means the same sort of thing to them as it does to anyone else.(51) The debate was part of the battle of ideas in the late 1940s in which Marxists argued that Marxist ideology should be freely discussed and dialectically examined in opposition to bourgeois ideology.

Some people have taken this position a stage further, and argued that tutors should show positive discrimination in favour of minority and unorthodox views, to counterbalance the prevailing orthodoxies or attitudes, and to correct the bias in teaching, which has already been noted, arising from tutors' inability to give a fair presentation of views with which they disagree or are not familiar. In English adult education for many years this meant that, in practice, even with the best will in the world and the greatest effort on the part of tutors to be objective, Marxist ideas received very little attention because most tutors were antagonistic or indifferent to Marxism, or ignorant of its theories, mirroring a more general ignorance in the wider society. As Professor Allaway once explained, 'many of the courses on economics and economic history paid no attention to Marxism at all ..... partly because the teaching staff ..... hadn't a clue about Marxism'.(52)

When this positive discrimination was openly adopted in the late 1940s, it was vehemently challenged – revealing a very real difference of opinion about how much prominence it was legitimate to allow Marxist ideas in adult education, particularly in trade union courses. Those tutors who looked forward to a radically alternative society believed that their political perspective should be presented within adult education's open forum (in the hope that such a perspective would thereby gain wider acceptance), without that contravening the liberal values of the adult education movement. Therefore, Marxist ideas should be introduced to the students as a credible alternative ideology, to confront the dominant bourgeois capitalist perspective. It was regarded as legitimate that adult education should help to combat the bourgeois tendencies in the Labour Movement, particularly through its trade union contacts, and that in the long term this should help to bring about a more socialist society. It was both legitimate and desirable in the battle of ideas that grew in intensity as political conflict sharpened after 1947, that adult education should help to deepen Marxist understanding in society generally, and among activists in the Labour Movement in particular. But the non-Marxists felt that Marxism should be presented only as a minority viewpoint, reflecting its current level of acceptability, and should not be allowed seriously to challenge the ideological orthodoxies of English society. When it appeared that this balance was threatened by positive discrimination, the WEA and university authorities reacted sharply to render extramural classes (particularly those provided by Oxford University) safely 'liberal' once more.(53)

This raises the whole question of what is meant by a liberal approach. It is a false definition of the liberal tradition to assume that adult education must reflect the balance of prevailing values in society. Indeed, it is arguable that where it challenges the prevailing viewpoint, which is overwhelmingly presented to the public in other areas of education, in the media, and in a thousand-and-one ways, adult education is most accurately fulfilling its liberal role. And those tutors who are sympathetic to alternative perspectives - Marxist or otherwise - are better equipped to ensure that the students receive an objective, total picture, rather than a one-sided, orthodox one, and to stretch their students' minds by challenging their existing prejudices, while other tutors are more likely merely to reinforce those prejudices in a far from liberal way.

Thus Marxism and the liberal tradition find common ground in adult education, always provided that tutors adopt a genuinely objective teaching approach. As G D H Cole said in 1925: 'Our tutors do not set out to convert students to their views, but to help them in forming their own. Those of us who are Marxians or Socialists hold this faith - that we are serving Marxism or Socialism better by this method than by turning education into propaganda'.(54)

More than half a century later, Hodgkin expressed the same philosophy:

> People have to find their own way to Marxism ..... A tutor can only be a mid-wife - to help

people to develop their own ideas. It is only ideas that you reach by your own processes of thinking, however much you may have been stimulated by others, that are any good to you.(55)

Or, as he said in The Highway debate in 1951: 'the essence of good teaching is that every student should be allowed to work his own way to his own conclusions'.(56) This might be taken as the essence of the liberal tradition in English UAE, encompassing, as it does, the notions of objectivity, social purpose and ideological commitment.

NOTES

1. Cited in Norman A. Jepson, The Beginnings of English University Adult Education, 1973, p. 144.
2. Ibid.
3. Central Joint Advisory Committee on Tutorial Classes, First Annual Report, 1910, p. 13.
4. J.A.Hobson, Free Thought in the Social Sciences, 1925, p. 271.
5. Harold A.Hodges, Objectivity and impartiality, 1946, pp. 12-15.
6. Or, in the words of E.H.Carr: 'It used to be said that facts speak for themselves. This is, of course, untrue. The facts speak only when the historian calls on them. It is he who decides to which facts to give the floor, and in what order or context'. E.H.Carr, What Is History?, 1961; paper back edition, 1964, p. 11.
7. Hodges, op. cit., p. 17.
8. S.G.Raybould, paper (written for a departmental meeting in 1949) entitled, Objectivity and Toleration. Raybould was Head of the Department of Adult Education and Extramural Studies at Leeds University from its formation in 1946 until his retirement in 1969.
9. E.P.Thompson, Against University Standards, Adult Education Papers vol 1, no 4, University of Leeds, Department of Extramural Studies, 1950, p. 27. Thompson was a member of the Leeds Department from 1948 to 1965 during which time he wrote William Morris, Romantic to Revolutionary and The Making of the English Working Class.
10. Thomas Hodgkin, Objectivity, Ideologies and the Present Political Situation, The Highway, vol 42, 1950-51, p. 80. Hodgkin was Secretary of the Oxford Extramural Delegacy from 1945 until his resignation in 1952.

11. Leeds University Adult Education Department seminar papers on the philosophy of Adult Education (1974-6).
12. Hodges, op. cit., p. 19.
13. G.Clark, introduction to The New Cambridge Modern History, vol. 1, 1957, p. xxv.
14. George Orwell, 'Looking Back on the Spanish Civil War', written in 1942-3, first published in England Your England, 1953, reprinted with Homage to Catalonia (1966), pp. 225-47, and in the Collected Essays, Journalism and Letters of George Orwell, ed. by Sonia Orwell and Ian Angus, vol 2. 1968, paper back edition, 1970, pp. 286-306.
15. Orwell, Looking Back on the Spanish Civil War, 1966, p. 236.
16. Ibid, pp. 235-6.
17. Ministry of Reconstruction Adult Education Committee, Final Report, 1919, p. 118.
18. PRO ED 24/1915, Lindsay to Lord Eustace Percy (nd, August 1925). Lindsay was Master of Balliol College, Oxford, and for many years one of the leading figures in Oxford and English adult education.
19. PRO ED 80/23, Board of Education Minute paper on Adult Education Controversial Topics, May 1940.
20. Ibid.
21. Thompson, Against University Standards, loc. cit. p. 17. The following section on the confusing of a particular labourist attitude with objective truth was first published in Roger Fieldhouse, The Ideology of English Adult Education Teaching 1925-50, Studies in Adult Education, vol 15, 1983, pp. 11-23 (pp. 12-13).
22. Ibid, pp. 23-5.
23. Karl Polanyi, What Kind of Adult Education, Leeds Weekly Citizen, 21 September, 1945.
24. Papers written by Raybould, 1949-50, entitled Adult Education and Democracy: Objectivity and Toleration;and Academic Freedom and Propaganda, in the archives of the Leeds University Department of Adult and Continuing Education, University of Leeds; S.G.Raybould, Objectivity, Ideologies and the Present Political situation, The Highway, vol 42, 1950-51, pp. 100-2.
25. Thompson, Against University Standards, loc. cit., pp. 25-7.
26. ADL, Where We Stand, The Highway, Vol. 17 1925, p. 51.
27. Hodgkin, loc. cit., p. 79.
28. Roger Fieldhouse, The Ideology of English

Responsible Body Adult Education 1925-50, unpublished Ph.D Thesis, University of Leeds, 1984, Appendix.
29. The WEA and Adult Education, published in (ed.) Rita Hinden, Tawney, The Radical Tradition, 1969, p. 90.
30. Raybould, Objectivity and Toleration, loc. cit.
31. Hodgkin, loc. cit., p. 80.
32. See Roger Fieldhouse, Voluntaryism and the State in Adult Education: the WEA and the 1925 TUC Education Scheme, History of Education vol. 10, no. 1, 1981, pp. 45-63.
33. Manchester University tutorial class reports, 1911/12, 1913/14 and 1914/15.
34. Quoted in W E Williams and A E Heath, Learn and Live, 1936, p. 206.
35. R.H.S.Crossman, The Place of the Tutor in the WEA, The Highway, vol. 30 (1938), pp. 113-4; PRO ED 80/22, Report of Annual Conference of the British Institute of Adult Education, 16-19 September, 1938.
36. Polanyi, loc. cit.
37. Hodges, op. cit., p. 11.
38. Raybould, The Approach to WEA Teaching, a paper prepared in February 1947.
39. Ibid.
40. G.D.H.Cole, The Task Ahead, WEA (Yorkshire District) Yorkshire Bulletin no. 20, 1925, p. 3.
41. Manchester University tutorial class reports, Northwich tutorial class, 1925-6.
42. ATAE, The Future of Adult Education, 1944, pp. 3-6.
43. Raybould, The Approach to WEA Teaching, and Objectivity and Toleration.
44. Ibid. (The Approach to WEA Teaching).
45. Hodgkin, loc. cit., p. 80.
46. Thompson, Against University Standards, pp. 25 and 36.
47. For the contrary view, see R W K Paterson, Social Change as an Educational Aim, Adult Education 45, 1973, pp. 353-9; and Values, Education and the Adult, 1979, passim.
48. C.A.Smith and Roy Shaw, Objectivity, Ideologies and the Present Political Situation, The Highway, vol. 42, 1950-51, pp. 105-6.
49. Henry Collins, ibid., p. 134.
50. Hodgkin, loc. cit., p. 154.
51. Thomas Hodgkin, interview with Roger Fieldhouse, 16-17 November, 1979.
52. A.J.Allaway, interview with Roger

Fieldhouse, 19 December, 1979. For detailed examination of this topic, see Fieldhouse, The Ideology of English Adult Education Teaching, loc. cit., passim.

53. For details of this struggle, see Fieldhouse, The Ideology of English Responsible Body Adult Education, loc. cit., Chapters 6 and 7; and Roger Fieldhouse, <u>Adult Education and the Cold War</u>, Leeds Studies in Adult and Continuing Eduction, forthcoming 1985.

54. G.D.H.Cole, The WEA and the Future, <u>The Highway</u>, vol. 17, 1925, p. 101.

55. Hodgkin, interview.

56. Hodgkin, loc. cit., p. 80.

Chapter Four

THE IDEOLOGICAL DETERMINANTS OF UNIVERSITY ADULT EDUCATION IN ENGLAND

Two factors above all others stand out in the history of general university development in Britain in the twentieth century: the rapid growth in the size and importance of the university sector; and the ever closer relationship between the state and universities on a number of levels. Both these trends have been considerably more prominent in the post 1945 period, but, equally, both have their roots in the earlier years of this century. A major contextual aspect of the development of the structures, attitudes and priorities of UAE has lain within the wider progress of its parent institutions. The first part of this chapter is thus devoted to a brief discussion of the ideology and structure of British universities in general in the twentieth century, with a special focus on the contemporary picture; and the second, and more detailed, section of the chapter concentrates upon the specific nature of UAE, with particular reference to contemporary developments.

THE IDEOLOGY AND STRUCTURE OF THE UNIVERSITIES

The orthodox view of the universities' role in society holds centrally to a pluralist conception of that wider society. In the 'classic' statement of this perspective Berdahl[1] argues that, whilst there is a necessity for social institutions to operate freely in a democratic pluralist society, there is also a paramount need for private associations to operate in such a way that they serve national needs. The growth in the importance and power of the state, arguably an inherent consequence of the development of advanced industrial societies,[2] was increased by the two World Wars. '..... Universities, like all other vital national assets, were mobilized on behalf of the War efforts in 1914, and even more thoroughly in 1939 ..... it is axiomatic in the nuclear age that the value of a university physics department can often surpass that of an aircraft carrier'.[3] However, such close alliance between state and university, which found its first formal expression in the formation of the University Grants Council (UGC) in 1919, is held not to be detrimental to the autonomy of universities. Although protagonists of this view admit that, by 1945, 'the "pluralist state" ..... has become much less "plural"',[4] it is argued that because of the tolerance, flexibility and fundamentally consensual nature of British society, university autonomy and the 'national interest' can and do co-exist with little friction. Thus 'the universities should form their educational policies with sensitivity for national needs and ..... after consultation with the appropriate governmental officers'. Should there be disagreements, 'the universities' judgement should prevail, with the understanding that they have the responsibility of demonstrating the wisdom of their decisions within a reasonable time .....'[5]

In the considerably harsher climate of the 1980s, such views may appear somewhat over sanguine. This is a specific point, to be returned to later. There is, however, a more fundamental long-term tension between Berdahl's formulation and historical reality, which the crisis of the universities in the 1980s has served to make explicit. This resides in the perceived needs of the state for an increasing emphasis upon science (especially <u>applied</u> science) and technology within the university sector, and the insistence of the universities, perhaps a rather more <u>qualified</u> insistence in the 1980s than previously, that their functions must remain the furtherance and dissemination of knowledge for its own sake. The universities have thus been generally reluctant to expand areas of immediate practical concern at the expense of those subjects whose 'relevance' was not apparent. In part, of course, this has resulted in pressure from powerful interests in society to move resources in universities away from arts and social sciences and towards the broadly scientific and technological subjects.

These are questions of central importance in any discussion of the universities' contemporary situation, and thus worth exploring in more detail. What, first of all, constitutes the traditional, orthodox university conception of its own role? For Minogue, universities must be seen as essentially and fundamentally non-utilitarian:

> Academic inquiry is a manner of seeking to understand anything at all, a manner distinguished no doubt by its motives and preoccupations, but distinguished above all by a quite different logic from that of practice. This means that there is a consistent difference in the <u>kind</u> of meaning that is found in academic discourse, by contrast with that found in the world at large. To ignore this difference, and to treat universities simply as institutions which provide educational services for society is like treating a Ming vase as a cut glass flower bowl: plausible, but crass.(6)

This is the contention underlying formulations such as Tress's: that the university's function is 'to acquire, to possess and to transmit scholarship'.(7) As Tress goes on to note, these are explicitly <u>elitist</u> conceptions: 'to speak of a repository of scholarship is to suggest something walled-up and safe, almost monastic, and this is deliberate'.(8) Indeed, linked though it is, and very strongly, to the defence of a pluralist, democratic society, this stance necessarily advocates an <u>elitist</u> rather than an <u>egalitarian</u> conception of democracy. As another leading exponent of the traditional view has put it, university graduates 'should not simply dissolve and disappear in the democratic melting pot: they ought to lead in every community ..... as a result of gravitation to the top by minds and characters that belong there'.(9) Thus the traditional view sees universities as essentially centres of scholarship,(10) and centres of intellectual excellence, with an explicitly elite role in society.(11)

This long established orthodoxy, however, is under increasing attack, as the demands of the state for utilitarian relevance become ever more insistent (and as, since the 1970s, financial constraints become ever tighter). For defenders of the libertarian view of the university, both from the Left and the Right, the departure from the liberal ideal is a cause of great concern. From the Right, a part of the contemporary problem stems from the rapid expansion of the universities in the 1960s. This has resulted in a deterioration, not so much in the quality of university students, as of <u>staff</u>. This is held to relate predominantly to two factors: the recruitment of university staff 'from those sectors less imbued with the culture of the intellect'; and, second, the declining status and prestige of academics that has taken place as a result of university expansion: 'to be an elite, with its burdens and rewards, a profession should not be too numerous'.(12)

Even more serious than this dilution of the elite, however, has been, it is argued, the increasing bureaucratisation of university life. There are two particular aspects of this process, both, on this argument, equally deleterious. There is, first, the trend towards bureaucratisation within the universities themselves. As Andreski has put it:

> ...... you can make sure that people stay in their rooms, fill in the forms and write reports, but you cannot compel them to think creatively. Only a high level of collective conscience and unmercenary and undiplomatic ruthlessness in debating intellectual issues can create a climate which is conducive to advancement of knowledge ..... (13)

And second, there is the encroachment to the verge, if not over it, of state control of the universities. 'Pluralism', wrote MacRae in 1975, 'in my sense is at risk. More and more, the UGC seems not the agent of the universities dealing with the State but, rather, the agent of the State vis-à-vis the Universities'.(14) Subsequent developments, discussed below, would seem certainly to bear out such a statement.

From the Right, therefore, university autonomy is now seen as under grave threat from the state and from wider utilitarian interests (not always, incidentally, co-terminous sources of pressure). From the Left, of course, the universities have always been regarded as bastions of privilege, and a mainstay of an elitist and hierarchical (and thus inegalitarian and unsocialist) social system. Moreover, as purveyors of the hegemonic culture, their wider socialising role has been held to be of primary importance in the maintenance of the capitalist system.(15) Nevertheless, the existence of the liberal tradition of university autonomy, or quasi-autonomy, and of the (relatively) free pursuit of knowledge, with all its concomitants (the considerable freedom to plan curricula, and priorities, in both research and teaching, etc) has been regarded as of key importance in allowing at least an approximation towards a genuinely free analysis and discussion of the whole range of knowledge. To the extent that this has been eroded by the advance of the complementary pressures of state influence and the demand for 'relevant' (and, increasingly, directly <u>vocational</u>) priorities for universities, the view from the Left has been sharply critical of trends in the 1980s. These are not points to be pursued in any great depth here as they will be considered in more detail in the context of the specific developments in UAE. However, it must be noted that here, if not elsewhere, the 'libertarians' of Right and Left are united in opposition to the present dominant trends in universities.

It was remarked earlier that one of the most prominent aspects of state (and other societal) pressure upon universities was the attempt to shift their emphases more towards scientific and technological priorities. There can be no doubt of the determination of the state (in this case, principally in the form of government and civil service) in the latter years of the twentieth century to continue 'the drive towards efficiency and utilitarianism',(16) and of the determination of Ministers of Education to encourage a shift of emphasis in universities towards the scientific and technological subjects.

Such views are by no means confined to governmental and related circles. Voices in both industry and in universities themselves have called for a reorientation of university priorities and activities along similar lines. Two educationalists (Professors Roderick and Stephens) have argued, for example, that from the nineteenth century onwards Britain has persistently clung to an outmoded, pre industrial set of educational priorities, dominated by Oxford and Cambridge and their attachment to the classical education model.(17) Despite the rhetorical support given to technological education in the 1960s (by Harold Wilson amongst others), Britain remained one of the lowest per capita investors in higher education in the industrialised world, and, in the late 1960s, the proportion of students in 'arts plus social studies ..... (at) 42.2% was just about the same as it ever had been since before the war'.(18)

Other critics have been somewhat harsher in their condemnation of what is seen as the obscurantism of the universities' attitudes. David Weir, for example, argues that:

> ...... it is the arts based culture which
> dominates ..... Since the late nineteenth
> century other advanced industrial societies
> ..... have developed educational systems which
> attach more priority to science than to the
> arts..... Engineering is neither arts nor
> science, but a third culture, that of technik
> (and these technologies) are even further down
> in the power structure of British society.(19)

And, such critics would argue, their analyses of the innate educational conservatism of the university sector were confirmed by the UGC 'package' of cuts imposed on the universities in 1981, and the subsequent continuing restrictions imposed upon universities. (The implications of the UGC cuts are discussed in more detail below).

Such, then, are the main outlines of the <u>perceptions</u> of different groups about the functions, priorities and purposes of universities in contemporary Britain. The orthodox, liberal but elitist conception of the university is under attack. At one level this attack comes from the state and from certain powerful industrial and economic interests, which want to make its provision and research more 'relevant' and utilitarian, and who see this being achieved at least in part by a shift of emphasis way from the arts and social science areas, and towards science and technology. From the other side, so to speak, are those who, equally concerned about the threat to university freedom and autonomy, and equally concerned to resist pressures towards wholly utilitarian models of university research and provision, are nevertheless extremely critical of the elitist concepts and structures which are rooted in the traditional view of the university. These critics argue that the structure and the processes of universities, as well as their dominant 'culture', need fundamental change, in order for them genuinely to be democratised. Richard Hoggart, for example, argues that:

> the agenda to the end of the century is clear.
> It is for higher education institutions to
> modify their over-rigid attention to 18 year
> olds, to be more open to their communities by
> day and night, to help establish out in their
> wider territories multi-level education centres
> for adults, to open themselves more to part-
> timers, to make better provision of all kinds
> for the educationally deprived .....(20)

How these various perceptions of universities have influenced UAE development is the subject of the second section of this chapter. Before embarking upon that discussion, however, attention must be paid to the historical development of universities since 1945, in order to compare the ideological perceptions already outlined, with the actual historical record.

The modern university system in Britain is very much a twentieth century, and, more specifically, a post 1945, creation. By the end of the nineteenth century there were only six fully-fledged universities in Britain,(21) and only six more were created in the years before World War I,(22) with one further, Reading, coming into being in the inter war period. The real expansion of the university sector has taken place since 1945. In the decade following 1945, Nottingham, Southampton, Hull, Exeter and Leicester all received university charters, followed in the late 1950s by Sussex, the first of the 'new universities'. Keele was created in 1962, and a further six new universities were also founded during the early years of the decade: East Anglia, York, Essex, Kent, Warwick and Lancaster.(23) With the addition of the 'technological universities' (formerly Colleges of Advanced Technology, CATs), and the Open University, there were, by the 1970s, forty-two universities in Britain, (including the five federal units of the University of Wales, and the eight Scottish Universities).(24)

This expansion was matched, of course, by marked increases in the numbers of students attending universities. In 1938/9 there were 50,246; by 1956/7 this had risen to 89,866; by 1958/9, 100,204; by 1964/5, 138,711; by 1970/1, 227,956; and, by 1980/81, 297,200.(25)

Nevertheless, the influence of the Oxbridge model and its educational assumptions, had remained very strong.(26) In general terms, this influence has been profoundly important in perpetuating a generally elitist model of university education, with an emphasis upon the cultural, rather than the vocational, aspects of tertiary educational experience, provided for a small minority of predominantly male, non-working class, late adolescents.(27)

Two related aspects of this general influence are particularly important in the context of this discussion. There is, first, 'the persistence of the British concept of the university as a community with moral education as its chief task'.(28) The result of this has been, amongst other things, the norm of relatively small departments, a high level of student residence, and high staff/student ratios (approximately 1:8). All this is under considerable threat in the 1980s, of course, as is discussed below, but such characteristics have been prominent features of university structure and practice in Britain over many years. The second aspect is the low status accorded to any form of vocational or technological education: 'the main path to parity of esteem with Oxbridge did not lead to emphasis on professional instruction; although higher-level technology held its place within the universities, their preeminent mission remained the education of gentlemen'.(29)

At the same time, there can be no doubt that the main motivation on the part of the government for encouraging (and very largely financing) the expansion of universities, in the post-war period has been the perceived need to increase rapidly and dramatically the numbers of scientists and technologists qualified at university level.(30) Through the 1950s the pressure continued for further expansion in science and technology (the virtual doubling in size of Imperial College, following pressure from Lords Cherwell and Woolton, for example(31)). However, with creation of the new universities, the UGC reiterated a basically traditional policy for development:

> the initial academic thrust ..... should be in the fields of arts, social studies and pure science. Existing institutions could provide doctors, dentists, agriculturalists and other strictly vocational student places. Extensive developments in the colleges of advanced technology as well as those in engineering departments of existing universities led the UGC to have reservations about the introduction of technology in the new institutions.(32)

There was thus some tension here between government priorities and emphases, and those of the universities, as expressed, in this period, by the UGC. It is important to note here the changing role of the UGC. At the outset, that is from the time of its creation in 1919 until World War II, the UGC's role was 'to stimulate the universities to plan their own development more comprehensively than they would otherwise have done'.(33) There was a significant increase in the UGC's power after the war: henceforth the UGC was asked to assist in 'the preparation and execution of such plans for the development of the universities as may from time to time be required in order to ensure that they are fully adequate to national needs'.(34) From this time onwards the UGC became a 'quango', (i.e. quasi national governmental organization) representing at least as much the interests of <u>government</u> as it did the interests of the universities. Nor should this be a matter for surprise. In common with the general and marked trend towards collectivism throughout advanced industrial society, the state's involvement in tertiary education increased rapidly through the twentieth century. On the financial level alone, the evidence speaks for itself. In 1920, the state's contribution to universities' finances was approximately one-third of the total; by 1945/6 this had risen to one-half; and by 1967 to three-quarters.(35) By the time of the 'university cuts' in 1981/82, the UGC had become predominantly the vehicle for executing the detail of governmental policy, rather than acting as the collective representation of universities' interests. Nevertheless, even here, it is significant to note that the UGC/government 'axe' fell, to a great extent, upon precisely those institutions which concentrated upon science and technology (e.g. Salford, Aston, Bradford, etc), leaving relatively unscathed the larger, older and more 'prestigious' universities.

Thus, despite its increasing control over the university sector, in part through the UGC, the government was not able to re-shape the universities, to the degree it would have liked, towards vocationally and technologically oriented programmes of study. Undoubtedly, this was a major factor in the creation of the binary system from 1965, bringing into being thirty polytechnics, and thus attempting to by-pass, to some extent, the problem of the universities' intransigent traditionalism. Altogether, argues Brian MacArthur, the result has been that the DES, 'has deliberately shrunk (the universities) position within the system'(36) while 'consolidating and substantially strengthening the non-university sector .....'(37) It should be noted, too, that there was a more straightforwardly political motivation behind the creation of the binary system: unlike the universities' position of at least quasi-autonomy, the polytechnics were under a much greater degree of centralised, and predominantly DES, control.

Finally, in this section of the chapter, what has been the impact of the famous 'Robbins Report' of 1963, and how have the principles and practices of universities changed in the light of subsequent developments? The first, and perhaps the most important, point is that the much vaunted 'Robbins principle' - that courses of higher education should be available 'for all those who are qualified by ability and attainment to pursue them and who wish to do so'(38) - which is often held to have been the catalyst of the subsequent rapid expansion of universities, was, in reality, the public announcement of an already agreed governmental policy.(39) According to Gosden, 'in retrospect the main significance of the Robbins Report appears above all to have been the effect it had in securing for higher education a much more prominent position in the public and political consciousness'.(40) Certainly, most of its more radical proposals were either shelved or rejected.(41) The net effect of their total and successful <u>implementation</u> would have been twofold: to extend the size, power and autonomy of the university sector very considerably; and to introduce a decisive shift towards science and technology within the university sector.(42) In the event, 'the most rapid growth was not in science and technology but in social studies and to a lesser extent the humanities'.(43)

The latter effect, plus the prominent radicalism amongst the newly important social science faculties in the late 1960s and 1970s, which, it has been claimed, 'seemed to begin to compromise the apolitical values (sic) of the academic profession',(44) were important contributory factors in the creation of the binary policy, and the ultimate diminution in the strategic importance of the universities in the government's eyes. Thus, the by no means coincidental combination of the rise of the new, anti-intellectual, anti-education Conservatism of Mrs. Thatcher and her cohorts, and the onset of prolonged and profound economic recession, was a lethal context in which universities had to operate from the late 1970s onwards.

The resulting UGC 'cuts' package of 1981/82 was only the most dramatic of the effects. There has been persistent government pressure for more intensive use of university teaching resources (e.g. the resurrection of the two year degree idea, the proposals for a far less generous staff/student ratio, etc.), and a far more insistent and explicitly political rationale for a shift away from social sciences (held, axiomatically, to be not only 'irrelevant', but inherently socialist, and subversive, and <u>un</u>scientific), and towards vocational and technological concentrations.

The resultant squeeze on the universities, mediated via the UGC, has led in the 1980s to a number of tendencies, as yet unresolved. There has been an increasing emphasis upon vocational, professional and scientific/technological courses, and a corresponding downgrading of the importance of social sciences (and to some extent the humanities). The overall elitist structure and attitudes of universities have not been altered, however: indeed, they can be argued to have increased in some respects. Thus one effect of the UGC's actions has been to create 'the first dim outline of a super-league of research universities, ten or twelve in number .....',(45) leaving the remainder as second or third tier institutions whose role will be to concentrate more upon the teaching of undergraduates. Finally, of course, there has been a marked decrease in university autonomy, and, more specifically, in academic freedom, as a result of the increasing government pressure. This has ranged from quite explicit <u>political</u> or ideological pressure (e.g. the downgrading of social science, the attack upon peace studies, etc.), to the equally serious administrative curtailments of academic freedom: the movement towards abolition of the tenure system for newly appointed staff, and the increasing practice of short, fixed term academic staff contracts.

The future of the university system is wholly uncertain: what is clear, however, is that the traditional priorities and structures of the universities are under greater attack now than at any time since their foundation in their modern, post war, form.

UNIVERSITY ADULT EDUCATION IN THE MODERN CONTEXT

UAE has developed within this overall university context, and has been profoundly influenced in terms of both its structure and its provision by the changing face of the wider university system. Nevertheless, one of the central characteristics of UAE - and indeed one of the most fruitful and fascinating, as well as problematic - has been the border territory between the university and the wider society which it has occupied. UAE has thus responded both to the 'culture' of its parent institutions, and to the very diverse and rapidly changing demands of the wider society. This section of the chapter attempts to analyse the ways in which UAE has in practice responded to, and sometimes reconciled, these competing demands.

The early years of UAE development, and the themes underlying that development, were discussed earlier.[46] The major concern of this chapter is with the development of UAE since 1945, and, specifically, with the contemporary profile of UAE. By the 1930s the embryo of the future debate over the proper role of UAE was already apparent: there was a realisation both that there was now a 'better educated populace who, frequently, did not feel any urge to reform society', and that 'vocational courses held great potential for the development of Extension work'.[47] UAE departments (or extra-mural departments as they were generally known at this period), of course varied widely in their perspectives and priorities, but all had in common their desire to broaden out from the tutorial class relationship with the WEA. In this they received the support of powerful voices within the universities. In 1945, for example, a conference of the vice chancellors of the universities of Oxford, Cambridge and London issued a statement proposing a new role for UAE:

> The Universities are convinced that they should ..... experiment in new methods, and that they should no longer be confined to certain types of course specified in Regulations. The distinguishing feature of University adult education should be its higher quality and this can be achieved by less formal methods ..... (UAE should meet the) special needs of those engaged in the professions or in industry.[48]

With the return of the Labour government in 1945, many of whose members and parliamentary supporters had direct experience of university or WEA adult education, and with the commitment to overall educational expansion as a result of the 'Butler Act' of 1944, it is no surprise that the decade following World War II saw not only a quantitative increase of significance in UAE departments and their provision, but also a qualitative change. In the post war period UAE departments 'came of age' and developed an identity of their own. It is to an analysis of this identity that attention is now turned.

Most of the major trends in UAE have been continuously present since the 1940s and 1950s. Of course, the context has changed, and differing priorities have been adopted at different times. And, equally obviously, individual universities and departments have varied considerably in their practices. (See, for example, Professor Raybould's emphasis upon the sustained three year course at Leeds, compared to Birmingham's concentration upon short courses). Nevertheless, general trends can be discerned.

One of the most important and most pervasive has been the decline of the sustained course and the increasing proportion of UAE provision in the form of short courses. Raybould, in 1951, presented clearly the case for the sustained course:

> Three years of part-time study under a university teacher affords time for the attainment of a good standard of work in a limited field, even by students whose initial equipment is very limited; provided that the teaching is systematic and that the work in class is backed up by regular and directed work at home by the students ..... Three year classes do not attain a university standard merely because they last three years, duration is not a guarantee but only a condition of good quality.(49)

He deplored the rapid increase in short courses not requiring written work, which had occurred since the immediately pre-war period.(50)

Since then this trend has accelerated. Between 1945/6 and 1961/2, the number of three year courses rose by 17%, compared with an increase of 156% in university one year courses and 254% in shorter university courses. 'By the 1960s ..... some three-fifths of university adult education consisted of (courses) lasting less than one year'.(51) (If sessional and tutorial classes are for statistical purposes combined, then the total for 1962/63 just outnumbers that for shorter courses, i.e. 2,708 as against 2,265 for courses of between three and nineteen meetings(52)). This trend continued and accelerated through the 1960s and 1970s. Thus, by 1968/9, the figures for the two categories given above were, respectively, 3,659 and 3,238 - with the number of really short courses, three to nine meetings, having increased by 160%. By 1975/6, this trend had become far more marked: for the first time sessional and tutorial classes combined formed less than half the total (47.1%)(53), whereas the number of tutorial classes alone formed a very small minority of the total provision.

Nor does this shift in the balance of provision show much sign of being halted. In 1982/83, the latest year for which figures are available, the Universities Council for Adult and Continuing Education (UCACE) reported that the number of three year courses had fallen from 724 in 1976/7 to 596 in 1982/83 (although this latter figure was in fact a marginal increase on the preceding three years). The general picture, then, is one of 'decreases in the total of three-year courses over the last six years'.(54)

There are several reasons underlying this decline. At the most general level, two contextual, societal developments in particular stand out. Through the 1950s and 1960s there was, as a result of the modest but continuous growth of material prosperity and the general overall stability, international as well as national, a quiescent and seemingly apolitical mood. Keynesianism appeared to have solved the economic problems of capitalism, the nuclear deterrent appeared to have stabilised, at the very least, the potential conflict between the Super Powers, and the consensual politics of 'Bulskellism', incorporating a mixed economy and a commitment to the Welfare State, appeared to have defused both class and political conflict.(55) One result of all this was to produce a society far less concerned with social, economic and political concerns. The thirteen years of Conservative government from 1951 to 1964 contrasted sharply with the immediate post-war period, when, for the first time, a majority Labour government began seriously to implement socialist, or social democratic,(56) reforms, and a generally radical, optimistic and 'political' mood predominated.

These macrocosmic events and attitudes had their effect within the microcosm of UAE, as they did elsewhere. In general terms, since the early 1950s, there has been a decline in the social purpose orientation of UAE and, as has been noted earlier, a broadening out of the universities' conception of their appropriate role(s) in adult education provision. Once it had been accepted that at least a proportion of UAE provision should be for the professional and post-experience sectors of the population, then the insistence upon the need for sustained courses in order to enable those who had not had the benefit of tertiary education to reach the appropriate 'university standard', became otiose. Even more important, once the social purpose orientation had become of less importance, and thus serious social studies courses had lost their centrality in UAE provision, it became easier for departments to cater for the popular market for less demanding, more leisure orientated, and shorter courses. This trend has been reinforced, of course, by the 'temptation' of higher enrolment numbers, larger programmes, and hence greater prominence (and potential access to a greater share of university resources), which shorter course provision can be argued to have provided.

Closely linked to this has been the trend towards 'instant knowledge' which has been so characteristic of Western post-war society, and has found particular expression through the mass media. One of the many deleterious aspects of the advent of mass television coverage of everything from cricket to Einsteinian physics, has been the marked disincentive to serious study - the easy assumption that the most complex and sophisticated of subjects can be mastered by a passive viewing of a few T.V. programmes (or the newspaper equivalent of the colour supplement pull-out). This is to say nothing of the enormous ideological power of the media(57), but merely to concentrate upon its debilitating intellectual and educational effects, in this respect at least.

UAE departments have thus been pressurised into conforming to a change, for the worse, in cultural standards, by offering easier options in the form of the short course. And of course both the universities and UAE departments have been influenced to an extent by these developments, in terms of their own priorities and perceptions of the proper provision.

This is by no means the end of the matter, however. To the extent that the sustained course, usually the tutorial class, has always been seen as the primary vehicle by which educationally disadvantaged, working class adults can develop the level of factual, disciplinary and conceptual knowledge appropriate to a university, its decline has heralded a diminished interest in the task of working class adult eduction.

It should hardly be necessary to add that this cannot be explained away by nationally rising

educational standards: it remains the case that the
majority of the population has no experience of
education beyond minimum school leaving age. And
the total number of adults involved in further,
higher or adult education, at any one time, has
recently been calculated at approximately 16% of the
total adult population of England and Wales.(58)
Much more important than even this evidence of
minority involvement in any form of post secondary
education, is the alienation from 'education' as
it is perceived by the vast majority of working
class people. It is a commonplace of secondary
education that, for the majority of school leavers,
the latter years at least of education at school
are alienating experiences, and that the much vaunted liberal ethos of the British educational system
has left little impression. There is no need to
labour the point: it is, simply, that for the majority of the population, the supposed boom in
secondary and tertiary education has not, in fact,
happened. Moreover, the overwhelming majority of
the 16% already mentioned is engaged neither in
university education nor in any form of liberal
adult education. In fact, the university has moved
away from the concentration upon the working class
and the educationally disadvantaged in its adult
education provision (as indeed has the WEA).(59)

Apart from the relatively specialist provision
for trade unions, and the recent attempts in the
field of community adult education, both of which
are discussed in some detail in Chapter 5, the UAE
departments have attracted to their courses the
better educated,(60) and have thus been able to
argue that, because of the changing nature of the
student population, there is 'a great desire to
study in depth within specialised shorter courses,
and a strong interest in research activities'.(61)
This is a vicious circle indeed, and it is impossible to disentangle cause and effect. The salient
point, however, is that the progressive decline of
the structure which put the tutorial class at the
centre of the universities' provision has combined
with the changing nature of the universities'
students to produce a programme and an orientation
whose central concerns do not focus on working class
adult education.

A related pattern of development in terms of
subject coverage in UAE can be detected in the
post 1960 period. Just as shorter courses have come
to predominate, and better educated students to
form a larger proportion of UAE's clientele, so

subject concentration has moved away from those areas which bear directly upon socio-economic analysis and political change: those subjects which, in other words, had been seen as the key disciplines providing the working class with the necessary conceptual and ideological equipment to achieve fundamental social change.

Comparing 1975/76 with 1968/9 Dyson came to the general conclusion that 'the social sciences are particularly badly hit with absolute declines in psychology, economics, industrial relations, international relations and geography ..... between 1968-9 and 1975-6 the social sciences had a static programme which represented a fall from 35.9% to 29% of the total'.(62) According to the UCAE, 'it appears that there has been no significant change' in the subject balance from the mid 1970s to the end of the decade.(63) However, by 1981/2 this trend had become more marked, and the UCACE Report for 1981/2 recorded that the percentage of social science courses in the total provision was around 20%.(64) Of the subjects in which more than five hundred courses were provided in 1975/6, and whose rate of growth was in excess of the average, the strong tendency was towards those with a directly participative dimension. Thus, history (predominantly local history), archaeology and the laboratory sciences headed the table in terms of percentage growth (compared with 1968/9 figures).(65)

Part of this has been the result, of course, of the creation and development of the Open University. As Dyson noted 'it is the traditional social science and humanities programme that has been checked in the 1970s and the participative activities that have risen so strongly. The former are a central feature of Open University provision whilst the latter are activities least appropriate to the concept of distance teaching'.(66) But it is also reasonable to argue that this trend represents a move away from involvement in social and political affairs in society at large. Whatever the merits of the Open University - and they are very considerable - it has attracted only a minority of working class adult students. Moreover, and more importantly in this context, the course structures and ethos of the Open University, understandably, do not have the same blend of social purpose with academic discipline which has characterised to a considerable extent the core provision of the tutorial class movement. (See Chapter 2).

The decline of this key area of extramural

study thus represents more than a mere shift in subject fashions: it has been a reflection of the changing social and political priorities in the wider society and, in particular, has been indicative of the widespread scepticism, cynicism and apathy which the social, political and economic environment has engendered in Britain in recent decades. The increased popularity of the participative subjects is thus at one level a microcosmic example of a general retreat from social and political reality: an unwillingness to confront major social and political issues and problems, and a desire to escape into self-contained, unthreatening subject areas where the individual's thought, work and participation (often in research) can be seen demonstrably to have an impact. It is, in other words, part of the increasing privatisation and atomisation of contemporary society, and a function of alienation from issues and pressures which seem, to most people, too big, too complex and often too terrifying to confront.

Many university adult educators are opposed to this trend and would concur with the priorities presented by Brian Groombridge in a discussion paper, to the Academic Policy Board of the University of London in 1979, where it was argued that, as a very high priority, UAE 'should relate or stem from ..... our life and times - the great issues of our epoch'. Later in the paper this is elaborated to include:

> such matters as: the pursuit of peace, a recognition that the new economic order calls for a profound transformation of relations between the northern and southern hemispheres; our passing through some kind of political-economic crisis, the nature of which is obscure; the uncertain future of democratic government; the prevalence of much psychic malaise (alienation, rootlessness)

Whilst the tables given in the UCACE Reports do not provide conclusive evidence of the level of such provision, it is certain that such subject areas form, at best, a small minority of UAE programmes; and that some of these subject areas, such as Peace Studies, are almost non-existent.

Within a context of the overall growth of provision, therefore, there has been a relative decline in the concentration upon specifically working class adult education, and a move away from the social science subject areas. In addition to the marked growth of short course provision, already noted, what have been the other major trends? Two in particular stand out: post experience continuing education for graduates working in specific professional and/or vocational fields who require short, intensive, high level courses to acquaint themselves with the latest relevant research and information; and professional adult education work, usually in the form of part or full-time postgraduate diplomas or Masters' degrees for those engaged in adult education work, in the widest sense, in the extra-university context.(67)

It is in the former field that the most dramatic and significant expansion has taken place, especially since the mid 1970s. In 1978/9 the UCAE reported that:

> many departments were turning to an increase in post-experience and residential courses to help maintain the remainder of their programme. Leeds ..... notes the substantial contribution which the Special Courses Division has made in financial terms both to the extramural department and to other departments of the University. The proportion of Non-Grant Aided work at Keele has increased. Leicester now had a Continuing Education Unit within its department. Loughborough (as a technological University wishes to organise) short courses that are relevant to the needs of industry and the public services ..... (68)

And so on: other universities report similar developments. Subsequent years have seen an acceleration of such developments, with the 1981/2 UCACE Report noting that 'the broad threshold of continuing education and post-experience work is a major area for report'.(69) Among the individual departments whose Annual Reports for 1981/2, or similar documents, note specific developments in this field as a major priority, were Cambridge,(70) Ulster,(71) Leeds,(72) Nottingham,(73) Bristol,(74) Keele,(75) and Loughborough.(76) All, in their various ways, echo Nottingham's statement of 1978/9:

> The Department is in a period of change .....
> The changes are not just local. For very practical reasons adult education i.e. of the liberal tradition ..... is being paralleled by a considerable national interest in

> vocationally-based provision. Skills and
> knowledge date fast ..... It is often the
> highly educated who suffer most obviously from
> the dating of their initial education, and
> because of this the University (is) increas-
> ingly involved in post-experience provision
> ..... what we must do as a University is both
> develop the programmes to meet the new and/or
> increasing needs of the economy in the post-
> experience field whilst also building on the
> remarkable provision long established in the
> liberal adult education area. No major
> healthy society can afford to neglect
> either'.(77)

There is no doubt either that most UAE departments are adopting, to a greater or lesser extent,
a continuing education dimension to their programmes. However, at the time of writing (1984), major
provision of post experience continuing education is
restricted to a relatively small number of UAE
departments. A 1983 UCACE working part on continuing education found that, in the nineteen UAE
departments which provided information about their
continuing education provision in 1981/2, 'the
number of students enrolled vary from none to
several thousand; five departments enrolled over one
thousand whilst nine had fewer than five hundred
student enrolments'.(78)

It is reasonable to surmise that other UAE
departments will develop rapidly such post
experience continuing education. But it is important to note that actual growth to date in this
sector has been achieved by internal university
departments. In 1981/2, of all adult and continuing
education provision by universities, 61.3% was
undertaken by UAE departments, 18.2% by medical
and dental faculties, and 21.5% by other departments. And, between 1980/1 and 1981/2, whereas
growth in student numbers in continuing education
provision was a modest 4% for UAE departments, it
was 23% for other internal departments (and 14%
for medical and dental faculties).(79)

It is clear that the prominence accorded to
continuing education, and the structure for its
provision, varies widely. As the UCAE Report for
1979/80 noted:

> ..... in some cases an existing department of
> extra-mural studies or Adult Education has
> extended its range to include the provision of

> all that University's continuing education:
> in other cases the existing department has
> remained responsible only for extramural work
> with other departments providing post-
> experience courses. Many of the newer Univer-
> sities operate on a third model: a department
> of continuing education set up to provide
> mainly post-experience courses of an extra-
> mural type.(80)

And, it should be added, a large proportion of such work was being undertaken outside the auspices of UAE departments.

For most of the larger UAE departments, and for many of those smaller departments which are not RBs, continuing education is potentially the major growth area. Moreover, departments are becoming aware of the need to move quickly into such work before they are pre-empted by internal departments, or university registries, or indeed by other non-university agencies.

This whole area of growth represents potentially not only a quantitative but a qualitative shift in the nature of UAE provision. There are practical and pressing financial motivations underlying this development. In a time of recession and severe and unprecedented cutbacks in university financing, the appeal of a potential money spinner to the university authorities is hard to resist. The recent (1981) decision of Leeds University to stimulate, organise and supervise continuing education of this type on a scale of profit-making that would enable this section of the department to become self-financing by 1987/88, is indicative of the prominence given to financial rather than educational criteria.

In fact the whole funding basis of UAE is in the process of rapid and fundamental change, which will have serious consequences for the nature and structure of UAE departments and their provision. The primary source of funding for UAE has come, since 1908, from a government grant (from the Department of Education and Science - DES). The grant has been to all universities with Responsible Body (RB) status, and has also been made to WEA districts in England and Wales which are also RBs. Originally made to Joint Committees of the university and WEA district concerned, with the creation in more recent times of UAE departments, it has been made directly to each RB university. The grant has been calculated according to the size of the population in the extramural area, the programme of provision by the UAE department, and, crucially, the number of full-time staff employed by the university in the UAE department. The grant has met 75% of the teaching and related costs of mounting the extramural programme; the remaining 25%, plus administrative and capital costs, has been met by the parent university. With the expansion of UAE in the post-war period, and the growth of professional and post experience UAE, however, this basic funding system has been supplemented by a variety of other outside sources. And, of course, many of the newer universities do not have RB status, and therefore their whole programme of work has to be financed in other ways. By the 1980s, therefore, the overall funding structure, and, partly in consequence, the overall pattern of provision, has become highly diverse.

It has been in this context that the DES's 'new formula' for the allocation of RB grant has been proposed in 1983/4. At the time of writing (late 1984) the announcement of the details of the new formula has yet to be made. Nevertheless, it seems certain that there will be a change from funding full-time staff posts and overall departmental programmes, to the allocation of funds largely on the basis of output, measured in student hours. The implications of such a change would be major indeed: an increased emphasis upon shorter, less demanding, and thus more 'popular', courses; a disincentive to engage in difficult and/or experimental areas of work; and, in the medium term, the undermining of the whole concept of an academic UAE department - in which full-time, specialist UAE staff undertook research, administration and teaching - and its replacement by a model in which UAE was administered by a small, non-teaching (and effectively non-academic) unit, with the teaching being undertaken by large numbers of part-time staff.

The implications of the proposed change in the financial structure of UAE are thus both wide - ranging, and, for those espousing liberal UAE, very worrying. Above and beyond these financial and structural concerns, however, lie equally fundamental factors. From the late 1960s onwards universities as a whole have been under increasing pressure, as was argued earlier, from within as well as outside, to tailor their overall provision far more towards the expressed needs of advanced industrial and commercial enterprise. Thus there has been pressure to expand business and technology related subject departments (e.g. computer science, operational research, marketing, accounting and finance etc.); and, equally, pressure to decrease activity within both social science and the traditional humanities subjects. In this respect the Thatcher government's attack on the universities, and in particular on the social sciences, is only the most extreme form of a long-running campaign by successive governments. This whole development is in this sense part of the growing determination to make education 'relevant' to the needs of an increasingly sophisticated (but increasingly problem-ridden) industrial society, where the pace of technological and social change is rapid and accelerating. Within this context, UAE departments have been seen increasingly as, principally, appropriate agencies for entrepreneurial liaison and servicing between the university, with its expertise, and the higher echelons of technocratic and managerial elites of industry, commerce, and government.

There is thus a parallel between the aristocratic, high culture elitism of the university in nineteenth and early twentieth century Britain, with its explicit intention of permeating the values, the arguments, the practices and the theories of the university throughout society via the Extension and Tutorial class movement; and the managerial, technological elitism of the contemporary university, with its equivalent intention of transmitting not only the hard information, but the ethos of technocratic, 'apolitical relevance', via continuing education. The <u>form</u> of UAE has thus in this respect changed radically, but its <u>content</u>, ideologically, has remained essentially elitist and supportive of the dominant soci-economic strata in contemporary society. This is not to say that continuing education, in the sense of post experience study at postgraduate level, is <u>necessarily</u> located in this technocratic context. There are, of course, numerous other areas in which such work could, and to an extent does, take place within the UAE context. There is no reason why there should not be advanced level, post experience courses in appropriate subject specialisms within the extramural DES programme of evening and day classes. However, although the provision of a small number of such courses may prove possible, there is little doubt that this will remain very much a minority part of the programme.

The case of professional continuing education

is rather different: although there has been some contraction because of the recession and the cuts, UAE departments continue to provide a range of important provision in the areas of applied social studies, principally for those engaged in the social care and social control agencies. Such provision has normally centred on the full-time postgraduate course carrying either a Diploma or Masters qualification, in addition to a Certificate Qualification in Social Work (CQSW). In addition, 'in-service' courses for magistrates, involvement with educational provision for both prison staff and police personnel, and intensive short courses or conferences for practising professionals across a wide field, have been provided. However, the clear trend during the 1970s and 1980s has been for such work to be diminished within UAE. Generally, it has been either transferred to a separate, internal university department (as at Southampton and Liverpool, for example), or reduced disproportionately in size, scope and priority as a result of the cuts (as at Leeds).

The original motivations for UAE becoming involved in such work included centrally UAE's commitment to involvement with the community, and its belief in the importance of the liberal educational perspective within professional, vocational education. Raybould, in particular, emphasised the importance of the liberal tradition in broadening out students' narrowly vocational outlooks.[81] As with the developments since the 1950s and 1960s in trade union education,[82] the general trend has been markedly opposed to such a liberal approach. The professional agencies themselves, the government departments concerned, and, not least, the universities, have moved increasingly towards a training orientation.[83] The net effect, as far as UAE is concerned, has thus been to minimise aspects of continuing education other than the technocratic post experience type already discussed.

There is, however, another sector of the universities' 'elite' work in adult education which has prospered and expanded: professional adult education. As Paul Fordham has argued, the study of adult education itself, and the provision of (normally postgraduate) courses for adult educators by UAE departments, resulted essentially from the rapid expansion of LEA adult education in the post-war period.[84] In the 1960s and 1970s the bulk of those attending such courses were LEA employees, although, again, the recession has affected adversely recruitment in the 1980s. Such courses have been focused upon the theory and practice of adult education, but have used a multi-disciplinary approach, combining psychology, history, sociology, philosophy and educational theory. Practice has varied greatly: in some universities (e.g. Manchester, Surrey) considerable emphasis has been placed on such work: in others, little real progress has been made.

At almost all universities, however, there has been a change of emphasis amongst staff orientation over the last two decades away from subject specialists, who were committed to the adult education 'movement' and, broadly, to the social purpose aspects of its liberal tradition, towards specialists in adult education per se. As Fordham has noted:

> unless they (i.e. UAE staff) are seen - and see themselves - first and foremost as specialist adult educators, then they will remain marginal and, ultimately, dispensible. The core activities for an adult education department must lie in the practice of educating adults and with the scholarly study of its context and its processes. (85)

Such developments reflect the increasing tendency of universities to discrete disciplinary specialisms, defined relatively narrowly, in contrast to the broader liberal tradition. It is significant that the large majority of the more recently appointed heads of UAE departments have been specialist adult educators, and that, generally, those departments with a greater concentration upon professional adult education and adult education research, have both more secure and more prestigious positions within their parent universities. (86)

Overall, then, the development of a professional adult education orientation has reinforced the tendency towards both professional and elite education, necessarily at the expense of other forms of UAE, and the liberal tradition orientation in particular. The combination of the post experience, continuing education developments within UAE, with the increasing emphasis upon professional adult education, had undoubtedly become the dominant forces within UAE by the 1980s. (87)

It is, however particularly in the field of post experience, primarily technological and scientific, continuing education that the primary emphasis is to be found in the 1980s. It is here that university authorities look for expansion, generally speaking. For many within UAE this appears to be a legitimate and desirable development. Others, however, have found the devoting of scarce resources to a process that is largely concerned with educating more highly the already highly educated, a wholly unacceptable development - especially in a society that is so riven with educational, social and economic inequality and injustice.

In sharp contrast to most of the dominant developments analysed in this chapter have been the attempts to articulate afresh UAE's original commitment to working class adult education within the context of the liberal tradition. The final chapter of this book is devoted to a discussion of how, if at all, such commitments can be reappraised and redefined in ways which are appropriate and viable in the contemporary contexts of UAE in both England and the USA. There have been two particular areas of development in recent years in the English context, however, which require analysis and explanation before any such concluding discussion can be undertaken. Since the early 1960s UAE has made a major contribution to the growth of industrial, trade union education, on a scale hitherto unprecedented in England. Perhaps even more significantly, since the 1960s a varied pattern of innovative community adult education, both within and outside UAE, has grown up, and now forms a modest but substantial part of UAE activity which stands in sharp contrast to the dominant trends with which the latter part of this chapter has been concerned. It is to a discussion and analysis of these and other related developments that Chapter 5 is devoted.

NOTES

1. R.O. Berdahl, British Universities and the State, 1959.
2. For a wide-ranging selection of views on the nature and role of the modern state, with an illuminating introduction, see eds. David Held et al, States and Societies, 1983. For the classic modern Marxist interpretation of the capitalist state, see Ralph Milibard, The State in Capitalist Society, 1969.
3. Berdahl, op. cit., p. 2.
4. Ibid. p. 185.
5. Ibid. p. 193.

6. Kenneth R. Minogue, The Concept of a University, 1973, p. 76.
7. Ronald C. Tress, The Universities' alternative in quaternary education, in eds. Stephens and Roderick, Higher Education Alternatives, 1978, p. 13.
8. Ibid., p. 14.
9. Brand Blanshard, The Uses of a Liberal Education, 1974, p. 24.
10. There is a distinction here, noted by Tress, op. cit., p. 14, between scholarship and research. Whereas the latter is concerned only with 'discovering new knowledge', the former in addition implies 'philosophical speculation and artistic creation'. It can also be argued that whereas research is concerned with extending the frontiers of knowledge, scholarship involves familiarity with the sum total of existing knowledge within a given subject area.
11. For a dated, but full-blooded and appealing, description of this conception of a university, see Dacre Balsdon, Oxford Life, 1957.
12. Donald MacRae, The British Position, in ed. Paul Seabury, Universities in the Western World, 1975, p. 178.
13. Stanislav Andreski, Remarks on Conditions of Creativity, in eds. Flood Page and Yeats, Power and Authority in Higher Education, Proceedings of the Society for Research into Higher Education, 11th Annual Conference 1975, published by SRHE, 1976, p. 60.
14. MacRae, op. cit., p. 179.
15. See Miliband, op. cit. (The State in Capitalist Society), Chapter 8, Section IV.
16. Editorial, Times Higher Educational Supplement, 30 September, 1983.
17. Gordon Roderick and Michael Stephens, The British Education System 1870-1970, in eds. Roderick and Stephens, The British Malaise: Industrial Performance, Education and Training in Britain Today, 1982.
18. Michael Sanderson, The Universities and British Industry 1856-1970, 1972, p. 365.
19. David T. H. Weir, Management Training and Education, in Roderick and Stephens, op. cit., p. 92. Weir goes on to argue that the Open University might be enlarged to cater for almost all arts and social science university education, leaving other universities free to pursue science and technology subjects exclusively. Whilst such radical ideas may not be immediate policy options, in the 1980s

they appear considerably less far-fetched than would have been the case in the 1960s or 1970s.

20. Richard Hoggart, Robbins: Bigger - but not better?, <u>Times Higher Education Supplement</u>, 28 October, 1983.

21. i.e. Oxford, Cambridge, London, Durham, Victoria (Manchester), and Wales. There were in addition, of course, the ancient Scottish Universities. Source: John H. Van de Graaff, Great Britain, in eds. Van de Graaff et al, <u>Academic Power: Patterns of Authority in Seven National Systems of Higher Education</u>, (USA), 1978.

22. i.e. the constituent colleges of Victoria University.

23. Source: Peter Gosden, <u>The Education System since 1944</u>, 1983, Chapter 5, The Universities, pp. 144-7.

24. Source: Van de Graaff, op. cit. See Chapter 1, p. 7, for a brief discussion of the foundation and purpose of the Open University.

25. Source: Gosden, op. cit., p. 136. (a full table of student numbers for each year from 1938/9 is given here).

26. This influence has not been only at the status and ideological levels, however. Because of their very size Oxford and Cambridge have continued to constitute a very large sector of the university structure. As late as 1961/2, 31% of British academics had studied at Oxford or Cambridge. Source: Robbins Committee Survey, cited in A. H. Halsey and M. Trow, <u>The British Academics</u>, 1971, and discussed in Van de Graaff, op. cit.

27. Despite the expansion in university student numbers since the 1960s the age participation rate (APR) of working class students has hardly changed. Professor Edwards has stated that 'the sharp escalation in numbers of students in the period from about 1955 - 1970 ..... was not accompanied by any closing of the gap between manual and non-manual workers. This means, of course, that the great majority of the increased flow of students came from the same social classes as before'. (E. G. Edwards, <u>Higher Education for Everyone</u>, 1982, p. 82).

In fact, between 1957 and 1975, the APR of sons of professional parents rose from 25.7% to 57.5% and for daughters of professional parents, from 10% to 38%, whereas the APR for the sons of unskilled workers rose from 0.6% to 1.4% and for the daughters of unskilled workers from nil to 0.8% (Source: Edwards, op. cit.)

A wealth of evidence suggests that these differences in the APR have little or nothing to do with differences in inherent abilities between the children of different social classes, but are the result of differing social environment.

28. Van de Graaff, op. cit., p. 87.
29. Ibid., p. 88.
30. Thus Gosden, op. cit., p. 141, cites the 'Scientific Manpower' Committee set up by Herbert Morrison, as early as 1946, because of 'the realization that industrial growth required more highly trained scientific and technological manpower ..... The Report recommended a doubling of the number of graduates in Science as soon as possible .....'
31. Source: Ibid, p. 142.
32. Ibid., pp. 145-6.
33. Van de Graaff, op. cit., p. 85.
34. Parlt. Deb. (Commons), 5th series, Vol. 246 (30 July 1946), col. 129. Cited in Berdahl, op. cit., p. 76.
35. Source: Van de Graaff, op. cit.
36. Brian MacArthur, Beyond 1980: the evolution of British Higher Education, New York International Council for Educational Development, 1975, p. 10, cited in ibid.
37. Ibid. (Van de Graaff), p. 99.
38. Robbins Report, cited in Gosden, op. cit., p. 152.
39. Thus, according to Gosden (ibid.) 'the decision to undertake rapid expansion of the University system and to set up new universities had been taken well before the Robbins Report appeared'. p. 149.
40. Ibid., p. 151.
41. See, for example, Peter Scott's summary of the main recommendations and the decisions taken on them, in The Times Higher Education Supplement, 28 October, 1983. Here, Scott cites thirteen major recommendations, nine of which were either not implemented, or have been unsuccessful.
42. Thus the following were major recommendations: i to promote the CATs to full university status; ii to create five Special Institutions for Scientific and Technological Education and Research; iii to promote sufficient regional colleges of technology to create six more universities; iv to ensure that a higher proportion of students should be on science and technology courses. Of these, only the first was implemented. Source: ibid.
43. Times Higher Educational Supplement, editorial, 5 August, 1983.

44. *Times Higher Educational Supplement*, editorial, 19 August, 1983.
45. Ibid.
46. See Chapters 1 and 2. For further details see Norman A. Jepson, *The Beginnings of English University Adult Education*, 1973.
47. John A. Blyth, *English University Adult Education 1908-1958: a unique tradition*, 1983, p. 109 and p. 156.
48. Cited in ibid., p. 160.
49. S. G. Raybould, *The English Universities and Adult Education*, cited in ibid., p. 249.
50. According to Raybould, ibid., an increase in such courses of 1000%.
51. Roger Fieldhouse, *The Workers' Educational Association: Aims and Achievements, 1903 - 1977*, Syracuse University Publications in Continuing Education (U.S.A.), 1978, p. 35.
52. Professor Roger Dyson, Determining Priorities for University Extramural Education (inaugural lecture), University of Keele, 1978, table 1. p. 6.
53. The corresponding figures for 1968-9 were: sessional and tutorial, 3954; courses of three to nineteen meetings, 4396. Source: ibid.
54. UCACE Annual Report 1981-2, Table 3(a), and p. 8 of the Introduction ('The Work of the Universities'). The 1982/3 UCACE Report noted that, although there was a general decrease in the longer courses, 'there was a slight increase in courses of three years duration. This may reflect the stability of those specific long courses which lead to named awards'. (p. 8).
55. On the broad question of consensual politics in the 1950s, see, for example, Daniel Bell, *The End of Ideology*, New York, 1960; Antony Crosland, *The Future of Socialism*, 1956; ed. R. H. S. Crossman, *New Fabian Essays*, 1952; R. A. Butler, *The Art of the Possible*, 1971.
56. See Ralph Miliband, *Parliamentary Socialism*, Chapter 9, (second edition) 1973, for an analysis of this and other questions relating to the 1945-51 Labour governments.
57. For discussion of this see: Ralph Miliband, *The State in Capitalist Society*, Chapter 8, op. cit.; Colin Pritchard and Richard Taylor, *Social Work: Reform or Revolution?*, Chapter 6, 1978; the Glasgow Media Group publications, *Bad News*, 1976, *More Bad News*, 1980, *Really Bad News*, 1982; and Graham Murdock and Peter Golding, For a Political Economy of Mass Communications, in eds. Miliband and

Saville, Socialist Register 1973, 1973.
58. This is made up of approximately 8% engaged in adult education, further education, community associations, women's organisations and youth and community service, and a further 8% in industrial training, and full and part-time higher education. Source: H. A. Jones and K. E. Williams, Adult Students and Higher Education, ACACE, Occasional Paper 3, 1979, p. 42.
59. See Fieldhouse, op. cit., passim.
60. The UCAE reported this to the 'Russell Committee' in its submission. For a discussion of this, and of a limited empirical survey conducted by the Durham University Department of its adult student population, see Dyson, loc. cit., p. 15.
61. Ibid.
62. Ibid., p. 12. Dyson also noted that in the humanities the situation was only 'a little better with very small below average rates of growth in Philosophy, Religion, Ancient Languages and Literature and the Visual Arts'. For full details see table V, p. 11.
63. UCAE Report 1979-80, p. 8.
64. UCACE Report 1981-82, Table 6(a), pp. 20-21. Included in social science are: psychology, economics, political science and government, industrial studies, geography, social studies and applied social studies.
65. Economics/industrial relations, social studies and the visual arts head the list of subjects whose rate of growth is below the average, with economics/industrial relations showing an absolute decline. Source: Dyson, loc. cit. See pp. 9-11 for more details.
66. Ibid.
67. There has also been some development in the part-time degrees field, but to date this has been restricted largely to a small number of UAE departments (e.g. Hull, Kent).
68. UCAE Report 1978-9, p. 5.
69. UCACE Report 1981-2, p. 7.
70. Board of Extramural Studies, University of Cambridge, Annual Report for 1981-2, where the development and potential of continuing education with the armed services, magistrates, the clergy, engineers, and business and industry, are noted.
71. Institute of Continuing Education, University of Ulster. In a letter to Richard Taylor, Professor Alan Rogers remarked that his was 'a University Adult Education institution faced with a hostile Continuing Education tradition and feeling

under very great threat.' Letter, 6 May 1983.

72. The Annual Report of the Department of Adult Education and Extramural Studies, of the University of Leeds, noted its change of title to the Department of Adult and Continuing Education, and the accompanying change of emphasis, with Continuing Education being accorded considerably more prominence than in the past.

73. In addition to the Report mentioned below, numerous other papers and books emanating from the Nottingham Department all emphasise the importance and centrality of continuing education (e.g. the Annual Report for 1980-1; ed. K. H. Lawson, The Grey Papers, 1979; eds. A. H. Thornton and M. D. Stephens, The University and its Region, Department of Adult Education, University of Nottingham, 1977).

74. Annual Report, Department of Extramural Studies, University of Bristol. This articulates clearly the commitment to continuing education as a priority of the Bristol Department.

75. In a letter to Richard Taylor, 5 May 1983, Professor Roger Dyson of the Department of Adult Education, University of Keele, stated that: 'The basic philosophy of this Department has been to maintain, protect and where possible to develop a highly subsidised non-award bearing liberal adult education programme for the general public with as broad a social catchment as possible ..... We have had to recognize, however, that we can only achieve this if we build our own financial protection for this programme. As a result, there has been a very substantial expansion at Keele in the volume of short residential and non-residential vocational courses ...'

76. Centre for Extension Studies, Loughborough University of Technology. Loughborough is in a rather special category, being, in the opinion of its Assistant Director, 'the pioneering centre in combining vocational training work with liberal adult education.' Letter to Richard Taylor from Morry Van Mentz, Assistant Director, 18 May 1983. In its 1981-2 brochure it is stated that, 'as is appropriate within a technological university, much of the Centre's work is concerned with post-experience vocational education and training.'

77. Introduction to the Report of the Secretary to the Delegacy and the head of Division of the School of Education for the session 1978-79, Department of Adult Education, University of Nottingham, p. 7.

78. Tim Bilham and Gordon Roderick, First Report of the Working Group in Continuing Education post-experience courses in United Kingdom Universities, UCACE, 1983.
79. Ibid.
80. UCAE Report, 1979-80, p. 6.
81. See Blyth, op. cit., p. 248.
82. This is discussed further in Chapter 5.
83. See Richard Taylor and Kevin Ward, Extramural work: different settings, common themes, Adult Education, vol. 54, no. 1., June 1981, pp. 12-18.
84. Professor Paul Fordham, A View from the Wall: commitment and purpose in Adult Education, inaugural lecture, University of Southampton, 22 February, 1983.
85. Ibid., p. 9.
86. There are, of course, many other variables of significance. For example, those universities, such as Hull, whose very existence stemmed originally from the extramural department, tend to regard their UAE departments as much more central to the university and its functioning than do other universities. See, for example, T. W. Bamford, The University of Hull, the First Fifty Years, 1978.
87. The changing emphasis within UAE is symbolised in the changes of title of departments over the years. At Leeds, for example, the department was originally entitled 'The Department of Extramural Studies'; this changed to 'The Department of Adult Education and Extramural Studies'; and, in 1982, to 'The Department of Adult and Continuing Education'.

Chapter Five

RADICAL DEVELOPMENTS IN UNVERSITY ADULT EDUCATION
IN ENGLAND: REDEFINING THE LIBERAL TRADITION

The dominant trends in post-war UAE have been of the post experience and professional type, described in the previous chapter. And these tendencies have become considerably more marked in the 1970s and 1980s. Nevertheless, there have been other developments which, although very much subsidiary to those major areas of activity, have formed collectively a substantial and significant body of work. Moreover, such areas of work have represented an attachment to a series of ideological positions concerning the proper role of UAE which differ sharply from those described in Chapter 4. Broadly, these approaches are concerned with devising ways of making educational provision for adults who have not had the benefit of tertiary education. Beyond this most general purpose, however, the approaches are very disparate in terms of both objectives and structures. Despite this disparity, all have a direct bearing upon the central conception of liberal adult education. Do these various approaches collectively constitute a new and separate UAE 'tradition', supplanting the previous concerns and structures of the old liberal tradition or, alternatively, do they represent a contemporary articulation of traditional liberal concerns, expressed in ways more appropriate to the radically changed social context?

This chapter is concerned primarily with two themes: the identification and analysis of some of the major aspects of this area within contemporary UAE; and a discussion of how far, if at all, such approaches are compatible with the core concepts of the liberal tradition, as discussed in Chapter 2.

There are two main areas and approaches within this sector of contemporary UAE: industrial studies provision for trade unionists; and community adult education developments of a wide variety. Both have in common their central concern with education for those who have had no educational involvement since leaving school at the minimum leaving age: that is, predominantly <u>working class</u> adults.(1) There have also been other innovatory and important areas of UAE development which relate to these objectives: in particular, the growth of daytime Second Chance to Learn or New Opportunities courses, intended primarily for women; and the various moves towards part-time degree courses. Both of these areas too are discussed briefly towards the end of this chapter.

UAE AND TRADE UNION EDUCATION

The most longstanding and firmly established aspect of such working class adult education has been the provision of courses for trade unionists. From the outset of the Extension and Tutorial movements the concept of a liberal approach to industrial studies education has been central. This broad-based approach to industrial education for adults reached its height, in terms of quantity if not, arguably, quality, in the 1960s, when the UAE departments provided a large programme of both day release and evening class work for trade unionists in a number of industries. Course length varied considerably, from short and basic day release courses through to three year day release or evening classes. From the late 1960s onwards the universities have been compelled, in effect, to reduce their commitment to this type of work, because the TUC has developed its own rationale and approach to trade union education, this move being represented organisationally by the replacement of the Workers' Educational Trade Union Committee (a joint WEA/Trade Union body), by the TUC scheme in 1966. The TUC then set up an Education Committee to supervise all education to which it gave financial assistance.

Whereas the universities' approach had been concerned with the discussion and analysis of industrial and trade union affairs within the various relevant subject contexts - economics, sociology, politics, law, history, the whole being considered within the liberal framework - the TUC's emphasis has been predominantly upon training, upon increasing the professional proficiency of the shop steward (and trade union rank and file members). For the TUC Education Committee the primary object of workers' education is 'training those responsible for conducting trade union affairs in the knowledge and skills essential to conducting those affairs efficiently'.(2) To this end, the TUC has tended increasingly to prepare specific and detailed syllabuses for its courses which are concerned exclusively with either factual information or with straightforward training in collective bargaining techniques. As John McIvoy has argued:

> trade union courses were not intended for the development of the whole person or for developing an understanding of how society operated. Trade union education (which was restricted primarily to shop stewards R.T.) was legally determined as having another end: the reproduction of collective bargaining agents in the interests of improved industrial relations and greater efficiency ..... The TUC again asserted its right to control education, "we claim the right to determine the training of trade union representatives on the achievement of trade union objectives. This is a principle from which we will not deviate"'.(3)

(There have also been quite specific programmes of industrial education related to particular pieces of legislation e.g. the Health and Safety courses of the late 1970s and early 1980s).

The overall context of this discussion must be borne in mind, however. It would be quite mistaken to suppose that the years of the WETUC in general marked some 'golden age' of trade union education. The numbers involved in both general working class adult education and specifically trade union education are far greater today than in the past.(4)

Moreover, there is a gross imbalance both in the scale of trade union education as undertaken in the shorter TUC courses taught by agencies other than the universities and the WEA, compared with the very small numbers involved in the latter's provision, and in the disproportionately high cost of the sustained courses provided through UAE and the WEA. Leaving aside the reasons for the paucity of resources for trade union education, the very practical point must be emphasised that, at present, there is no possibility, within existing funding, of providing sustained liberal adult education courses for large numbers of trade unionists. In addition, whilst the training emphasis has been predominant for the TUC, it is, however, important to note that both the WEA and UAE departments have often been able, in practice, to teach TUC syllabuses within the liberal framework. As the authors of a recent article have concluded: 'the experience (of) many of those closely involved in trade union education has been that it is possible to provide genuinely liberal adult education within the post-1966 framework; that some of the work (e.g. health and safety courses) has stimulated significant social and political education in the best traditions of the WEA; ..... and that the TUC courses provide at least a starting point for liberal adult education for the working class .....'(5)

However, although some universities, and some WEA districts, have adopted a great deal of such TUC work, the tendency has been for the TUC to use other educational institutions which are more prepared both to engage in a more mechanistic training role of this type, and to surrender academic autonomy in the sense of teaching to a syllabus over whose drafting and content they have no control.

Some trade unions do remain outside the TUC schemes, and some UAE departments provide significant numbers of courses for such unions, with syllabuses and approaches agreed between the department and the union concerned. Thus, for example, the UAE departments at Sheffield, Nottingham, Hull and Leeds, all have substantial commitments to traditional heavy industry unions, such as coalmining and steel, where sustained day release course provision is organised between unions, employers and departments.

Generally, these courses fall within the liberal tradition of working class adult education. The objective is seen not as role training but as worker education. The courses are designed to introduce trade unionists to the social, economic, political and cultural context within which trade unionism and its industrial relations practices have evolved and developed. The structure is thus multi-disciplinary, with the unifying thread of concern being the interaction of trade unions, and the general labour movement, with the wider society.

The whole process is seen as one in which students' perceptions of society are broadened in as many ways as possible. Not only is a variety of subject disciplines brought to bear upon industrial studies, a number of often conflicting analytical frameworks and ideological models are discussed.

Given the problems associated with objectivity, as discussed in Chapter 3, it should be emphasised here that the intention in such courses is not to promulgate one particular ideological viewpoint to the exclusion of others (as was the case with the generally crude Marxism of the NCLC), but rather to examine as large a number as possible of competing explanations. That said, there is such an overwhelming preponderance, in contemporary society, of essentially pro-capitalist ideology, that particular attention must be paid to elaborating, analysing, discussing (and criticising) alternative conceptions. This is a theme to be returned to in the final chapter. Here, we need to stress the central point that, in this example and in others of a similar nature, the primary purpose is to broaden out students' perceptions, to 'open doors' educationally and culturally. Given the context, it has been through the development of social studies that such UAE industrial studies work has taken place. The emphasis has thus been upon individual and collective 'education for citizenship'.

Such provision is very much in the minority, however. Most trade unions either work through the TUC, or have their own, more role oriented, educational programmes. UAE (and to an extent WEA) trade union provision is thus under attack from two directions: the general move in the educational sector towards a more vocational, role oriented, training approach; and the attempt by the TUC to centralise control over trade union education and standardise course content along role training, industrial relations lines. The overall result has been to marginalise the RB sustained course approach to industrial studies provision. As a recent commentator on RB industrial studies has observed:

> on the whole the vast majority of trade unions are perfectly happy to plug into the TUC's provision partly because they lack funds themselves and partly because they do not have any explicitly formulated educational policy of their own.(6)

In such circumstances, which are not of the university's making but again reflect the increasingly instrumental and ostensibly apolitical approach which has been characteristic of much recent corporate development in Britain and elsewhere, the role of the universities in industrial education has thus become severely limited, and is likely to become increasingly so. The effect of this on UAE programmes has been to undermine the connection between the universities and the organised Labour Movement, and more generally, to decrease still further the contact that universities as a whole, and UAE departments in particular, have with the working class.

The argument should not be left there, however. It would be both unrealistic and unimaginative to imply that the only viable role for UAE was to replicate the rather formal and traditional course structure and approach outlined above, however excellent of its type such a course may be. There <u>are</u> other possibilities for trade union educational development within the liberal context. Discussions are beginning to produce suggestions for innovative work of a more informal type, aimed at particular groups of trade unionists with special concerns: women trade unionists and ethnic minorities, for example. Many of the lessons learned in other spheres in recent decades are beginning to be applied to trade union education: the emphasis is becoming more upon the local, personal and immediate situation (as a starting point at least) and less upon macro, subject based study. And linked to this is the recognition of the need for <u>membership</u> education in trade unions, rather than a concentration exclusively upon the activist and committed elites.

Such discussions and experiments are at an early stage, but they do represent one potentially important area of development for trade union education, and one in which UAE could have a major role to play.

UAE AND COMMUNITY ADULT EDUCATION

In contrast to the long-established, but seemingly declining, industrial studies sector of UAE provision, has been the rapid though modest growth of 'community adult education'. The conceptual roots of community adult education lie in the growth of libertarian ideology in the 1960s. In the general educational sphere this found expression in the influence of the work of Illich, Freire, and in Britain, such writers and practitioners as Bob Ashcroft, Keith Jackson, and Tom Lovett (and, later, of Jane Thompson). In the UAE context, however, this influence was mixed in with community work experience and ideology, and with the neo-Marxist legacy of the late 1960s, to form a rather different amalgam.

The basic motivation for UAE departments

developing such programmes has been the longstanding problem of the predominating middle class composition of the student body. UAE:

> departments provide an opportunity for the local community to make use of the resources and research of the university. That 'community' has, in the main, however, been predominantly middle-class and the relationship one that is dominated by, on the one hand their needs and interests and, on the other, a narrow definition of what is and what is not the proper domain of UAE.(7)

As consensus politics began to break down in the 1960s, and poverty, deprivation and inequality were 're-discovered' by academics and, more importantly, decision-makers, so various community-based projects within the social work/social services sector were developed (e.g. the Community Development Projects). 'Participation' became an increasingly popular concept in the 1960s: 'community development' blossomed. According to Tom Lovett, the process began 'as a straightforward modernisation of social work designed to deal with the more intractable aspects of "urban deprivation", which the standard battery of welfare services seemed unable to cope with'.(8)

This took place in the wider context of the restructuring of the public sector in the 1960s, involving increasing centralisation of services through the state at both national and local levels. At the same time there was a mounting emphasis upon the need for participation and community involvement (see, for example, the Skeffington Report on Planning). Whether this was the result of a genuine pluralist and democratic desire on the part of the state to avoid bureaucratic centralisation, or rather was illustrative of the contradictory processes of modern capitalist structure, is an issue which need not concern us here.(9) The fact remains that, for whatever reasons, community involvement and participation very rapidly became the order of the day.

At the outset this took the form of mutual support amongst disadvantaged groups in the community but, as budgets became tighter, some statutory services were 'off-loaded' onto community and voluntary groups. At the same time, partly as a result of the rapid growth in the late 1960s of the libertarian socialist politics of decentralisation and quasi-anarchistic ideas, 'action groups were appearing ..... in working class residential areas all over the western world'.(10)

This can be seen as a part of a general process that Ralph Miliband has termed de-subordination,(11) in which both the organised working class, and other potentially radical and/or disadvantaged groups, combined to challenge the hegemony of the governing class and its ideology. A crucial part of this movement, or series of movements, has been the growing importance of a stratum of radical <u>middle</u> class opinion. There has been a considerable expansion in the number of radical, tertiary-educated, professional and intellectual employees, whose public sector occupations and general background of 'critical thinking', have resulted in an ideological stance opposed to the market individualism of competitive capitalism.(12) There have been three major groupings within this stratum: trade union activists in the 'white-collar' unions; 'new artisans' (i.e. a set of often college-trained young people denied access to bureaucratic occupations because of the recession, who have turned instead to petty commodity production - in wood, textiles, paint and so on)(13); and welfare bureaucrats (those working in schools, hospitals, welfare agencies, etc., who, as Cotgrove and Duff have observed, have rejected, at least to an extent, the ideology and values of industrial capitalism and opted instead for 'careers outside the market place').(14)

It has been this last group, plus the development of working class community groups themselves, which has given rise in the 1970s and 1980s to a whole new area of community action and community development. Generally, such community activity has been of two types. Those forms of community action emanating from within communities themselves can be termed 'spontaneous'. But, equally important, have been those 'sponsored', or state financed and structured programmes (e.g. the Community Development Projects, and the growth of Community work projects generally in the 1960s and 1970s).(15)

It is within this context that community adult education must be seen. In the 1970s, various responses were made in the adult education sector generally to these new initiatives:(16) there was a new realisation of the urgency and priority of adult education that was not only working class but which tried seriously to match provision to the needs of local working class people.

For some, community adult education was the panacea. Jack Tivey, for example, juxtaposed the problems of the modern age with the potential educational solution:

> we try to come to terms with material power such as there never was, matched by an individual uncertainty of soul unparalleled since the Black Death ..... The problem (is) ..... one of controlling events rather than being at their mercy, and our society can only hope to do so if it can find the means of turning itself and its institutions into learning systems which can bring about their own transformation ..... A flexibly constructed community education service is called for (incorporating both UAE departments and the Open University). (17)

Others, however, have taken a less sanguine view. To begin with, community adult education is a very nebulous concept - very much 'all things to all men'. Eric Batten has argued that community adult education is by no means necessarily a radical, reforming concept: indeed, it:

> is likely to be tolerated only when it does not significantly affect elite control over knowledge accreditation and distribution; whilst it remains a ghetto activity ..... participation is by no means always a radical influence ..... until the debate is joined about the humanist socialist ethic in education..... community education will be an authoritarian conservative influence. (18)

Leading on from this position, Keith Jackson has argued, from a socialist viewpoint, that community adult education is limited both politically and educationally. The central perspective of community adult education - that there should be positive discrimination in favour of educational provision for the 'disadvantaged' - can lead, in Jackson's view, to a static, 'quietist', view of society, in which it is assumed implicitly that levels of economic and political inequality are fixed and permanent. (19)

It can also lead to an introverted, microcosmic focus, where attention is fixed upon exclusively _local_ interests and problems, and potential collective solidarities and macro-cosmic solutions to problems are effectively ignored or dismissed. This has been part of a longstanding problem within adult education generally: it has been argued often by radicals that the very process of withdrawing from 'action' in order to undertake abstract 'study' is of itself retrograde, because it substitutes analysis for change. On the other hand, and perhaps more persuasively, other radicals from within the socialist tradition have argued, following Marx, Lenin and Gramsci, that, without adequate theory, there there can be no effective practice. As always, the 'solution', within the radical context, is to obtain an appropriate interaction between theory and practice, to produce a socialist praxis.

Within contemporary community adult education there has been an awareness, usually, of such problems - though by no means always within this specifically socialist context - and one of the central concerns of practitioners within the WEA and UAE sectors has been to develop structures of provision which encourage links from the local to the national, and from the specific to the general.

Many of the advocates of community adult education have thus been both suspicious and critical of what they have seen as the essentially conservative tendencies of the liberal tradition. In the hands of the 'educational establishment', it is argued, community adult education is in danger of being incorporated and integrated into the predominant bourgeois, individualistic model of adult education. Community adult education thus becomes either 'a means of providing remedial education for the disadvantaged',(20) or a means of enabling the determined and/or talented working class individual to rise above his or her deprived state into the middle class, privileged world. The liberal tradition is criticised 'for its individualistic, essentially middle class ethos; its belief that educating individuals eventually helps the broad mass of the working class; its acceptance of the prevailing pluralist ideology'.(21)

In contrast to this (assumed) conservatism of the liberal tradition, radicals within the community adult education field have constructed various models which attempt to combine concepts of community _action_ with concepts of radical adult _education_. Lovett, for example, categorising various community education models, appears to find fewer disadvantages with the 'Social Action/Education' model than with other models.(22) The point is made strongly by such critics that, whereas the liberal tradition concentrates exclusively upon the <u>individual</u>, community adult education must concern itself with <u>collective</u> advance. The Council of Europe's interim report on Permanent Education summarises this view:

> Whereas the aim of social advancement is to reduce individual inequalities but the social environment which produced them is left intact (on the assumption that those inequalities are due to an inadequate education effort on the part of individuals, or the state, or to inequality of education gifts) the aim of collective advancement is to give individual education and at the same time influence the social context in which the individual lives. An effort is made to involve as many persons as possible in the education campaign. It will always be based on the concrete problems encountered by communities in real situations ..... <u>without collective advancement there can be no genuine individual advancement</u> but only uprooting.(23)

Complementary to this individualist/collectivist division is the reformist/structural conflict division. Lovett has distinguished usefully between the two fundamental aspects of community adult education as it is conceived in British UAE departments:

> One stresses the specific role that adult education can play in the community action process, acting as its "education arm". The other emphasises the role of adult education as a general "community education service", meeting a wide variety of needs and interests in the community, not only those concerned with community action.(24)

The bases of these positions are rooted firmly in wider ideological traditions, both of which stress the need for a greater emphasis upon working class adult education, but for different reasons, and therefore with different objectives. Thus, the latter of the two views expressed is reformist/liberal in approach in that it:

> has a conception of social purpose which emphasises a commitment to the working class as a group so that they can avail themselves of adult education resources and opportunities

> ..... this concept of reform is popular in
> adult education circles because it enables
> those concerned to reject a consensus view of
> society without necessarily endorsing a more
> radical model. This position is a pluralist
> one, viewing society in terms of the
> "competition" between various interest groups
> for power and resources ..... the problem of
> adult education and the working class is seen
> as co-ordination and more effective use of
> existing resources.(25)

The other approach, however, adopts an implicit conflict model of social change, not necessarily Marxist but certainly with a strong collective class action emphasis. Thus, community adult education is seen as one aspect of community action, which in turn is seen as a central part of the grass roots, working class movement of opposition to capitalist society. The stress here is on collective consciousness and collective action to achieve social change.

Whilst many of those involved in community adult education do <u>not</u> have a radical orientation, and are more concerned with ostensibly apolitical attempts to involve local communities in a range of leisure and recreation educational activities, within the RB sector those who advocate a radical approach have been predominant. For J. E. Thomas, radicals in adult education have had two primary aims:

> to question the very assumption on which
> organisations, institutions and society itself
> rest ..... radicalism is the expressed inten-
> tion to attack the foundations of a system,
> complemented by a visible, manifest effort
> to do so, whether or not that effort is
> successful.(26)

And, second, to engage in a genuine search for the truth:

> the education purveyed by the system distorted
> the very Truth with which, allegedly, edu-
> cation was concerned. They (i.e. the radicals)
> did not, therefore, see education as a crude
> tool with which to capture power. Rather did
> they believe that if education really did
> occupy itself with Truth, then the capitalist
> system would collapse. It was not just a

> revolutionary tactic ..... it was, at its
> most idealistic, a desire to introduce honesty
> and <u>real</u> enquiry into the educational
> process .....(27)

It is at this stage of the argument that we should refer back to one of the central themes of this study: that the liberal tradition in English UAE encompasses both the individualist <u>and</u> the collectivist, social purpose orientation, and that these reflect both middle class and working class perspectives on the nature and purpose of UAE. It is true that these variants have co-existed somewhat uneasily, and that for most of the twentieth century the collectivist and working class perspective has been the secondary, minority strand within UAE. As was argued in the preceding chapter, it is also the case that, in recent years, the tendencies within UAE have become much more heavily professional and post experience in orientation, and <u>all</u> aspects of the liberal tradition are under attack. Nevertheless, it is quite erroneous to <u>ignore</u> this minority collectivist strand within UAE. From the outset of the Extension movement in the 1870s, this perspective has been continuously present, and has been seen, in its various guises, as being a part of the liberal tradition. The fact that, as was argued in Chapter 3, the practice of UAE has not conformed always to its principles - especially in relation to those operating on the Marxist or quasi-Marxist Left - should not blind us to the fact that central to the radical part of the liberal tradition spectrum has been precisely the commitment to objectivity and the 'search for truth', referred to by Thomas in the passage cited above.

Those radicals within UAE who have advocated a community adult education approach, have held generally that liberal adult education and community adult education are, virtually, mutually exclusive. Jane Thompson, for example, has argued that:

> the liberal tradition ..... has progressively
> abandoned any early commitment it might have
> made to "really useful knowledge" concerned
> with social change. Its roots in academic
> scholarship and the patronage of the leisured
> and genteel classes in the nineteenth century
> has contributed to the sense of detachment
> from contemporary society. Current defenders
> of this legacy still advocate it in preference

to the "practical instrumentalism" which they associate with recent developments (sic) like trade union studies and community education, preferring adult education's "traditional role of general cultural diffusion and personal development through studies on a broad perspective" (K. H. Lawson).(28)

Given these opposing conceptions of the nature of the liberal tradition in its relationship with community adult education, what has been the reality? How has community adult education developed within UAE? The first point to make is that community adult education within UAE (and, for that matter, within the WEA and the LEA sectors) accounts for a very small percentage of the total adult education work undertaken. Generally, such work has been regarded as rather separate and 'experimental' (see below for discussion of the work at Liverpool and Leeds). Most of the UAE work has continued to fall within the tradition of individual, intellectual development, as a cursory glance at the programmes of the larger, well-established UAE departments will confirm. (This pattern of provision is likely to change, given the proposed radical alterations to the RB grant formula, under discussion at the time of writing. See chapter 4 and chapter 8).

Many of those within UAE <u>reject</u> the viability of any community adult education dimension to the programme of UAE departments. Gordon Roderick, in his inaugural lecture at Sheffield University in 1976, commented that, although there had been a 'new urgency ..... given to meeting the needs of the deprived of all kinds', it would be 'simplistic to equate educational deprivation with (the) working class', given that only 4% of the adult population attended adult education of any type; and he argued for a more balanced approach to UAE development.(29) Michael Stephens of Nottingham University has expressed somewhat similar views about the immediate future of UAE. Writing in 1977, he argued that:

> it is probable that the need for continuing education will be pressing firstly among those who have already had more than their fair share of education, and notably those who are graduates or their equivalent ..... those with the least education will find their education outdating in job terms less than those

with the most education.(30)

Both of these are contingent, practical arguments concerned with planning for UAE in the 'real world', rather than statements of principle or ideological commitment. Thus, in the same paper, Stephens goes on to comment that these priorities and tendencies take 'no account of social needs and injustices. (However) it would seem likely that considerations of the economy in England will continue as paramount in education during the next few years'.(31) They do not, therefore, indicate any rejection per se of community adult education for working class people, but rather the administrator's recognition that predominating trends are otherwise.

However, there are those who reject explicitly and in principle the whole notion of social purpose adult education, and certainly any involvement in community adult education of the type discussed earlier. R. W. K. Paterson has been among the most prominent of such advocates. Paterson, described by Thomas as the 'heir to the Newman tradition',(32) has claimed that study for its own sake is, a priori, the exclusive criterion for UAE (as for other education). He has rejected explicitly any utilitarian model of education, and particularly that which has a radical social or political orientation. 'No-one', Paterson has argued:

> would seriously wish to dispute that adult education can in many ways make a notable contribution, perhaps an indispensable contribution, to the remedying of many specific social problems and to the general betterment of our social life ..... however, it is one thing to acknowledge that adult education can incidentally make a notable contribution to the accomplishment of many worthwhile social purposes. But it is quite another thing to view adult education as essentially or primarily an instrument to be utilised in the service of such purposes. This latter conception of adult education is clearly fraught with danger, not only to the deepest values of adult education, but also to the deepest values of society itself.(33)

From this stance:

> to view adult education as an instrument for the attainment of some favoured social purpose

> is to treat that social purpose as a given and unquestioned starting-point, as an original and basic datum ..... But there are and can be no social objectives which are so <u>manifestly</u> just or benign that their desirability is absolutely beyond question ..... Adult Education, then, cannot take sides on any social question.(34)

Such 'purism' is atypical, however. It is reasonable to assume that most contemporary adult educators in the UAE sector concur with the Russell Report's moderate, reformist, and above all, pluralistic, view of the proper function of UAE departments. Until the potentially disruptive, if not destructive, series of moves by the UGC and the DES in the early 1980s threatened its equilibrium, liberal adult education within UAE departments remained within the framework outlined in the preceding chapter. In this context the salient point is the position of community adult education within this structure of provision. In no department has the community adult education programme been more than a relatively small part of the overall activity. And by no means all departments have taken any initiatives at all in this area. At Nottingham, for example, it has been argued that the large majority of 'working-class adults will only seek education if it is <u>for</u> something' (broadly speaking, either for social change or for improving the individual's qualifications, etc). UAE for the working class should concentrate, it is argued, upon 'provision outside and after day release', oriented towards 'knowledge for power'. 'It is not necessary', argued G. F. Brown of Nottingham, 'and probably not desirable either, in many working-class areas to resort to recently fashionable and often ill-thought-out "community adult education" approaches'.(35)

Leaving aside Tom Lovett's work in Northern Ireland, which is necessarily rather different in kind,(36) the major initiatives in community adult education in recent years in Britain have taken place at Keele, Leeds, Liverpool, Sheffield and Southampton. Predominantly, these have been radical, community-based programmes attempting to construct innovative provision appropriate to working class people.

Attention here will be concentrated upon two somewhat contrasting experimental programmes as examples of the provision, which have particular relevance for this discussion of the liberal tradition in relation to community adult education: Liverpool and Leeds. Liverpool's work, and the educational philosophy underlying its approach, has been described and analysed in some detail elsewhere,(37) and there is thus no need here to replicate such discussion. The central thrust of the Liverpool approach has been threefold: to stress the importance of <u>community action</u> in relation to community adult education, and, within this; to emphasise the conceptual and practical centrality of class analysis; to reject notions of 'informal community education' in favour of rigorous and relatively high level work ('..... not only does theory not hinder practice; it informs practice and makes success more likely .....'(38)); and to argue for working class <u>control</u> of the educational process.

From the outset the Liverpool project was insistent that educational concern with local issues exclusively - even if linked into community action - was not enough:

> Local issues are essentially manifestations of societal problems, and action leading to social change will emerge from an awareness that this is so ..... Similarly, highly localised community action which is not related to a much broader class movement is more likely to benefit active working class areas at the expense of the apathetic working class, and not at the expense of existing elites.(39)

All these approaches were exemplified well in the case study, which formed the basis of a subsequent article by Bob Ashcroft and Keith Jackson,(40) of the developments in Liverpool around the Housing Finance Act in 1972. It was decided to hold a mass meeting to offer a factual but critical, and in effect socialist, analysis of the Act. In the leaflets advertising the meeting no mention was made of the sponsoring educational bodies (the WEA and the Institute of Extension Studies at the University), because:

> the theoretical framework we have adopted requires a definite rejection of "educational imperialism" in favour of an attempt to create working-class control of the operation. We should prefer to be considered as educational advisers and consultants and for people

locally not to feel obliged to adopt our
institutional forms.(41)

Following this meeting, several smaller groups
were established, and one eventually became an
organised adult class on social theory and social
problems. As Lovett has noted subsequently, there
was in the Liverpool project 'a constant emphasis
on the need to engage the residents in relevant
education of a high standard, making few concessions
to what was regarded as second class informal
community discussion methods or learning through
doing exercises'.(42) Initially, this was regarded
by the Liverpool project as quite clearly the
primary aim. But other provision, of the more traditional recreational and leisure variety, _was_ also
organised; and, also, more community oriented courses in housing, finance, unemployment, etc., were
provided. As a result of all this a 'Second Chance
to Learn' project was initiated in 1976, with working class students studying full-time on day
release. However, as Lovett has noted, 'there is
some evidence that this is creaming off bright
working class leaders who regard it as a means of
individual, not collective, development'.(43) In
1978 a Liverpool Inner Areas Consortium was established to link in the 'Second Chance' scheme to a
range of other opportunities, including the Northern
College at Barnsley (an adult residential college
where Keith Jackson, one of the initiators of the
Liverpool project, is now Vice Principal).(44)

The Liverpool approach has thus been to concentrate UAE provision upon high level adult education in the social sciences for a relatively small
number of working class people. Although this objective has been linked to a perspective of working
class advance through a Marxist notion of praxis,
the _reality_ has contrasted, to an extent, with this
ideal. The project has necessarily developed _other_
areas of adult education provision which have not
been 'political' in nature - certainly not explicitly so; and, as noted above, there has been a tendency for the 'high level provision' to encourage
some of the more intellectually - and politically-
sophisticated (and perhaps the more intelligent)
students to take the opportunity to develop _individually_, through access to higher education, better
jobs, etc., rather than as part of a collective
class and community advance.(45)

In wider political terms there must remain a
question, too, over the viability of such a

potentially 'vanguardist', if not elitist, educational model. If the objective is, in part, to stimulate a decentralised, socialist democracy, are such educational schemes not divisive and partially counter-productive? Finally, on a more pragmatic note, given the (regrettable) paucity of UAE resources, is UAE justified in concentrating these resources so heavily upon such a small minority? These are, of course, all <u>open</u> - not rhetorical - questions: whatever the reservations that might be made about the Liverpool project, there is no doubt that it has represented a significant advance in both UAE and community adult education. And, whatever the other questions which the Liverpool project may provoke, there is no doubt that it falls directly within that radical, working class tradition in UAE, which itself has been so important a part of the liberal tradition.

The objectives, provision and structure of the Leeds Pioneer Work project have been rather different. The broad purpose has been similar: to construct programmes of liberal adult education provision appropriate to a university and of relevance and interest to working class adults in an urban environment.(46) The more detailed objectives and structure of the Leeds project have differed somewhat, however. Strong emphasis has been placed upon the need for educational innovation and experimentation within a wholly community-based programme. Almost all provision has been made on an inter-agency basis, ranging from work with voluntary groups to joint courses with the LEA and the local colleges; and the whole programme has been provided at various non-institutional, local and accessible locations, rather than in central, 'educational' buildings. Fees for all courses in the Pioneer Work programme have been remitted, and almost all courses have been held in the daytime.

Part of the purpose of this inter-agency, community-based provision has been to develop a close, collaborative system, within which initiatives begun within Pioneer Work can be handed over to other agencies when appropriate. Inter-agency provision has also been considered important, however, because the project has given high priority to constructing courses that were based genuinely within the community, and emanated from the needs of that community, rather than being imposed from outside. For both these reasons, courses have tended to be concerned with issues, rather than subject disciplines: thus, for example, there have been numerous courses on welfare rights, housing issues, etc., rather than on social policy or social administration per se.

It was decided at the outset of the project in October 1982 that certain 'target groups' should be identified. Whilst these were not mutually exclusive, this selection did provide some focus for the allocation and administration of resources, both human and financial. The groups selected were: working class unemployed people; working class women; working class retired people; and the ethnic minority communities in Bradford and Leeds.

The decision to focus on specific groups in this way was related closely to the strong emphasis put upon research and monitoring within the project. At one level, the whole project is an exercise in 'action research', with the provision forming the essential empirical information upon which analyses of the most appropriate and successful models for development are based. This is regarded as absolutely central to the project's viability: in this sense the Leeds project is at one with Liverpool in arguing that far too much provision in community adult education has been without real purpose or structure and has been largely ad hoc response to particular needs randomly expressed. The research emanating from the project thus has considerable practical importance, not only for the future development at Leeds itself, but also in other analogous contexts elsewhere.(47)

In terms of the provision, the work with the unemployed has been by far the largest section of the Pioneer Work project. In 1982 the DES agreed to fund a special three-year full-time lectureship to develop work with the unemployed, and the appointee has been responsible, within the overall Pioneer Work structure, for this aspect of the project. In 1982/3, a total of 116 courses was provided, enrolling 1,193 students. Four different approaches were adopted, deliberately, from the outset, partly in order to facilitate comparative analysis, and partly to exploit to the full the inter-agency network of contacts possessed by the project teams of full and part-time staff in Leeds and Bradford. These four approaches were:

    organisation   (e.g. liaison with centres for the unemployed; and other organisations for

	unemployed people).
community	(e.g. liaison with local community organisations).
institutional	(e.g. liaison with the LEAs in Leeds and Bradford and local educational institutions, with officers and councillors in the authorities; and with non-educational institutions and agencies such as Probation, MIND, NACRO).
trade union	(e.g. liaison with full-time and lay representatives of trade unions).

In 1982/3, the first category accounted for over 40% of provision, the second for just under 20%, the third for 30%, and the fourth for just 3%.(48) In 1983/4 an approximately similar sized programme has been provided, although in Bradford, with the granting of an additional £14,000 from the District Council for development, a significant increase is expected in the size and scope of the programme towards the end of 1984. In late 1984 funding for two specific co-operative projects was also obtained from the newly established national Steering Committee on Adult Unemployed Projects (SCAUP), administered by the National Institute for Adult and Continuing Education (NIACE). The first of these is for development of a community-based education programme in conjunction with a voluntary agency, Harehills Housing Aid, in a disadvantaged area of Leeds. The second project, organised jointly with Leeds LEA, is for the extension of educational provision in the Leeds City Centre area. The grants obtained, which are both for two years, will be used to employ full and part-time educational workers to organise and teach a programme of appropriate courses.

Also in late 1984, the DES allocated additional funding to the Leeds department to appoint a Research worker to analyse in more detail the nature, effect and 'learning outcomes' of the programme of Pioneer Work for unemployed people.(49)

Provision in 1983/4 has been concentrated rather more in the 'organisational' and 'community' sectors, as those had proved not only successful in enrolment terms but had involved the most innovatory inter-agency approaches. More than 90% of those attending had had no educational involvement since leaving school at the minimum leaving age.

In 1982/3 provision for the other target groups in the Pioneer Work project was much more modest but the foundations were laid for significant expansion in 1983/4. On the basis of two courses in 1982/3 provided for working class retired people in Bradford, a further ten courses were developed in the area for other working class retired groups (ranging in subject matter from psychology to history and literature, and an 'Opportunities for Retired People' course). As a result of this programme, a University of the Third Age (U3A) branch was established in Bradford, centred on the working class students who had attended these courses. The U3A branch is part of a new and international voluntary movement, organized by and for retired people, with educational provision as a centrally important function.

Indications for the future are that such provision will continue to increase, resources permitting, and that there are opportunities for courses that bridge the gap between this programme and that for the unemployed.

Whilst a large proportion of the provision for the unemployed and the retired discussed above has involved women, there is a need to address the specific problems of women who are housewives and mothers, and the growing numbers of women who would like to find paid work but do not consider themselves unemployed.

Educationally and socially disadvantaged women in this group, for whom Pioneer Work provision is intended, experience particular problems that need to be taken into account: the need for child care, timing of courses to take account of family commitments, lack of money, lack of transport, and social and family attitudes towards women's education.

Staff responsible for developing this area of work in Bradford adopted in 1982/3 a dual approach linking community and estate-based morning or afternoon classes on the one hand, with a centrally located, one day a week course on the other, this latter being organised jointly with the Education Advice Service for Adults (EASA).

In 1983/4 this programme has been developed and eight further courses have been provided, including two very successful, short 'Opportunities for Women' courses - again, organised jointly with EASA. Approximately half of this whole programme has been organised for Asian women in Bradford, each in conjunction with voluntary agencies in various localities of the city, and dealing with a variety of subjects (e.g. healthcare, women and society, etc.).

Later in 1984, with the appointment of a new part-time organising tutor specifically to develop work with the Asian community, a number of courses for male Asians was provided - including black history, drama, and welfare rights. There have also been joint initiatives with both the West Indian Parents' Association, and the Centre for Ethnic Minority Health Studies.

What conclusions can be drawn from the experience of the Leeds Pioneer Work project over its two years of existence, bearing in mind, of course, that the full implications of the project cannot be assessed at so relatively early a stage? The project has illustrated a considerable need and demand for liberal adult education, as understood within the RB framework. As a crucial corollary to this, however, the importance of solid preliminary preparation and, even more important, an outreach and community network approach, has been amply demonstrated by the project's success. Without doubt, any programme that had been centrally based and advertised through conventional channels would have failed. The four approaches to work with the unemployed, and the inter-agency co-operation which has also characterised the other aspects of the project's operation, have all had in common their community network basis and have relied heavily upon building through local contacts before embarking upon any formal provision.

A further element of importance has been the project team approach whereby full discussions on all aspects of the project's functioning have taken place regularly between full and part-time staff, and decision-making has been very largely on this co-operative model. Such a framework is labour intensive and very time consuming: but the project's success is indicative of the importance of the team approach to work of this type.

In research terms the project has already demonstrated that there is a significant, urgent, but largely latent, demand for provision of the type that has been made. What sort of approaches are successful and which types of people come to which types of course, are among the questions that have begun to be examined (and answered) empirically. The development of differing models of inter-agency co-operation to ensure the most efficient and beneficial use of scarce resources has also been investigated, not only in terms of theoretical models, but *in practice* in the differing contexts of Leeds and Bradford.

These and other areas of investigation have indicated that, in research terms, there is much of value to be learnt from the project's operation over the next few years, and the research work to be undertaken in the new DES funded research project should yield results of interest to all those involved with community adult education development.

What of future plans for Pioneer Work development? In the short-term there will be concentration upon a number of issues: the construction of programmes which bring together this part of Pioneer Work with the other areas of priority (see below); the development of more intermediate courses which link in Pioneer Work initiatives to the mainstream liberal adult education programme; the further integration with other agencies so that, beyond the initial pioneering stage, course programmes can be located with those agencies which are most appropriate; and an intensification and deepening of the research programme in order to ascertain the effects, for both students and tutor, of the Pioneer Work educational experience.

All this leaves aside, however, the central question of whether activity of this type is appropriate to a university. Moreover, and of particular relevance to this analysis, can this sort of provision be regarded as legitimate within the liberal tradition? At the extremes, can six week courses in photography or welfare rights or health care *really* be appropriate for UAE?

It is argued at Leeds that there are four main reasons, in ascending order of importance, which do make Pioneer Work a viable activity. First, and most obviously, the university has access to unique expertise in terms of up-to-date research and resources in areas of direct relevance to much of the subject matter of Pioneer Work (e.g. social policy information, new technology equipment and expertise, and so on).

Second, given the institutional and academic flexibility of both universities *per se* and the DES/RB system as it applies to UAE departments, such departments are well placed to develop a variety of inter-agency provision on flexible bases. Moreover, these departments, despite some 'incursions' over the last few years, still maintain a high degree of freedom to engage in educational provision which other agencies might feel was too sensitive politically (e.g. the possible reluctance of LEAs to become involved in housing or other local issues which may be of direct concern to their political paymasters).

Third, universities are uniquely qualified to undertake rigorous research; and, as has been argued, this type of work requires detailed, regular and critical analysis if it is to develop on valid and viable lines. Without such research, provision becomes merely <u>ad hoc</u> response to almost randomly expressed demand, and no clear policy for future development can be formulated. Moreover, given the dispersed and disparate nature of the provision in a community-based programme, it is essential to have built in from the outset both a commitment to reporting and monitoring by all tutors, <u>and</u> the full-time staff who are adequately qualified to bring together and analyse the research material. Thus, in the Pioneer Work project, not only the full-time staff involved, but both the University and the DES, have given high priority to the research and monitoring aspects of the project.

Fourth, and finally, it is only within the UAE and WEA sectors of adult education that it is possible to develop <u>critical</u>, <u>liberal</u> adult education. It is here that the nub of the earlier series of questions is reached. It has been regarded as entirely valid for the Leeds UAE department to engage in subjects and areas usually regarded as outside its brief, provided that two criteria are rigorously applied. The provision must be planned rationally with the objective of some appropriate longer term outcome (either for the University itself to provide, or, equally tenable, for the provision, once established, to be handed over to another and more appropriate agency). And further, any subject provided must be taught within the liberal framework. For the purposes of this project, provision must not only be understood to conform to the objectives outlined earlier, and be concerned with individual and/or group development rather than recreational or vocational or training or qualification oriented courses: it must also involve some attempt at <u>critical analysis</u> of the subject matter within a wider context. It is only if both of these criteria are met that courses such as photography <u>et al</u> can be justified as UAE provision. Does the course, however it begins, succeed in the end in broadening out the students' interest in the subject to include some critical analysis of the social (or literary or cultural or economic etc) context within which the specific recreation or skill is located? And does it lead at least some of the students onto more sustained study or educational activity? If so, such courses can be regarded as legitimate for Pioneer Work, within the UAE framework, beyond the initial short, innovative stage. If not, then, beyond this initial stage, provision should be handed over to a more appropriate agency. Indications after the first two years of the Leeds Pioneer Work project are that there <u>has</u> been some considerable success in combining these aspects, but any final judgement must await the completion of the research at present underway, as well as the detailed reporting on future work.

There are, finally, other ancillary but important questions surrounding the Pioneer Work project which bear upon these considerations of viability. Pioneer Work at Leeds - perhaps in contrast to the Liverpool approach - has always regarded its contribution as being 'educational' rather than 'political'. It has been argued that, whilst there is an explicit commitment to educational innovation for the working class, as discussed above, there must be strict adherence to the pedagogic methods of objective study as outlined in Chapter 3. If UAE is to maintain its <u>educational</u> function it must not become merely an <u>instrument</u> of a particular political position, however worthy that position may be held to be. As was argued in Chapter 3, the notion of ideological neutrality in teaching approaches is wholly spurious, and has been used generally to mask deeply pro-bourgeois ideological stances in UAE. However, as was also stressed in Chapter 3, there is a legitimacy, indeed an absolute need, for certain practices in teaching methodology which protect and extend the educational function, above and beyond the purely polemical and propagandist level.(50)

How viable is this view of UAE's proper function, given the need, as stressed in the Liverpool project, 'to establish a position of <u>solidarity</u> with (the working class residents in the community)'?(51)

On the more directly pedagogic level, the viability of the Pioneer Work project depends also upon two related factors. First, the extent to which provision <u>inappropriate</u> to UAE can <u>in fact</u> and with success be passed on to other agencies; and second, whether or not successful intermediate course provision, bridging the gap between Pioneer Work and mainstream UAE provision, can be devised, and at least some Pioneer Work students make the transition successfully.

Neither of these is a new question for UAE, of course. Since its inception UAE has had to grapple with problems of role, inter-agency co-operation and, most important and difficult of all, the transition for adult students from innovatory and academically elementary work to sustained and serious study. What is distinctive in the present situation, however, is the context of community-based UAE which takes as its starting point the response to expressed needs in the local community and constructs (normally issue-based) provision accordingly. In this sense, therefore, work of the type undertaken at Leeds can be argued to be more solidly grounded in the local communities and their culture than previous experimental UAE provision.

As yet, however, there is insufficient evidence on either of these points to make any clear judgement. However, should either (or both) prove ultimately not to have been satisfactorily fulfilled, this, arguably, would undermine the long-term viability of the Pioneer Work approach within UAE.

More serious, perhaps, than either of these problem areas, is the perceived effect of the provision upon the students. Of what benefit - personal, collective, intellectual, educational, political or whatever - has the educational experience been? Of course, such questions can and should be put to the 'consumers' of mainstream adult education, and indeed perhaps of all education. But the point is especially germane in an experimental area of provision, where the educational contact period is frequently brief, and the 'normal' UAE students' educational expectations and motivations often do not apply. It is to an examination of these, amongst other questions, that the recently established research project funded by the DES will be addressing itself. At this stage, therefore, the question must remain open.

All in all, therefore, whilst the Leeds Pioneer Work project can claim justifiably some significant achievements, there remain many questions - both empirical and conceptual - which require further analysis and research before any confident claims can be advanced concerning the long-term viability and expansion, within UAE, for work of this type.

We should now return, briefly, to consider further the question posed at the opening of this chapter: how far are these approaches, examples of which have been discussed above, compatible with the liberal tradition as described in Chapter 2? Alternatively, how far do they represent a new variant of UAE which lies outside that tradition?

REDEFINING THE LIBERAL TRADITION

As was indicated in the earlier discussion of industrial studies, there has been a long, centrally important and continuous, though minority, tradition of UAE within a critical liberal framework, and designed specifically for working class, trade union students. To the extent that this provision persists - as it does, despite powerful opposing pressures both from within the TUC and from the wider society - it forms unambiguously a continuation of the liberal tradition. However, indications are that this provision is under severe threat. As argued earlier, trade unions and the TUC are generally moving over to a more role oriented, 'apolitical' (i.e. consensual, uncritical, and implicitly conservative), perception of workers' education and training. Within UAE itself, however, the trend in industrial studies education has also been away from critical, liberal study and towards more role oriented work. Equally important, there has been a marked tendency towards shorter courses of a less rigorous and demanding academic level within which the main emphasis has been upon 'practical' aspects of industrial relations. In brief, then, whilst industrial studies within UAE remains, without any qualification, a part of the liberal tradition, it is somewhat beleaguered, diminished in quantity and prominence, and has been undermined internally in the 1970s and 1980s by the development of provision that is more in tune with the vocational and pragmatic temper of the time.

The relationship between the liberal tradition and community adult education is considerably less clear. It has been argued throughout this book that the liberal tradition is not monolithic but is rather a continuum or spectrum, containing certain common elements, but highly disparate in its priorities and concerns. Within this continuum there has always been an important place for working class adult education, within the critical liberal framework. The argument that the liberal tradition has concerned itself <u>exclusively</u> with education of a bourgeois, individualist type, is therefore quite erroneous, both conceptually and historically. Community adult education, however, has not yet shown that it can develop substantial programmes of working class education of a standard, and in subject areas, appropriate to universities. Both the Leeds and Liverpool projects described here have yet to overcome these problems. Both have adopted firmly the criteria and objectives inherent in the liberal tradition; but, unless and until they can fulfil the criteria discussed earlier, it must remain an open question as to whether they fall genuinely within the liberal tradition of adult education, and thus, in the context of the argument here, properly within UAE provision as a whole.

There is no doubt, however, that both projects, and most other UAE experimental ventures in this field, are based upon the _ideology_ of the liberal tradition. And, despite the frustration of many of those staff concerned with the projects with the relatively low priority given to such work within UAE, and the overall conservatism and elitism of universities _per se_, staff involved frequently see their function and long-term development very much within that liberal tradition.(52) The _form_ which community adult education in the UAE section has taken - its decentralised, informal, and issue-based structure - clearly owes much both to the contemporary radical theorists of education (Illich and Freire in particular), and to the general development in western society since the 1960s of libertarian socialist ideologies and movements.(53) But the institutional context of the universities, _and_ the over-arching ideological tradition of UAE, have ensured that this has been ancillary to the objectives and criteria of the liberal tradition.(54) Whether this will continue necessarily to be the case, in the light of mounting pressure in other directions in the 1980s from both government and the universities, is discussed in the final chapter of this study.

NEW DEVELOPMENTS IN UAE FOR WOMEN AND IN PART-TIME DEGREE WORK

It would be wholly misleading to conclude this chapter, which has been concerned centrally with radical developments in UAE, without acknowledging other innovative areas of UAE which have contributed in the post war period to the liberal tradition. The broad trends of provision were outlined and analysed in the previous chapter. What such analysis omits, however, is the range of _structural_ developments within UAE provision, and these have a direct bearing upon our concerns here. There have been two such developments of particular importance in the 1970s and 1980s: the programme of 'Second Chance to Learn' (or similarly titled 'access' courses); and part-time degree provision. Both have been responses to changing social and cultural pressures, and both, like community adult education, have involved UAE in changes in the format and structure of provision. But, generally, both have conformed to the objectives and criteria of the liberal tradition, though of course given the breadth of this continuum, practice and priorities have varied widely between departments.

'Second Chance' courses have had several central purposes: to enable women to break away from the subservient and domestic roles which have been allocated to them via the culture of a male dominated society; and to gain understanding, confidence and group cohesion, by coming together in an informal but serious educational context. The popularity of such provision has been a part of the expanding consciousness of women in the period since the early 1970s, and to that extent these courses reflect social and political, as much as educational, needs. It has been a persistent contention in this study, however, that at its best the liberal tradition within UAE combines such socio-political concerns within a properly educational context. And this has been the case generally with the Second Chance provision, which has combined the 'feminist interest' with subject discipline study, and with counselling and study skills components. In the Leeds department, for example, a number of models of provision exist, ranging from the short Pioneer Work provision already mentioned, to one year courses meeting once a week for six hours each day; and from courses restricted entirely to women, to those which are open also to men, and which are taught by male as well as female lecturers. A considerable emphasis within these programmes has been laid upon access to higher education, and to professional or voluntary training in various fields (e.g. social work). Without entering into the whole debate over the discriminatory, sexist nature of contemporary society and how best to open up such attitudes to critical analysis from the general adult population, (55) it must be noted that there has been a tendency in most of this provision to recruit broadly middle class women. In more recent years there has been considerable effort made to construct provision attractive to working class women and some modest but notable progress has been made (especially at the Southampton(56) and Leeds UAE departments).

Some UAE departments have developed part-time degrees as a substantial part of their activities (e.g. Hull, Kent(57)), whilst others have found their parent universities rather less enthusiastic. There have been numerous models of provision but almost all have embodied a collaborative structure involving the UAE department and appropriate internal departments. Such provision falls within the liberal tradition for UAE departments, insofar as its objectives are to provide access for mature students to part-time degree level study, which is itself based upon liberal precepts. However, as in other contexts, the pressures within the universities and the wider society have led to increasingly vocational orientations in these as in other internal course structures. Perhaps even more important, these schemes have thus far tended to attract predominantly middle class students: as with the Open University, the enrolment from working class adults has been generally disappointing. Again, therefore, there are problems surrounding the long term development of the part-time degree structure, assuming that the criteria and objectives of the liberal tradition are accepted.

An interesting and important project, which has combined the access to higher education orientation with the opportunity for adult students to progress to degree level study, has developed in North West England from the late 1970s. The 'open college' idea originated with the Nelson and Colne College, and has involved a range of institutions in the area, most especially the University of Lancaster and Preston Polytechnic. The course, according to the 'open college's' own description, 'is intended to offer mature students a route into higher education other than by taking 'O' or 'A' level examinations, and also to provide courses of study worth taking for their own sake by those who do not wish to proceed to higher education'. Introductory Stage A units, intended to introduce adult students to skills, basic concepts and methods of study, are followed by Stage B units on a range of subject based courses. Four Stage A units, each involving fifty hours of tuition, must be satisfactorily completed before progression to Stage B: the successful completion of two Stage B units, of one hundred hours tuition each, is regarded by the University and the Polytechnic as 'A' level equivalents, and entitle students to be considered for entry to degree courses.

Several hundred adults have passed through this system, and many have gone on to higher education. Analysis of the evidence suggests that a high proportion of the students involved have had few previous educational qualifications. The scheme thus represents a good example of institutional 'networking' which has enabled a significant number of adults to progress into higher education.

CONCLUSION

The cumulative effect of the developments described in this chapter - industrial studies, community adult education, and the areas briefly mentioned above - has been to change the nature of UAE provision. But it must again be emphasised that all these, and especially perhaps community adult education, are very much minority trends within UAE, sub-themes within the overall pattern which has been dominated by quite opposite tendencies, as discussed in the preceding chapter.

Whilst the balance _within_ the liberal tradition of UAE has been changed quite considerably, other 'non-liberal' areas of UAE have assumed dominance, as was discussed in Chapter 4. This process has been indicative, among other things, of the accelerating pace of change within UAE. Never before, however, has the future for UAE been so uncertain, and the volatility, in terms of ideological orientation, of the decision-makers so marked, as in the 1980s. The future of UAE is the focus for the discussion in the final chapter. But what must be noted here, as a basis for that discussion, is that the effect of all these changes on the liberal tradition continuum has been to emphasise those aspects of UAE which could traditionally have been seen as on the fringes (community adult education, 'second chance' work, etc), or, even more significantly, outside it altogether (post experience work, professional adult education, etc), whilst relegating the traditional core of UAE provision to an almost ancillary position (i.e. subject discipline based courses in the whole range of arts and social sciences).

Of course, this must not be exaggerated: the bulk of UAE provision remains, for the short terms at any rate,[58] in these areas. But, equally, there is no doubt that the move away from this pattern has been persistent and continuous for some years, and that it shows every sign of accelerating. Whether or not a viable liberal tradition can survive into the longer term if this basic core diminishes further, is one of the key questions to be discussed in the final chapter. Before moving onto this discussion, however, attention must be turned to the experience of the USA.

NOTES

1. The whole subject of the definition of class and of social stratification is both large and contentious. For a good empirical account see Ivan Reid, <u>Social Class Differences in Britian</u>, 1981; and, for a comprehensive socialist analysis, see John Westergaard and Henrietta Resler, <u>Class in a Capitalist Society</u>, 1975.

In the context of adult education the term 'disadvantaged' is often used in an attempt to avoid the pitfalls of class definitions. However, as Tom Lovett has argued, 'the term disadvantaged is used ..... to cover the working class and other minorities suffering from physical and mental handicaps. Its use as far as the former is concerned, implies certain negative connotations and judgements regarding their lifestyle and general attitude to education. The term working class community can be interpreted in a much more positive fashion implying a distinct set of social relationships, values, attitudes and culture .....' (Lovett, Adult Education and Community Action: The Northern Ireland experience, p. 145, in eds. Fletcher and Thompson, <u>Issues in Community Education</u>, 1980).

The practice here, then, follows Lovett, and for broadly the same reasons.

The definition of 'working class' itself is of course problematic. In this context we adopt a primarily educational criterion: that is, we define as working class those people who left school at minimum school leaving age, and use occupational experience as essentially ancillary to this central educational yardstick. This is not to dismiss the complex debate over social stratification, and still less to ignore the marxist concept of class as related essentially to the ownership and control of the means of production. But it is to claim, in this context of educational debate, that this simple educational criterion is accurate enough to define our main target group for educational provision.

2. G. F. Sedgwick and D. Winnard, Trade Union Training - Is it a Dead End?, WEA News, Vol. 1., No. 4, 1971, pp. 4 - 5.

3. John McIvoy, Adult Education and the Role of the Adult in The TUC Education Scheme 1929 - 80, Studies in Adult and Continuing Education (forthcoming 1984). The internal quotation given is from the TUC Report 1975, p. 443.

This article gives a detailed and impressive critique of the training orientation of the TUC Education scheme from the perspective of the radical liberal tradition of UAE.

4. See, for example, Michael Barratt Brown, Trade Union Education and the Residential Colleges, The Industrial Tutor, Vol. 3, No. 9, Spring 1984.

5. Roger Fieldhouse and Keith Forrester, The WEA and Trade Union Education, The Industrial Tutor, Vol. 3, No. 9, Spring 1984, p. 14.

6. Bernard Foley, Trade Union education: some recent developments, The Tutors' Bulletin for Adult Education, Vol. 4, No. 2, Autumn, 1981, p. 6.

7. Tom Lovett, Adult Education and Community Action: The Northern Ireland experience, p. 145.

8. Tom Lovett, Chris Clarke, and Avila Kilmurray, Adult Education and Community Change, 1983, p. 15.

9. For a discussion of this latter perspective see Cynthia Cockburn, The Local State: Management of Cities and People, 1979.

10. Lovett, Clarke, and Kilmurray, op. cit., p. 16.

11. Ralph Miliband, A State of De-subordination, British Journal of Sociology, Vol. XXIX, No. 4 (1978), pp. 399 - 409.

This article is cited in Lovett, et al., Adult Education and Community Change, pp. 16 - 18. An earlier version of this paper was given to a Staff Seminar, Department of Adult Education, Leeds University, in 1973. (For other aspects of the arguments within this paper, see Chapter 2, p. 18).

12. For further discussion, see David Coates, The Context of British Politics, 1984.

13. Ibid., pp. 134-5.

14. Steven Cotgrove and Andrew Duff, Environmentalism, Middle Class Radicalism and Politics, Sociological Review, Vol. 28 (2).

15. Again, whether this led to genuine participation, and thus to a more democratic society, or rather was a form of social control, need not concern us here. The salient fact in this context remains that such expansion of community action did

take place. For a comprehensive account of one of the CDPs, see Kevin Ward, Batley Community Development Project: a case study in Community Action, M.Phil. thesis, University of Bradford, 1979.

16. See in particular The 'Russell Report' (Advisory Committee on Adult Education, Adult Education: a plan for development, HMSO, 1973).

17. Jack Tivey, An Education Service for the Whole Community, in (eds) Costello and Richardson, Continuing Education for the Post Industrial Society, 1982.

18. Eric Batten, Community Education and Ideology: A Case for Radicalism, in (eds) Fletcher and Thompson, op. cit., p. 30.

19. Keith Jackson, Some fallacies in community education and their consequences in working class areas, in (eds.) Fletcher and Thompson, op. cit.

20. Lovett, Clarke, and Kilmurray, op. cit., p.3.

21. Jane Thompson, cited in ibid., p. 3.

22. See ibid. (Lovett), pp. 36 - 41.

23. Council of Europe, Permanent Education - Evaluation of Pilot Experiments, interim report, Council for Cultural Cooperation Steering Groups on Permanent Education, Strasbourg, 1974, cited in ibid., p. 8 (emphasis in original).

24. Tom Lovett, The Challenge of Community Education in Social and Political Change, Convergence, Vol. XI, No. 1, 1978, p. 43.

25. Ibid., p. 46.

26. J. E. Thomas, Radical Adult Education: Theory and Practice, Nottingham Studies in the Theory and Practice of the Education of Adults, Department of Adult Education, University of Nottingham, 1982, p. 13.

27. Ibid., p. 16. Thomas goes on to cite E. Reimer, School is Dead, 1971, p. 14:
'True education is a basic social force. Present social structures could not survive an educated population, even if only a substantial minority were educated ..... People are schooled to accept a society. They are educated to create or recreate one'.

28. Jane Thompson, Women and Adult Education, in (ed.) Tight, Education for Adults, Vol. 2, Opportunities for Adult Education, 1983, pp. 152 - 3. The quotation from K. H. Lawson is taken from, Community Education: a critical assessment, Adult Education, Vol. 50, No. 1, NIAE, 1977.

29. Professor Gordon Roderick, inaugral lecture, 1976, 'Tradition, Change and Challenge in Adult Education', University of Sheffield,

Division of Continuing Education, 1976, pp. 9 - 12.

30. Professor Michael Stephens, Some National Trends, in (eds.) Thornton and Stephens, The University in its Region: the extramural contribution, Department of Adult Education, University of Nottingham, 1977, p. 187.

31. Ibid.

32. Thomas, op. cit., p. 48.

33. R. W. K. Paterson, Values, Education and the Adult, 1979, p. 255, cited in ibid., p. 48.

34. Ibid., (Paterson), pp. 255 - 8.

35. G. F. Brown, Working Class Adult Education, in (eds.) Thornton and Stephens, op. cit., pp. 57 - 63.

It is interesting to note the editorial comment at the end of this article: a good example of the more orthodox liberal educational perspective on working class adult education. 'If adult education can be said to have still a "social purpose" then surely this might be it - to equip able men and women in knowledge and in skill to take an active and constructive part in the life of the community. Let no one despise a contribution which is not only an enrichment of the region but is also a service to the wider causes of social and industrial stability and political democracy'. (p. 64, emphasis added).

36. See Lovett, Clarke, and Kilmurray, op. cit.

37. Keith Jackson, Adult Education and Community Development, Studies in Adult Education, Vol. 2, No. 2, 1970; Bob Ashcroft and Keith Jackson, Adult Education and Social Action, in (eds.) Jones and Mayo, Community Work One, 1971.

38. Ibid., (Ashcroft and Jackson), p. 44.

39. Ibid., p. 52.

40. Ibid.

41. Ibid., p. 57.

42. Lovett, Clarke and Kilmurray, op. cit., p. 35.

43. Ibid., p. 35.

44. This information is taken from ibid, and from Martin Yarnit, Second Chance to Learn, Liverpool. Class and Adult Education, in (ed.) Jane Thompson, Adult Education for a Change, 1980.

45. There have been claims that the Liverpool project has moved away from its original objectives and practice. In an unpublished paper, Mark Turnbull, a tutor on the course since 1977, levels a number of criticisms, reminiscent of the NCLC/WEA disputations, at current practice. The objectives

must be, he argued, twofold:'to equip working people with the ability to comprehend their adversary (i.e. the British ruling class)'; and to enable working people to take their own decisions and control their own environment.

By 1983, Turnbull argued, the course was failing to fulfil these aims: it 'has an academic approach which fails to relate to working-class activity. It is concerned with examining "both sides of the argument" and so abandoning our partisan cutting edge'.

Similarly, the course was concerned, by 1983, primarily with enabling students to gain access to higher education, whereas the course's aim should be to 'abolish capitalism, ... not to "open up" the education system and leave capitalism fundamentally untouched'.

Mark Turnbull, Second Chance and the Independent Working Class Adult Education Movement, unpublished paper, Liverpool 1983.

46. Predominantly for reasons of scarce resources, the decision was taken at the beginning of the project, that, at least for the first stage of the project's development, Pioneer Work would be confined to Leeds and Bradford, and not extended to other parts of the Leeds department's extramural area.

47. In the first two years of the project the following journal articles have been published.

Kevin Ward, A University Adult Education Project with the Unemployed, <u>Studies in Adult Education</u>, Vol. 15, September 1983.

Rob Imeson, Unemployed Adults and Education, <u>Bulletin of Social Policy</u>, No. 14, Autumn 1983.

Richard Taylor and Kevin Ward, University Adult Education and the Community Perspective: the Leeds Pioneer Work Project, <u>International Journal of Lifelong Education,</u> Vol. 3, No. 1, 1984.

Kevin Ward, Free and Relevant Education: A University Response to Adult Unemployment, <u>International Journal of University Adult Education</u> (University Congress Journal), 1984.

In addition, a lengthy report to the DES on the work with the unemployed was submitted in November 1983. (Kevin Ward, <u>Beyond Tokenism: Unemployed Adults and Education,</u> Department of Adult and Continuing Education, Leeds University, 1983).

48. For full information, see ibid. (Ward, <u>Beyond Tokenism</u>).

49. The DES has agreed to fund a one year research project in the first instance (£10,000),

with the possibility of an extension for a second year.

50. This is of course a contentious view, both in radical and 'establishment' circles. For the former, see, pre-eminently, Paulo Freire, The Pedagogy of the Oppressed 1972; and for the latter, Paterson, op. cit.

51. Ashcroft and Jackson, op. cit., p. 55.

52. See, for example, Ward, op. cit., (Beyond Tokenism).

53. For example, the Peace Movement, the 'Greens', and the Women's Movement. See Nigel Young, An Infantile Disorder? the Crisis and Decline of the New Left, 1977; Richard Taylor and Colin Pritchard, The Protest Makers, The British Nuclear Disarmament Movement of 1958 to 1965, Twenty years on, 1980; and Sheila Rowbotham, Lynne Segal and Hilary Wainwright, Beyond the Fragments, 1979.

54. Community adult education as organised and provided by other agencies is not subject, of course, to this ideological amalgam. Their orientations are both diverse and, to an extent, oppositional to the liberal tradition. This is one of the important reasons for inter-agency co-operation over this sort of work, where the different frameworks are complementary, and provision can be accordingly diverse.

55. See Jane Thompson's earlier book in this series, Learning Liberation - Women's Response to Men's Education, 1983.

56. See ibid.

57. And of course the Open University, but this is different in kind from the UAE work under consideration here.

58. Indications are that both the DES and the UGC, for different reasons, are intent on eroding further this core area of UAE work. See Chapters 4 and 8.

Chapter Six

THE LIBERAL PERSPECTIVE AND THE SYMBOLIC
LEGITIMATION OF UNIVERSITY ADULT EDUCATION IN
THE USA

> The American Association for Adult Education
> is dedicated to education – to the dissemina-
> tion of knowledge and to the open discussion of
> life's issues. Its activities illustrate the
> democratic process. All men and women may
> take part in them. All branches of knowledge
> may be drawn into consideration. All concep-
> tions and interpretations of human affairs may
> be presented. All expounders who respect the
> rights of others to be heard have their day
> in court.
>
> By implication, the future of the Association
> depends upon the future of democracy. If
> liberty of inquiry, exposition, and discussion
> comes to an end; if force is made to reign,
> then democracy dies. At that hour the doom of
> the education we promote is also pronounced.[1]

Charles A. Beard, President of the American Association for Adult Education (AAAE), writing in 1936,
revealed the essential connection, in the perception of leading Americans at that time, of liberal
ideals, democracy and adult education. Socially
progressive leaders saw adult education as the means
to the realisation of liberal democracy. This
occasion was the tenth anniversary of the AAAE;
Beard's works opened the Association's anniversary
publication, <u>Adult Education and Democracy</u>. Noteworthy is the symbolic legitimation of adult education in terms of democracy. That 'liberty of
inquiry, exposition and discussion' are crucial to
democracy, and education within a democracy, would
be readily agreed to by adult educators then and
now. In principle, most would agree that this means
all branches of knowledge, all adults, all

conceptions and interpretations, all expounders. In practice, qualifications abound, systematically limiting the egalitarian 'all' by pragmatic and elitist interpretations of 'appropriate', particularly for university work. This disjuncture, between liberal rhetoric and the historical development of UAE, is the basis for this inquiry into how the liberal tradition has been manifest in the USA.

The American experience of UAE illustrates the ironies of liberal thought in the USA as manifest in the bonding of education to democracy. A difficulty in researching the liberal tradition is that a philosophy of liberalism in adult education has not been articulated as a distinct approach to practice. Instead, liberalism has been assumed, and every variety of activity undertaken in its name. While the interconnectedness of liberalism, democracy and education has at times been perceived to be threatened, until the present their linkage has been assumed as an essential 'good'. Where there has been controversy it has been over meaning and means of one or the other term, within the liberal frame of reference, and within the assumption that the USA is the liberal democracy. This liberal world view is a much broader consensus than that represented by any particular political group. It is part of the American's taken-for-granted reality, typically not even named as liberalism. It exists in the unformulated frame through which the world is viewed. To outsiders it might be identified as ideology: to insiders, it simply is.

The liberal consensus in the USA is crumbling: 'neo-conservatism' vies as an alternative worldview, and a political force with which to be reckoned.(2) Ironically, conservatives herald liberal values as they carry the banners of 'progress' and internationalism. Blaming the liberals for the failure of social programmes, they promote greater privatism in the name of individual freedom and economic rationality. Liberals, for the most part, readily echo the mood of the day, calling for accountability, competency-based education, high academic standards, all in the name of excellence, the promotion of social mobility, and improved social services.

The thesis of these chapters on UAE in the USA is that the neo-conservative stance is not new: it marks the ascendance of elite pragmatism over egalitarian values within liberalism. As played out in UAE, the liberal tradition represents a history of two main conflicting stances, one elitist and the other egalitarian, joined together in an uneasy truce by the pragmatic requisites of survival. The contradictions inherent within liberalism are rooted in capitalist democracy.

The contradictions in liberalism scream out for attention. The mounting critiques of science, education and the liberal reform tradition have left adult education relatively untouched. Indeed, the connections from these critiques to everyday life are tenuous, left to the imagination or the world of abstraction. To the extent that the critiques remain restricted to the language of critique, of logic, rationality, abstraction - that is, in academic discourse - they remain disembodied, alien to lived experience, locked in the rational structures they confront.

In considering how the liberal tradition has been manifest in adult education, one begins to see how that tradition has operated in an arena of everyday practice. Some may dispute that the contradictions attributed to liberal ideology, and between ideology and practice, are properly attributed to the liberal tradition, arguing instead that inconsistencies represent misinterpretations or deviations from liberalism. Is the American tendency to eschew questions of philosophy and embrace the practical, properly considered to be within the liberal tradition? It is argued here that it is: for this is the way liberalism has been actualised in the USA, and this is its great dilemma. The humanitarian ideals of liberalism have been reinterpreted in terms of service to American democracy and its institutions. Thus, rather than democracy as an ideal, liberalism in the USA has been attached to a particular set of institutions and power relationships, and hence functioned much more as ideology than as philosophy. Ironically, liberalism, as structured in American democracy, has become, in many ways, the antithesis of liberal values.

It might be argued that adult education in the USA is not of the liberal tradition. In contrasting American and British adult education, S. G. Raybould noted:

> ..... the different ways we defined 'adult education'. The North American definition was literal and logical: adult education is any education undertaken by adults. My definition, brought with me from England, was much more restrictive: adult education is the liberal education of adults; other studies undertaken

by adults are 'further education' - and never the twain shall meet .....

..... The adult education programmes of the British universities consisted entirely of non-credit non-vocational courses of liberal study. In North America courses of this kind occupied a very minor place in Extension programmes as a whole, the main constituents of which were credit courses on the one hand and courses of professional study on the other.(3)

While Raybould's observation is important, it does not take into account the peculiarly American character of liberalism as an assumed world view. Liberalism in the USA has been pragmatic. In adult education, it has been a matter of extending the opportunity to earn degrees and credits to all who could so benefit, and of promoting the interests of democracy and social efficiency, both of which were perceived to be essential to the good life. It has become individualistic, firmly grounded on the premise of equal opportunity. 'Social purpose' has meant expanding access to education, not working toward social transformation.

The influential President's Commission on Higher Education, reporting in 1947, captured the liberal world view which has underlain educational policy:

The first goal of education for democracy is the full, rounded, and continuing development of the person. The discovery, training, and utilisation of individual talents is of fundamental importance in a free society. To liberate and perfect the intrinsic powers of every citizen is the central purpose of democracy, and its furtherance of individual self-realisation is its greatest glory.(4)

In this chapter, the connection of liberalism, democracy and adult education is considered. This leads to a discussion of the key ideas within liberalism that form the taken-for-granted assumptions which frame UAE, providing an ideological gloss for the contradictions within liberalism, as well as between liberal values and practices undertaken in their name. In the following chapter, the use of liberal ideology to annihilate left social thought as a valid part of adult education - indeed, of social experience in the USA - is portrayed.

Democracy, equality, service and excellence - these are the ideas that have served symbolically to legitimise UAE. They are the taken-for-granted assumptions of the liberal tradition that provide the legitimising basis for adult education in the university. Historically, the unversity's responsibility for the education of adults has been argued in terms of the university's democratic mission to serve the people and the country by providing the highest in educational quality, and by the dissemination and application of knowledge produced by its faculty. What is agreed upon is that adult education is a means of realising the university's democratic mission; the precise meaning of this has been the subject of considerable controversy in the past. Depending upon one's stance, the meanings of equality, service and quality have often been construed to be opposed to one another. Their co-existence as values within UAE has spawned some peculiar twists of logic and an operating mentality described herein as 'elite pragmatism'. The process has been one in which the idealistic, egalitarian values within liberalism have given way to the elitist values, also within the liberal frame, in order to survive within the university. Furthermore, it is argued that pragmatism has always been present as a factor within mainstream American liberalism, where the preservation of liberalism has been seen to be synonomous with the preservation of American political and economic institutions.

In the USA, UAE is not as clearly defined a field of practice as it is in England. While university extension is the work most clearly associated with UAE, adult education has been part of other aspects of university work, through graduate training in adult education, professional schools, evening colleges, agricultural extension, specialised institutes, etc. Then, too, the lines between UAE and the rest of adult education are not always clear; until recent times universities have tended to dominate the field through their influence in graduate training, professional associations, government agencies and foundations. In this work, UAE is loosely structured to mean the university in adult education, with university extension serving as the working arena through which one can begin to see how liberalism is manifest as a set of ideological practices.

THE KEY TO DEMOCRACY

Key to understanding the liberal tradition in the USA is its absorption by the American democratic experiment. Presumably unfettered by history, the rich new soil beckoned proponents of liberal democracy. How to operationalise the ideal? How to have a truly participatory governmental process that would be enlightened, informed, true to the principles of liberty, equality and social justice? Education has been the key: knowledge – informed choice – replaces force as the <u>modus operandi</u>. Knowledge is power: epistemology becomes politics.

Perceived as central to democracy, adult education has taken on different meanings. The earliest ideal is that knowledge is power; through the use of 'his' intelligence 'man' would find a way to promote peacefully the greater good; with education, the rational capabilities of 'man' would be developed, spilling into the political arena where rational processes would prevail. The only way to move toward a more egalitarian society was through the civilising influence of education. For some, the connection between the educational and the political is taken for granted as an article of utopian faith; for others, the faith is less utopian, their more pragmatic approach to education is as a means of social control. The premise is that the masses will be less unruly if they have access to economic mobility, use their leisure time wisely, know how to exercise their vote responsibly, and understand American democracy and culture, as well as the perils of authoritarianism, socialism, or communism.

The idealistic view of knowledge as power has co-existed with the pragmatic view of education as a means of social control. While the rhetoric of adult education is caught up in the missionary ideal of education as the key to social transformation, programmatically, the emphasis has been pragmatic: education for citizenship, Americanisation, vocational education, higher and continuing education, etc.

With the interpretation of knowledge as power, and power as knowledge, liberalism moves from a political philosophy into a unifying ideology grounded in a set of educational practices which conceal the contradictions between an egalitarian belief system and a hierarchically structured society. Education holds open the promise of possibility – it locates the 'problem' of inequality in individuals or inadequate educational 'solutions', avoiding structural issues. The focus upon the voting citizenry conceals the implicit racism and sexism in the knowledge as power concept, for not all are - or have been - voting citizens. As a system of schooling, a way of thinking, a path to social mobility, and a tool for the promotion of government interests, education has been crucial to the liberal as the primary means of maintaining American democracy.

The pragmatic linking of liberal thought to education and democracy was born of the highest ideals. Education was the means by which a new social order could be created. American liberal leaders had a deep sense of mission - some were radicals in their time. The missionary zeal of the American democratic experiment and the perceived centrality of education to its actuality, were vividly depicted by Alexander Meikeljohn in 1924:

> I think America, more than anything else, and more than any other nation that ever existed, is a vision, a spiritual adventure, a desire for something better, a purpose, an inspiration, a determination, an enterprise into which a hundred million people have thrown themselves. And I don't believe you can understand America unless you interpret it in those terms.
>
> It is what America wants to be, what she intends to be, what she is determined to be, what she is leading the whole world toward being, that is what you have to think of when you try to understand anything in America. I believe that America intends to be and must be a democracy. That is our mission, that is what we are living for, that is our opportunity.
>
> What is this democracy? As I understand it a democracy is a community which is committed to the principle that every person who comes into our human society is to have, just in so far as we can bring it about, an equal opportunity with every other for what life has to give .....
>
> My theory of democracy is this: Democracy is education. There is only one thing people can give to its citizens safely. There is only one thing a community can give to its members on a large scale and do it successfully, so far as I know, and that is education. In so

far as we can educate the people, in so far as we can bring people to understanding of themselves and of their world we can have a democracy. In so far as we cannot do that we have got to have control by the few.

..... Epictetus summed it all up a couple of thousand years ago when he said: "The rulers of the state have said that only free men shall be educated; but God has said that only educated men shall be free".

..... We have got to find out how a hundred million people can think together on the same question and make their thoughts fit into one another's thoughts in such a way that taken together they make sense as a total judgement.

..... We have got to learn intellectual interchange, so that out of a hundred million minds by some way or other, by some scheme or other, one mind, the mind of America, may be made.(5)

The passage is lengthy, but useful in the way it brings together the central themes of liberalism as manifest in the linking of democracy to education. Critical is the idea of community support for personal fulfilment and the perception that education is the only safe means by which to provide equality of opportunity for every young person. For adults, education is the means of intelligence; through the exercise of intelligence will come understanding, freedom, control, unity - the making of one mind, 'the mind of America'. Noteworthy is the curious blend of the ideas of individualism and unity, freedom and control. Implicit is a pragmatic shift from the ideal of freedom to the political need to attain unity, the desire to use safe measures, the faith in education as the vehicle for developing an adult intelligence that will foster American democracy.

Adult education, as a means of promoting democracy, moved from the realm of informal advocacy to official support in World War I. As the war ended, concern for the Americanisation of the foreign born gave way to a more broad-based approach to adult education as a means of promoting democracy. Carnegie Foundation funding for adult education, beginning in 1924, played a formative role in developing a national movement for adult education. Historically, the period was ripe for it. Out of the ravages of World War I, the USA's optimism had been shaken. In the effort to ward off communism and the appeal of socialism, adult education was made a more explicit instrument of democracy. The sense of urgency was intensified by the Depression and then World War II. In these years the institutional foundations of adult education were firmly established.

The links between adult education and democracy are not officially articulated as a specific government policy, rather they are present as a pervasive tone in the thinking about adult education. The prevalent question in the Journal of Adult Education during the inter war years concerned the relationship of adult education to democracy. While there were disagreements as to how to maximise the relationship, its significance was accepted as crucial.

Rationality must prevail against emotional attachments to propagandistic ideologies: this is a refrain that runs through the literature. Dissemination of scientific knowledge, deliberation and discussion, are the key tools in the process. The ideal model has been the American forum. Sponsored by the Carnegie Foundation in co-operation with the U.S. Office of Education, the forums were promoted by John Studebaker, U.S. Commissioner of Education, the only high-ranking government official in the history of the USA to develop a national plan for adult education. According to Studebaker, in Education for Democracy, 'forums equip citizens of civic intelligence to cope with the problems of our nation and our day'.(6)

In her probing study of the forums, Mary Ely has questioned whether the forums actually developed the capacity for intelligent critical thought that their promoters claimed to be their goal. The programmes consisted of public lectures followed by audience questions. In only a few instances did anything approximating a dynamic discussion of issues occur. Democracy was the key theme of the forums:

> As I went about from one forum meeting to another it was borne in upon me with cumulative force how completely, how passionately, our people are committed to the cause of democracy ..... Everywhere I found also that forum leaders and the people who make up the forum audiences, are pointing to democracy as the one bright star of hope in our firmament ..... the solemnly renewed pledge that we will hence

forth lead a more righteously democratic
life - it was this unifying thread of devotion
to democracy that bound together all the forum
programs that I heard.

This I saw and felt.

At the same time, throughout my forum visits,
there was always in the background of my mind
the oft-repeated declaration of our most
ardent forum advocates that the forums are not,
and must never be, the agencies of propaganda
for any conceivable cause what ever. "They
seek to establish no particular theories of
politics, economics or social organization",
are the exact words that Mr. Studebaker uses
in one of his open letters to the citizens of
Des Moines. No propaganda. Democracy. No
particular theory of social organization.

This I puzzled over.(7)

Paradoxically, democracy is not taken to be a
'particular' theory of social organisation. In the
USA, it is taken for granted as the only legitimate
form of social organisation. It is the only theory
accessible to most people - that is, the only one
taught or presented in other than horrific glosses
by the media and educational authorities (some
advanced university seminars being the only possible
exception). There is thus the anomaly that, for the
vast majority of the population, democracy is truth,
all else is propaganda.

The Carnegie Foundation declared itself to be
neutral. The Foundation organised and funded the
AAAE 'to promote the development and improvement of
adult education in the United States and to co-
operate with similar associations in other countries'. Morse Cartwright, Executive Director of
the AAAE, stressed the alleged neutrality of the
Association:

> It has consistently adhered to its policy (a)
> of serving as a central clearing house for
> information and (b) of sponsoring and conduct-
> ing studies, experiments and researches in
> adult education.
>
> ..... A sincere and compelling desire to pro-
> ceed conservatively and constructively, even
> if slowly, has ever been uppermost in the minds

> of staff and committees. This policy has prevailed in the face of numerous opportunities to strike publicly for various phases of adult education which, while perhaps meritorious in themselves, did not make directly for a safe, sane and careful upbuilding of the central idea of adult education as a continuing cultural process pursued with ulterior purposes.
>
> ..... If the ultimate ends of adult education are to be reached, the Association which represents the movement must be directly in the middle of the road; it must veer neither to the right nor to the left, although it must have sufficient strength of purpose and of character to deal fairly and dispassionately with those organizations and individuals which happen to be progressing upon the edges of that selfsame road.(8)

Writing a year later, Cartwright underlined his view of the liberal approach:

> A few years later, the report makes a plea for liberalism, paying its respects alike to communism, fascism, and hidebound conservatism in relation to educational matters. Those who seek to emotionalise the content of education, the indoctrinators for whatever cause, are declared unworthy of the adult education trust. The efforts of those who seek to seize control of our curricula for children and adults, either to overthrow or to uphold, are decried.(9)

The vision of a middle path in the midst of controversy is fundamental to the liberal policy of gradualism and neutrality as etched out in adult eduction. Through the AAAE, Carnegie sponsored a variety of programmes and studies, including everything from the cultural to the vocational, the urban to the rural, the education of workers, education for the foreign born, citizenship education, forums, community studies, and a series of projects entitled 'Emergency Education and Cooperation with the Federal Government'.(10)

With Carnegie's funding, the ideal of adult education as the key to democracy, subtly, but significantly, shifts in meaning. From the abstract ideal of knowledge as power comes the goal of promoting national unity, consensus within the USA's democratic framework. Education of all adults, providing for their continuing effort to overcome ignorance, is the key to avoiding conflict.(11) If adults know 'the facts' they will come to the right conclusions; this is the power of knowledge. In this respect, the American development paralleled the English, as has been discussed in Chapter 3.

Not all adult educators have been in favour of the middle-of-the-road position. Edward C. Lindeman, in his classic, <u>The Meaning of Adult Education,</u> raised some questions about the facilely assumed relationship between knowledge and power. Science, the great liberal tool of social progress, is not an unmitigated good in Lindeman's view:

> Science, curiously enough, furnishes grounds for both our expectations and illusions ..... Nevertheless, our power over nature, such as it is, has been achieved by intellectual processes. Scientific method is a discovery, if not an invention, of man's mind. Moreover, this power which utilizes natural forces has come to be the most potent manipulator of our lives ..... The hiatus between a life dominated increasingly by science and a life rationalized in terms of unscientific or anti-scientific thought represents one of the most appalling deficiencies of our civilization ..... Adult education presumes, then, to serve as one of the means by which the mind may be kept fresh for the assimilation of that knowledge which is snyonymous with power .... We are capble of developing sufficient intelligence to secure at least partial control over things and we know how to govern people by coercion. But we have thus far failed completely in devising intelligent procedures for socializing power.(12)

While Lindeman has great faith in the capacity for human intelligence, he recognises the dynamics of power, and urges that the power of science be democratised. The socialisation of power and the encouragement of critical reflection are central to his social philosophy. His social reconstructionist stance is not typical of adult educators, but he does represent a significant strand within the movement.

James Earl Russell, President of the AAAE for

the first four years of its history, is also concerned about the relationship between knowledge and power. Russell's concern is that in a society where mass education is promoted, not everyone can be a leader: the paradox of education in the USA is to educate leaders and followers through the same system. Instead of socialising power, his concern is with social control. According to Russell:

> ..... (we can)..... resolve our educational paradox by ignoring it or denying its existence. So far as the safety of the State is concerned, agencies are at work which secure a high degree of voluntary standarization and vocational efficiency - agencies quite as effective as the efforts used generally in the old world to enforce caste and class distinctions. And just as in the old world the schools have been used to attain their ideal of docile, obedient subjects of a monarchical state, so our schools are striving to train citizens who will voluntarily subject themselves to expert leadership in a democratic society.(13)

While it is unusual to suggest openly that class and caste serve important functions of social control which can be promoted by education in a democracy, Russell captures the prevailing concern about social control. Of course he sees his position as a 'neutral' one. Agreeing with the stance taken by Cartwright and the Carnegie Commission, Russell concludes 'it follows, therefore, in promoting adult education that this association should not be partisan'. The objectives of adult education as he sees them are to develop leaders, which Russell defines as knowledgeable experts, to promote social control through vocational training, and to provide guidance for voluntary standardisation.

EQUALITY OF OPPORTUNITY

Equality of opportunity is the ideological means to the promotion of voluntary standardisation. Not only has the public mind been made to believe that there is equal opportunity, but the process of acquiring it has pushed all along the same educational conveyor belt. Demands for social reform are mediated by opening up educational access. In the nineteenth century, the ideology of opportunity applied primarily to children; in the twentieth century, especially in the years from World War I to World War II, the ideology was extended to include adults as well.

The doctrine of equality of opportunity is central to the USA's liberal framework. In this land of plenty, equality has been perceived to be a function of a liberal political process rather than an economic problem. Economic opportunity has been assumed, left up to the prerogative of the individual. The transition in thinking, from equality as a social goal to equality of opportunity, is significant in shifting attention from the idea of equality of condition as a right, to the idea of providing the individual with the opportunity to change his or her condition, theoretically the only limitation being the individual's capacity or motivation. The significance of this shift in focus from social condition to individual advancement must not be underestimated. The ideology of the USA as the land of unlimited opportunity, the myth of the self-made 'man', personified by Horatio Alger, has glossed over structural inequalities and permitted the merger of an egalitarian political ideology with a hierarchically structured economic system. As Richard de Lone has pointed out in his work on the limits of liberal reform:

> There is, as many writers have observed, a deep tension in liberal thought between the political and economic traditions. The political tradition emphasizes equal rights of all individuals, rights conferred by the natural law from which human reason draws its strength. The economic tradition emphasizes not so much the rights as the prerogatives of individuals in the pursuit of self-interest, e.g. the accumulation of property and wealth. Rights and prerogatives often clash. The political tradition of rights embraces equality while the economic tradition of prerogatives leads to inequality.(14)

De Lone proceeds to argue that the ideology of opportunity shifts the focus from adults to children who become the 'Bearers of the Dream'. Education is overwhelmingly child centred; in their future lies the hope of liberal democracy. The deferred dream hides structural inequalities that are integral to patriarchy and racism, as well as capitalism. Certainly, education in the USA (as in England) has always been predominantly child centred, yet there have been times when adults have also been an educational target in the realisation of the American dream. The idea that adults must learn to participate as good citizens in American democracy has been there from the time of the Revolution. In the 1890s adult education became a vigorous assault on 'foreigners', solidifying into a nationwide Americanisation campaign around the time of World War I. Since World War II, adults have also been part of government policies that have used education as the means to promote equality of opportunity. For workers, 'illiterates', minorities and, most recently, women, adult educational provision is rationalised in terms of providing equality of opportunity. The cardinal premise has been that such education must not be 'separate'; that inequality is taken care of by expanding existing educational opportunities, not to workers as workers, or women as women, or blacks as blacks, etc., but to each individual as an American adult. Through opening access to education, each will gain access to the possibility of advancement through the American economic system.

Opportunity is the right to individual advancement for those who can seize the prerogative to do so: in a significant way, the individual is decontextualised from the social historical context, treated as though one of a mass of other individuals, and given the opportunity to see how far up the ladder he or she can climb. If one does not go far, the problem is an individual one, lack of motivation or capacity. The problem is not conceived as one born of unequal conditions, a human condition which is integral to the capitalist economics on which democracy in the USA has come to rest.

Equality of opportunity has also had critical consequences for adult education in its effect upon the amount of resources put into childhood as contrasted to adult education. Unless they are categorised as 'deprived' and therefore as needing further opportunity, adults must pay for their education, on the premise that as mature, responsible people, they will appreciate their education much more if they assume personal responsibility for the cost. The doctrine of personal responsibility has been extended to include the idea that adults must continue their education over their lifespan in order to maintain their right to opportunity and to keep abreast of change. The educator's job is one of making sure programmes are provided, and that they are available to all adults willing to participate.

Psychological research into adult learning has

played a central role in the reinterpretation of equality of opportunity in adult education. To the assumption that adult learning is critical to democracy, there is now scientific proof that some adults are capable of learning well into their fifties. Ironically, this premise has contributed to the unprecedented expansion of opportunities for adult education through hierarchically structured educational institutions, indirectly giving voice to the elitist impulses in adult education. Edward Thorndike's pioneering research on adult learning played right into the democratic/elite tensions so prevalent in the contradictory myth of equality of opportunity: now it could be scientifically justified to say that the opportunity was for those who could benefit by it.

In <u>Adult Learning</u>, Thorndike discussed the practical applications of his research for adult education. Thorndike's theory is that nobody under forty-five should attribute to age the failure to learn. Instead, such failure should be attributed to lack of capacity, lack of desire, inadequate methods of learning, or the unwillingness to alter personal tendencies that interfere with learning. As to implications for teachers and administrators of adult education:

> In general, teachers of adults aged 25 to 45 should expect them to learn at nearly the same rate and in nearly the same manner as they would have learned the same thing at 15 to 20. What that rate and manner will be depends upon the general intelligence and special capacities of the individual. Men and women of the dull half of the population will not at any age learn after the fashion of high-school pupils, who are, almost without exception, from the bright half. Individuals in this country who leave school to go to work at fourteen are in general much duller than those of the same community who leave at later ages. Those of them who return to study later in evening schools or correspondence schools are probably much brighter than those who do not so return, but their exact status is uncertain.

> Those in charge of enterprise for adult education ought to be provided with the means for administering a system of admission and classification that will be even more searching and decisive than is customary in schools for the

young. The variability of the applicants is likely to be wider than at any point of admission, promotion, or classification of the young. The failure to exclude incapables is more likely to degrade the instruction given to their level, because general standards to guide the instructor are lacking.(15)

Thorndike's work in World War I and the years immediately following has been critical in establishing the idea that adults have the capacity to continue to learn, if they have the desire and requisite ability to do so. His research is a landmark in the development of a scientific professional basis for adult education policy. It has laid the basis for establishing differential approaches to adult education policy. Until the 1960s, 'the dull half' of the adult population was ignored. Clearly, adult education was for those with education, or the very few bright ones who might have missed it in their childhood. It is significant that Thorndike was president of the AAAE in 1934-35. In 1935, Graduate Study in adult education was initiated at Columbia University under the leadership of Lyman Bryson. The scientific basis of graduate training has been drawn from psychology and management theory. At that time, Columbia was also the home of Morse Cartwright and the Carnegie Foundation Project on Adult Education.

Ironically, equality of opportunity found a scientific basis in the psychology of individual development, which sanctioned the mass institutionalisation and legitimation of inequality: now equality of opportunity should be made available to those able to benefit from it. The onus of failure shifted from social conditions to individual shortcomings - the lack of individual motivation as the never-ending dilemma. Adult education became a matter of matching individual abilities and motivations to educational opportunities. However it played into the justification of inequality in the name of equality, the idea that adults can learn was revolutionary for its time and was to have a tremendous impact.

Proclaiming its goal as the 'Education of All', the Truman Commission studied the results of IQ testing during World War I, and concluded that:

1) At least 49% of our population has the mental ability to complete 14 years of schooling with a curriculum of general and

vocational studies that should lead either to gainful employment or to further study at a more advanced level.

2) At least 32% of our population has the mental ability to complete an advanced liberal or specialised professional education.(16)

This 'national pool of talent' included adults. For the first time in the USA's history, federal policy explicitly named adult education as integral to its political and economic objectives. A programme of mass higher and adult education was expounded as crucial to democracy. 'The Goal - Equal Opportunity':

Equal educational opportunity for all persons, to the maximum of their individual abilities and without regard to economic status, race, creed, color, sex, national origin, or ancestry is a major goal of American democracy. Only an informed, thoughtful, tolerant people can maintain and develop a free society.

Equal opportunity for education does not mean equal or identical education for all individuals. It means, rather, that education at all levels shall be available equally to every qualified person.(17)

Policies to promote equality of opportunity place the emphasis upon adult access to regular degree programmes. Most of these opportunities have been directed toward men, either in the armed forces or through the G.I. Bill. Since World War II, one of the best ways for a 'disadvantaged adult' (working class male) to acquire a higher education has been through the military. While this has changed with the dismantling of the G.I. Bill, the 1980 Amendments to the Higher Education Act authorised a study of 'the extent to which Federal student assistance may be used to promote the recruiting of individuals to serve in the Armed Forces and to retain members of the Armed Forces'.(18)

The promotion of adult access to degree programmes has meant that a major aspect of UAE has been undertaken outside the domain of university extension. In the post-war years, degree-related education was frequently offered through university evening colleges. To accommodate returning veterans, these grew in unprecedented proportions during the late 1940s. The most significant experiment in the history of liberal education for adults was partially a response to the chaotic development of these colleges and the many problems they posed. In 1951 the Center for the Study of the Liberal Education of Adults (CSLEA) was funded by the Ford Foundation's newly created Fund for Adult Education. The Fund was also concerned to protect the USA's democratic institutions by seeking to encourage a return toward more traditional educational values in the conservative post-war era. The CSLEA stressed non-credit, liberal programming for adults, but could not stem the tide toward degree credit. Moving away from the conventional subject centred definition of liberal education, the CSLEA's focus put 'man' at the centre. As one observer noted:

> No matter what approach, content, method, or organization is used, the distinguishing feature of liberal education is its view of man as the central figure in a ground of things. When liberal educators are doing what they ought to be doing, they are worrying not so much about poverty as about poor people, not about perfecting systems but about producing people who can cope with systems, not about making a good society, but about developing good men.(19)

By 1954, the CSLEA had lost its basic grant from Ford Foundation; its mantle was picked up by the Higher Education Act of that year which, for the first time in history, provided federal funding for Community Service and continuing education programmes. For a decade, 'equality of opportunity' would be pursued with unprecedented fervour, but this time under the guise of individual need fulfilment. Firmly grounded in the concept of individual need, adults, especially those from 'disadvantaged' populations, were encouraged to continue their educations. As Nell Keddie has suggested, need is the mirror image of achievement: 'the emphasis on individual need in both adult and primary education blurs the competitive edge of the ideology of individual achievement which informs secondary and higher education'.(20)

More recently, there has been a marked shift away from the welfare liberalism of the 1960s. Most significant is the trend toward the privatisation of education. Nowhere is this more noticeable than in UAE, which must survive on a self-support basis. As the economic crisis has hit the universities, forms of indirect support to extension have been eroded progressively. Indirect support, such as office and classroom space, long taken for granted, is threatened as university administrators look for every possible way to trim budgets. Extension's precarious position is made even more precarious as universities move into the adult 'market', not through extension, but through regular campus departments, ever on the lookout for new sources of students.

The Higher Education Act Amendments of 1980, passed just before the Reagan takeover, reflected these transitions in UAE. Couched in the ideology of 'equality of opportunity', Title I of the Amendments is dedicated to equality of access, freedom of choice, quality, responsiveness 'to rapidly changing social and economic needs', and the efficient use of resources. Significantly, Title I is now relabelled 'Continuing Postsecondary Education Program and Planning'.(21) Whereas the 1965 Act stressed community service '..... to assist in such areas as housing, poverty, government, recreation, employment, youth opportunities, transportation, health and land use',(22) the 1980 amendments begin from the premise:

> ..... that institutions of higher education in our Nation and their human and intellectual resources are critical to the future of American society and that the Nation's economic potential, its strength and freedom, and the quality of life for all citizens are tied to the quality and extent of higher education available.(23)

Noteworthy is the direct link between higher education and the economy, the paramount theme of the Amendments as post secondary education is repeatedly linked to labour force preparation; need is clearly perceived as employment. A related aspect of the Amendments, significant also in terms of the privatisation of higher education, is the inclusion of business, industry and organised labour as major participants in the control, co-ordination and execution of the provision for post secondary education. At the same time, a primary concern is clearly with the maintenance and support of institutions of higher education as efficiency, co-ordination and planning are repeatedly stressed. The Amendments explicitly provide for outreach to adults, particularly women wanting to re-enter the labour force. It is stated explicitly that 'with declining population growth rates, the future of post secondary education in the United States is largely dependent upon its ability to respond to the challenges of new student populations'.(24)

The use of adult student markets to soften the feared effects of declining enrolments has become accepted policy. At the same time, the hierarchically tiered system, inherent in the very concept 'post secondary education' is maintained. Note how the Amendments provide for the 'disadvantaged':

> ..... to meet the unique problems and needs of adults who are disadvantaged in seeking access to post-secondary educational opportunities, resources must be marshalled from a wide range of institutions and groups, including community colleges, community-based educational institutions, business, industry, labour, and other public and private organisations and institutions.(25)

Missing is any mention of higher education or the university, which are mentioned throughout the other Amendments. By adapting post secondary education to the conception of 'need', the social order is maintained through differentials in institutional responses to need fulfilment. Differences in need legitimise differences in education. Efficiency means that the appropriate institution responds to the appropriate need as manifest in different categories of the population. Differences in condition mandate differences in response, if some degree of efficiency is to be realised. In an era of declining resources, efficiency is essential to serve as many as possible. Equality of opportunity requires different treatment for conditions vary, resources are limited, and excellence must be maintained. So inequality is perpetuated under the guise of equality, in the name of difference - or 'unique problems and needs'.

It is not insignificant that equality of opportunity as a goal tends to wax and wane with the status of the economy, in part to maintain a <u>status quo</u> in the labour force and in educational enrolments. After World War II, the G.I. Bill was a means of keeping returning veterans from flooding the labour market. True, they then flooded educational institutions, initiating an expansion that did not subside for decades. During the economic growth period of the 1960s, equality of opportunity kept the economy going; in the 1980s it is helping to fill over-expanded educational institutions, alleviating the strain on the depressed labour market. Through financial aid to students, the strain on welfare is eased, and the financial status of higher educational institutions enhanced. But as financial aid is cut back and tied to draft status, and as fees are increased, the financial burden progressively falls upon the individual student.

Even in its heyday, equality of opportunity, as conceptualised within the framework of liberal ideology, was limited. Equality is for those who seek to enter the mainstream on the terms laid out by the dominant white male establishment. The suppression of the Black Liberation Movement and the backlash against feminism are testimony to the limits of equality as practised in the USA. The defeat of the Equal Rights Amendment (ERA) suggests that the fears of 'real equality', even as limited to 'rights', run deep. Laying bare the patriarchal bias of liberalism, Zillah Eisenstein has outlined the ideological twists in logic that have been used to keep women in their place:

> If liberal capitalist society cannot abide real equality between the sexes, and if equality of opportunity is subversive to itself in that once it is accepted as a 'right' it leads to further expectations about a more substantial equality, and if feminism ..... has been the major political movement in the 1970s to highlight the inadequacy of liberal ideology for creating real equality, then the importance of neoconservatives reembracing the notion of so-called sexual difference in an attempt to reassert the necessity of (a form) of inequality in the race of life becomes clear. The concept of sexual difference is being used to curtail and define an acceptable notion of equality - meaning equality of opportunity and not equality of conditions. And the particular import of using the concept of sexual difference is that it can be used to underline and justify the notion of difference <u>as natural and necessary</u>. Once the race of life between men and women <u>as a specific</u> is justified as natural, the epistemological and political base of equality of opportunity in <u>general</u> is made. The natural differences (inequalities) in the (sexual) race of life justify the inequalities of the

economic and social race of life.(26)

THE IDEOLOGY OF SERVICE

'The urgent necessities of world-wide understanding and cooperation cannot be postponed ..... it assumes responsibility for a program of adult education reaching far beyond the campus and the classroom'.(27) In the conservative periods following each of the world wars, adult education became a national priority, turned to out of the sense of urgency that democracy might not survive a generation while waiting for the impact of childhood education. It could be argued that the neoconservatism of the post Vietnam period is a continuation of this tendency to turn to adult education as a means of peaceful post-war reconstruction. In each instance, democracy is perceived to be threatened, both internally and externally, by the forces of radicalism, socialism, communism or fascism. The economic and political supremacy of the USA stands challenged. An intelligent citizenry and a national pool of highly trained manpower become national priorities to meet this challenge - and to absorb the labour excesses occasioned by post-war demobilisation.

So epistemology meets politics in yet another way. Concern, or an 'informed citizenry', is intensified by the challenges to American institutions and supremacy posed by wartime opposition. This has led to the explicit use of adult education as an instrument of government policy and a major arena for Foundation funding. Significantly, post-war conservatism results in a return to traditional, elite, liberal education, as well as specialised vocational/professional/technical education. These tend to go hand in hand, as a means of promoting national cohesion, strengthening the social order, re-establishing the USA's economic and military supremacy, and redirecting manpower into new economic sectors. More progressive elements within liberalism (i.e. people working through the CSLEA), unintentional though this may be, join more conservative elements in the call for excellence, unity and the revitalisation of democracy through the development of individual intellectual capacity. Institutional redirection is called for in the name of service - service to the individual, to the community, and, above all, to further the interests of democracy.

The ideology of service represents another critical element in the interconnection of liberalism, democracy and education. Service is the peculiarly American interpretation of the liberal ideals of social purpose and professional responsibility as discussed in Chapters 3, 4 and 5. The utilitarian construction of service captures the curious blending of the pragmatic and ideal in the American liberal tradition as it responds to the pressures of egalitarian democracy within a capitalist economy. Inherent in the service ideal is a tension between the populist vision of democractic control by the public, and the elitist vision of the professional providing for public need. As universities expanded and the professoriate professionalised, new consumer needs had to be constituted to create a demand for academic services, to secure the economic stability and monopoly of the university within the public market place. University extension played a key role in this process.

While the meaning of service changed dramatically in the period of World War I, it was not a new conception. The idea that knowledge in some way should be made practical and serve political interests was institutionalised with the passage of the Morrill Land-Grant Act in 1862 which stipulated that proceeds from the sale of federal lands were to be used by each state for:

> the endowment, support, and maintenance of at least one college where the leading object shall be, without excluding other scientific and classical studies, and including military tactics, to teach such branches of learning as are related to agriculture and the mechanic arts, in such a manner as the legislatures of the states may respectively prescribe in order to promote the liberal and practical education of the industrial classes in the several pursuits and professions in life.(28)

In accentuating the education of the industrial classes, the Act has been significant in laying the basis for the idea that higher education has a responsibility in providing for equality of opportunity. The meaning of that education was left ambiguous, however. Should it provide industrial classes with access to traditional higher education to which would be added a few practical subjects, or should it alter drastically the content of higher education to serve the practical needs of agrarian and industrial workers? The more practical solution was to accept the former interpretation and expand access to higher education. With the development of science and technology, agricultural and mechanical arts were removed from the province of the industrial classes to the middle and even upper classes. In the development of the sciences of engineering and agriculture, the university etched out a viable role for itself.

The Morrill Act turned out to be a critical element in establishing at least one, and more often two, public universities in each state, as federal funds were augmented by state funds. The institution of public universities, dependent upon a mixture of state, local and private funds for survival, accentuates the idea of 'public service' as a major function of the American university. Along with practical and popular mandates go the dimensions both of propinquity, that is, the notion of service to the residents of the state, and of pragmatism, that is, service to those interests upon whom support depends - government, big business, and the paying public.

The ideology of service weds liberal ideals to practical concerns for survival. With the economic base of university support shifting to government, responses to political and public pressure are rationalised in terms of the ideology of public service. When the economic base shifts to private capital, academic priorities are legitimised as serving the public through furthering economic development. Pragmatic initiatives are legitimised in terms of liberal values - the promotion of the common good. As has been suggested, the idea of serving individual needs by providing access to higher education has been integral to the ideology of equality of opportunity, the American interpretation of the liberal values of human rights, social justice and equality. The problem has been in identifying which individual needs to serve, who will identify what the individual needs, and how to provide for their being met. This has given rise to the central controversies in adult education over content, method and audience. There is an egalitarian/elite split in adult education which is intensified by its location in the university. This split, a manifestation of the tension between liberalism and democracy, is discussed below.

The utilitarian aspects of the service ideology are not necessarily in contradiction with liberal ideals. Integral to the idea of service is the goal of improving the quality of life, manifest in the notion of university responsibility to apply its knowledge for the betterment of society. The

Progressive reform movement at the dawn of the twentieth century saw liberals advocate the use of expert knowledge to promote rational government planning and decision-making. University men were taken by the idea of disseminating academic knowledge, and applying newly developing scientific understanding and methods in the physical and social sciences to the improvement of social conditions and political decision-making processes. Science, social mission and professionalisation were united in the ideal of service as social reform. The liberal ideal shifted from that of the gentleman reformer to the image of the scientific expert. Academics as expert advisers to government, business, and industry emerged as a critical phenomenon. So too were initiatives for commissioned research, which would drastically change the shape of the American university.

Adult education in the university was born of these various pressures to serve the public. Disgruntled farmers and mechanics after the passage of the Morrill Act argued that the university was not responsive to their needs. Rather than radically shift the university's conception of purpose, extension courses were added to quieten the demands of influential publics not directly considered within the university's purview. Next, pressure for extension came from the university itself to meet the challenge of developing a coherent system of high school accreditation so that it would have a pool of highly qualified students to draw upon for admissions. This required the education of a cadre of teachers, and this was extension's first official mission in the 1890s. When forces in various localities throughout the state organised to found local institutions of higher education, extension outposts were established to stay public pressure, increase access and maintain university hegemony in the state. Typically, egalitarian pressures for university expansion were met first through extension: recently, however, declining enrolments have spurred the university proper to pursue and develop an adult market. That the university used extension to promote its interests is hidden in the record: initiatives were always justified in terms of the loftier goals of public service or social advancement.(29)

Just as the university's pragmatic interest in survival and expansion gave impetus to extension work, so too did the idea that the university had a key responsibility for social advancement through the dissemination and application of scientific knowledge. In the merger of science and politics, the university has played a key role. To the earlier liberal ideal of extension as the means for disseminating academic knowledge, has been added the goal of direct social service through research, consultancy, planning and public education. Alain Touraine, in comparing the university's role in the USA to its role in Japan and France, has noted that:

> the United States - where the university's role as producer of knowledge is more important, at least since the First World War and especially since the Second World War - is more accustomed to an ambiguous type of academic rhetoric that is progressive and conservative at the same time and goes beyond a flat abstract liberalism.

The concept of need is an example of this form of rhetoric. Touraine also observed that 'the American academic system has more often served the power structure's ideology'.(30) Service is the ideology that blends the conservative and the progressive, concealing and yet providing the link between the university and the power structure.

The history of adult education in the university has been caught up in the democratic and elite tensions of higher education. The zenith of its democratic expression has been during major periods of social reform. In the Progressive reform era the idea gained ascendancy that the university had a responsibility for the education of all people in whatever form or subject was necessary. Key was the idea that maximum social efficiency would be advanced through the widest possible diffusion of knowledge. An influential speaker for this position was Lester Frank Ward:

> ..... Knowledge is science ..... it is a power as soon as it is possessed by the mind. It is as useful to one mind as to another. It is the only working power in society, and the working power of society increases in proportion to the number possessing it - probably in greater proportion. Only a few minds possess any considerable part of it. <u>All are capable of possessing it all</u>. The paramount duty of society therefore, is to put that knowledge into the minds of all its members .....

> But society has never and nowhere been so
> organised as to transmit the products of ach-
> ievement to more than a small fraction of its
> members ..... Of all the problems of applied
> sociology that which towers above all others
> is the problem of the organisation of society
> so that the heritage of the past shall be
> transmitted to all its members alike. Until
> this problem is solved there is scarcely any
> use in trying to solve other problems. Not
> only are most of them otherwise incapable of
> solution, but this primary problem once solved
> all others will solve themselves.(31)

Like Lindeman, Ward saw the primary problem to be the breakdown of the monopoly of knowledge and power. Their egalitarian views about the capability of all stand in sharp contrast to Thorndike and other equality of opportunity advocates: inequities are due to hierarchical social organisations, not differences in individual ability or motivation. For Ward, there were no limits to the potential of science - the key to egalitarianism is its accessibility to everyone.

Ward's ideas of intellectual egalitarianism and social efficiency were influential in Wisconsin, where the state university provided a uniquely American alternative to the English model of extension lectures. Under the banner of 'service to the people of the state in every practicable manner', Dean of Extension Louis Reber explained the 'Wisconsin Idea':

> Right or wrong, you find here a type of Uni-
> versity Extension that does not disdain from
> the simplest forms of service. Literally
> carrying the University to the homes of the
> people, it attempts to give them what they
> need - be it the last word in expert advice;
> courses of study that carry university credit;
> or easy lessons in cooking and sewing.(32)

The Wisconsin model, which included departments of class and correspondence instruction, public lectures and entertainments, debate and public discussion, information and social welfare, provided the basis for the 'revivification' of extension in the USA prior to World War I.

The world wars and Depression years saw the universities actively put themselves in the service of democracy; because of its relative oppenness, adult education was seized to meet manpower and civic education needs. For example, during World War I, the University of California's Board of Regents resolved:

> That through the public service efforts of the University of California, the university should exert powerful leadership in the crystallization of public thought in defense of American institutions and American ideas, and this work should especially be recommended to the attention of the Department of Agriculture and University Extension Division.(33)

Service is a complex concept that has been used in many ways to legitimise the expansion of the university. Throughout its history, extension has been legitimised in terms of the university's responsibility for service. The meaning of that service has varied depending upon the audience. To the public, service in its interests has been stressed; to the university administration and faculty,(34) extension's service to the university has been stressed.

In the university, the meaning of service has shifted according to pragmatic demands of survival. Basically, extension has been tolerated in the university, not because of some abstract vision of social transformation or commitment to the education of adults, but because it is seen as useful in promoting the university's interests in the state. From the perspective of the university faculty and administration, extension's purpose has been to serve the university. In California, Extension initially was seen as a means of developing a pool of talented high school students for University admission. In later years Extension would actually perform preparatory functions for the University. In the first half of the twentieth century, Extension played a key role in checking the establishment of potentially rival state institutions which were feared as a threat to the University's dominance in the state. During the Depression years, Extension was actively used to perform a public relations function for the University. During World War II, Extension was used as a key agency for government training in the armed forces and in defence industries. Following the war, it continued this work under the guise of continuing professional education. The public relations role of Extension has always been crucial in the University administration's convincing the faculty to let it continue to exist. Though the faculty, for the most part, could see no reason for Extension, it could appreciate that Extension reached influential audiences: the powerful and wealthy of the locality.

The pragmatic view of the service ideology distorts to a large degree the ideals of some of its adherents. In California, there have been Extension leaders who have argued rigorously in terms of fairly radical public service ideals - two were dismissed when their more populist interpretation of service differed from the University's more traditional sense of mission as teaching and research. The first Extension dismissal was Ira Howerth who attempted, unsuccessfully, to import the Wisconsin model to California in 1912. The second was Paul Sheats who ultimately resigned in 1968. While the forces involved in Sheats's resignation should not be reduced to conflicts over public service, controversial service activities undertaken during his administration were a key factor in the opposition of the University administration to his position as University-wide Dean for Extension.

As early as the 1950s, Sheats stressed the importance of Extension's role in community development. When the Ford Foundation began to experiment with public service programming in 1962, Extension, under Sheats's leadership, quickly succeeded in securing funds for a new type of programming. Most controversial was the Oakland project, the goal of which was to have a direct effect upon the urban decay of the troubled city. Project workers moved away from the original intention of working through government agencies: as they found their efforts increasingly frustrated in working through official channels, they moved toward grass roots civil rights efforts, working with independent citizen action organisations, and touching off a major controversy within the university. Disillusioned project workers concluded:

> It is ironic that most of the University's resources are irrelevant when confronting the immediate problems of the poor. At best the University can address these problems in a secondary manner. That is, the University can 'teach the teachers', or 'consult the consultants', or 'plan for the planners'.(35)

University Extension continued to work in the public service area, but confined its work largely to this secondary function - that is, training people to work in communities. Title I of the 1965 higher Education Act was central to opening up this possibility. The stipulation that activities must be 'consistent with the institution's overall educational program and ..... appropriate to the effective utilisation of the institution's special resources and the competencies of its faculty',(36) reinforced the 'training of trainers' concept. Nevertheless, vital social programmes were mounted which otherwise could not have been. The point is that public service programmes cannot be expected to pay for themselves, either because people do not have the money, or the money they do have to spend on education is more apt to be spent on activities that they perceive to be of personal benefit. Public service programmes, in the highest sense of liberalism's concern for social purpose, received unprecendented support through Title I of the Higher Education Act; with the conservative redirection of those funds toward post secondary and continuing education, funds for social purpose programmes are virtually non-existent, and their demise is evident everywhere.

The consequence of the shift in funding for extension from the public to the private sector has had serious consequences for programming. To succeed, extension must be integrally tied into the economic base of the community. The movement is away from not only public service, but also general interest courses, and toward career oriented and/or contract courses that are indirectly supported by business and industry, or directly through personal funds. As one extension Dean observed, a programme entitled 'Peace and the Children' might be very well-intentioned, but 'where's the money in that? There are no dollars - no support. You need ties to the economic base of the community to survive these days'.(37)

Practice is defined by marketing strategies; the consequence is the 'commodification' of extension. Curiously, the language of marketing and the language of service exist side by side. Or not so curiously: according to Magali Larson, anti-market service ideology is central to the development of a professional market:

> As I have emphasised, the need to establish social credit for markets of services ..... involved shaping the need of the consumers .... The production of new needs, or the direction

153

> of largely unrecognised needs toward new forms
> of fulfilment, is a civilising function, to the
> extent that it does not obey first to the
> profit motive, but seeks first to improve the
> <u>quality</u> of life ..... they could not secure the
> market without guaranteeing the high quality
> of their services.(38)

In severely restricted economic times, even the sense of responsibility to serve the educational needs of adults is shifting. Whereas in the past Extension Deans have been in the position of advocacy for adult students not served by the university, a new breed of administrator is shifting focus to those markets that can bear the high fees necessitated by self-support policies. As an Extension Dean in the University of California system explained it:

> instead of being an advocate of students not
> served by the University, Extension must res-
> pond to the University need for ties with
> business and industry for support ..... my
> educational mission is to contribute to the
> larger teaching, research and public service
> role of the University, not to provide an edu-
> cational alternative for adults ..... We've
> chosen to go after an elite population our
> faculty can relate to.(39)

Extension has always been in a marginal position in the university, its economy dependent upon shifting course enrolments. Though at times it has been looked upon more favourably, it has never been conceived of as a primary function; it has not enjoyed a stable base of fiscal, faculty or administrative support. Extension is peripheral to the university's primary goals of teaching and research; it is tolerated as long as it does not interfere with the university's image and can be justified as enhancing the university's base of public support. Neither adult education nor public service are conceived of as major university goals, although at various times in the past they have been supported, often to lure funds, whether in the form of student enrolments or federal and state appropriations. In California, there are signs that the University is assuming greater control over Extension programming as Extension fights decentralisation to the departmental or school level, appointments of University administrators to Extension posts, and complete integration into academic structures.

Public service is less integral to the academic sense of mission than ever before. Where it is alluded to, it is in terms of the application of research, usually through specialised institutes or the indirect effects of teaching. In the academic mind, extension has little to do with public service; it is seen as adult education, and tolerated for purposes of public relations. But then, the meaning of public service has never been clear. Recently, one of the more applied campuses in the University of California system deliberated establishing an Organized Public Service Council. Former Extension Dean Glen Burch writes of his 'uncomfortable' feelings with the deliberations:

> We realised only at the end that there can never be agreement about just what public service means; the discussions reminded me of arguments about the nature of the Holy Ghost in that other sacred trinity. Everybody is convinced it is important but nobody is quite sure what it is.[40]

Nevertheless, the service ideology lives on in UAE. It means providing education opportunities that respond to adult learning needs and interests. Service is operationalised in the form of needs assessment, letting communities, educational groupings or individuals determine what is to be learned. The service ideology is that adults, as mature individuals, know what they need to learn best when education is directly relevant to their problems. The service ideology also lives on in the emphasis upon serving the needs of government and economy. Emphasis has been upon learner centred programme design and teaching methodology, or social needs, not questions of social purpose. The utilitarian process orientation of the needs assessment approaches have appeared to be inconsistent with the idea of content. In adult education theory, the learner knows what he or she needs; in practice, influential sectors of society (for example, employers, government officials, educators) often determine what is needed - in either case, the subject matter is interpreted as secondary. This gives rise to one of the biggest controversies within the liberal tradition: process vs. content. Concerns for quality and standards have been perceived to be in direct contradiction to the ideology of service.

FROM EXCELLENCE TO MARKETING

> There is so much talk of service in these times that we have come to feel that we must teach everyone whatever he wants to know. Consequently our university announcements of courses look like a Sears-Roebuck catalogue. Let us be more discriminating. (41)

The elite/egalitarian tension within the liberal tradition has been a fundamental source of conflict within UAE. At stake are questions of epistemology, that is, what constitutes legitimate knowledge, and politics, that is, who determines and controls knowledge. Elitist conceptions of knowledge are in conflict with egalitarian values of social justice; elitist conceptions of differences in human capability are in conflict with egalitarian notions of innate capacity. As already discussed, the provision of mass educational opportunity for those who could benefit from it has been the liberal way out of the contradiction. Another way has been to set up a system of hierarchically tiered educational institutions. In the case of UAE, the inevitable 'solution' has been to appeal to the most highly educated adults in the population. This has been necessary, in order to survive financially, in order to appease the faculty, in order to achieve status in the community, and in order to appease inner conflict around the desire for excellence.

Liberalism in the USA is grounded in an epistemology of rationality. Its methods and discourse are those of philosophy and science, or scientific reason. The idea of excellence derives from an idealistic conception of knowledge which posits that one can, through study and deliberation, come to know the truth, and that truth will set one free, for appropriate behaviour flows from objectively knowing what is true. The idea of excellence also suggests a hierarchy of knowledge which might be thought of as moving from the instinctual to the realms of myth, common sense, practical reasoning, intuition, and, at the apex, scientific reasoning. Current theories of lifespan, cognitive and moral development are built upon the premise of an implicit hierarchy. The educational system and, to some extent, the labour market, are structured accordingly. Clearly, head knowledge has a much higher value than hand, body, emotional or common sense ways of knowing. The point is not that the ascendance of rationality is mistaken, but that it is used to legitimise the hierarchical structure of society; UAE is caught in this process.

Because of its ties to the labour market, as well as to state and professional bureaucracies, the social organisation of knowledge serves to reproduce the class relations of society. The universities play a key role in this process by establishing and standardising the cognitive, scientific production of knowledge which serves as the basis for professional organisation and monopolisation. For the universities to allow extension to counter the scientific premises upon which its legitimacy rests would be unlikely: in fact, the very opposite has been the case as extension has been legitimised in terms of the unique academic knowledge resources to which it has direct access. However, throughout its history, there has been a tension in extension between its more pragmatic, egalitarian, need oriented conception of knowledge and the university's more elitist, scientific, theoretical stance. This tension between theoretical and practical conceptions of knowledge continues to pose a central conflict for extension.

The tension between the theoretical and the practical runs much deeper than extension. There is a hierarchy in the market of knowledge production which sees the producer at the apex, the consumer at the base. The very different worlds in which knowledge production and everyday practice occur sets up a tension that is not easily overcome. The discourse and professional accountability structures for the academic are very different than for the practising professional, and even further removed from the world of everyday life. Rather than look at the educational problematic posed by these differing realms of discourse, and diametrically opposed accountability structures, attention has been upon the preservation of academic excellence through the enforcement of university standards. As Magali Larson has pointed out, with:

> advances in the unification and standardization of professional knowledge ..... 'theoretical' and 'practical' knowledge becomes distinct. The organisation of centers for the production of knowledge sharpens the bifurcation and tends to subordinate the practitioners who 'apply' knowledge to those who produce it. This subordination is magnified when the centers of cognitive production become, as well, the principal agencies of professional training.(42)

The mythology of adult education is that it is democratic. It is democratic in terms of population, content and method. In the words of Charles Beard, quoted at the beginning of this chapter, 'adult education involves all men and women, ... all branches of knowledge, ... all conceptions and interpretations of human affairs .....'

Despite rhetoric to the contrary, all adult educators are not in agreement over the meaning of democracy: and some have been openly elitist. Everett Dean Martin challenges the idea that adult education must 'appeal to the man on the street .... Can we as physicians minister to the great masses of people without contracting the diseases of prejudice and ignorance from which they suffer? The danger is grave'.(43)

Adult educators do not talk of elitism, they talk of motivation, capacity and excellence. The timeless question is whether the missionary sense of responsibility 'to educate everybody' is at odds with values of excellence. In 1934, Everett Dean Martin invited Lyman Bryson to participate with him in a dialogue about the aims of adult education. The article they produced is entitled, 'To Educate Everybody'. Their dialogue focussed on the question of excellence, and whether everybody can be educated into excellence. They agreed upon the broad meaning of excellence as the classical values of wisdom, temperance and justice; they also agreed 'that there are a few people whose aesthetic intellectual and ethical judgments are superior to the great multitude', but Bryson insisted 'that such superiority is not, as (Martin) seems to imply, inherent in a few minds but may be developed in many minds through education and cultivation'. According to Bryson: 'the task for adult education is not merely to make excellent people more excellent but rather to offer opportunities to all people in order that they may, in greater or less degree, each according to his own capacity, be imbued with excellence'. Martin maintained that 'we should not delude ourselves into thinking that everybody would be equally educated by any particular effort we made'. Bryson preferred to end with, 'we shall try, so far as we possibly can, to educate everybody'.(44)

Like Bryson, most adult educators do not experience a contradiction between their view that the 'masses' are inferior, and need education, and their egalitarian values. They do not say that the masses are inferior, but that they need education. Their good intentions are to make the excellence that resides in the elite accessible to the masses. The challenging voice of Harry Overstreet is very unusual:

> ..... We visualise the 'dutiful' citizen, the sternfaced individual who does what he knows he ought to do although he would much prefer to go fishing ..... We virtuous adult educators mean to save the civic souls of these rapscallion neighbours of ours. We will establish forums. We will induce these irresponsible neighbours to come to meetings, to listen and to learn, and to go forth civically regenerated. Adult education has had too much of this soul-saving citizentry. Come therefore, ye of little education, and we shall make you into the hope of democracy.(45)

The idea of excellence carries a mystique that blurs the fact that it consists of a set of concrete organisational practices to control what is offered through the university. The ideology of liberalism and its constituent ideologies of democracy, equality, service and excellence are constituted in a set of ideological and organisational practices which define extension work. These practices fall into two major categories: academic control and marketing. The burden under which extension must labour is that these practices tend to be opposed to one another - and yet, as noted earlier, the establishment of a professional market depends upon convincing the public that it is receiving the highest quality in professional service.

To develop fully the ways in which these practices define everyday operation is beyond the scope of this study, but some insight can be acquired by considering the institutional conflicts and controls over Extension work instituted by the University of California. As the largest Extension Division in the USA, it could be argued that California has served as the pacesetter for the rest of the country. If it has had a more difficult road to travel due to the elite academic standards of the University faculty, it has also set the pace in sophisticated marketing and programming. Furthermore, while specific practices may vary, the general picture is that extension must be accountable to the university faculty for the quality of what it offers, and to the university administrator for a balanced budget - or, in the case of some private institutions, bringing in a surplus.

In the university, the democratic/elite tensions of adult education have been pronounced. The battleground has been over the issue of standards. The history of Extension at the University of California has been riddled with conflict between University faculty and administration and Extension administrators over the standards of Extension work. On at least four occasions in its history, university-wide committees have been established to deliberate the continued existence of Extension in the University. The faculty's first priority has been to preserve its academic integrity, and Extension work has been perceived to be a constant threat to its conception of excellence. Extension has been caught in the University's conflicted sense of mission in trying to walk the middle line between elitist and egalitarian conceptions of democracy. The contradiction has been captured by Charles Mills Gayley, an influential Professor of English and the first head of Extension at the University:

> ..... the University should not adopt the ideals of the community. It should set the ideals. The American University is, and ever must be, democratic. It offers education to all who can profit by it. But education itself is aristocratic - of the best and for the best. The educated are those who, having striven are the chosen few.(46)

The initial work of Extension was conducted by the academic faculty of the University. Their goals were mixed: to spread learning and culture, and to educate teachers for the rapidly developing secondary schools. The public demand was for access to higher education, for the establishment of local institutions of higher learning which would be practically oriented, not for 'cultural uplift'. Responding to public pressure and fearful of multiple institutions of higher education competing for limited public funds, the President of the University succeeded in getting state funds to establish extension 'outposts' around the state. For the first time, an outside extension specialist was brought in to administer the work. Ira Woods Howerth was head of Extension from 1912 to 1919 - perhaps the most controversial period in Extension's history.
Howerth was committed to an egalitarian, utilitarian conception of public service which was in direct conflict with the faculty's simultaneous drive to raise academic standards. In Howerth's view,

'Extension offerings must be geared to the practical need of the people for help to a higher degree of industrial efficiency, and a fuller pay envelope'.(47) The faculty rigorously opposed offerings which were below college grade; Howerth argued that to so limit offerings would be to cater exclusively to an elite.(48)

The conflict that emerged in this period has been critical to the definition of extension in the USA. Excellence in extension work has been defined in terms of university equivalence; whether above or below, inside or outside university standards for academic credit, the defining criterion has been the traditional university credit course: the accepted goal is that all university sponsored work be at university level. To Howerth, this was a critical error, for even if extension confined its offerings to college level work:

> ..... it is always certain to lose the respect and sympathy of those who are disposed to judge it by its success in maintaining the recognised university standards rather than by its actual service to the people. For to succeed beyond the provision of instruction for the select few, it must adapt its methods and the subject matter presented, that is, in a certain respect, lower its avowed standard, and thus make it something different, if not less than what it pretends to be.(49)

With the imposition of University standards, the regular faculty of the University gained the right to control Extension; it defined acceptable course content and instructor qualifications. The shape of Extension came out so that, at the very least, it could create the illusion of mirroring regular university work, which greatly affected what was offered, who taught, and the population served. When Howerth was fired, he argued that the 'true cause' of his dismissal was his belief that 'University extension of necessity involves enlargement of the scope of University service ..... (it) is nothing more or less than Democracy in the so-called higher education; that is to say, University education is the common right of all, not the exclusive privilege of a favoured few'.(50)

In Howerth's view the very conception of university education needed radical redefinition. His dismissal dramatically points to the contradiction in the liberal values, which undermine any form of adult education that challenges the existing order. The liberal standard of excellence was defined in terms of a method and content of knowledge which was controlled by an academic elite, distributed to the public who were determined to be worthy recipients through what would become an elaborate set of hierarchically structured educational institutions. This hierarchically structured vision of knowledge was critical to the use of education as a means of distributing social status. Ironically, twenty years before being fired, Howerth had written:

> It is contended by the authorities that there is complete liberty, and the claim is logical, for they make a careful distinction between liberty and license. Thought is free so long as it is sound, and the authorities have their own convictions in regard to what constitutes sound thinking. While freedom of thought is doubtless increasing in all our institutions of higher learning ..... yet it is probably true today that there is not a college or university in the country that would long tolerate an active and formidable advocate of serious changes in the present social order. He would be required to go and the occasion of this removal would not be avowed as opposition to intellectual liberty, but to his own incapacity as evidenced by his vagarious opinions.(51)

Bringing extension back into the University fold, the appointment to follow Howerth was a professor of Latin, Leon Richardson. His goal was 'to make the university extension service adequately represent the university'. He accomplished this by limiting Extension to instructional activities that 'resembled university level work'. Regular university faculty and instructors with equivalent qualifications were actively recruited to teach in Extension, and an elaborate system of faculty controls over all Extension work was institutionalised: each Extension offering had to be approved by the faculty through an Extension Advisory Board, the relevant university department, and, in the case of credit courses, the Committee on Courses of Instruction. Except for modifications due to bureaucratic restructuring, these regulations continue to be operative, with the addition that all Extension instructors must also be approved.

The Richardson appointment marked the legitimation of faculty control over Extension work, a return to more traditional liberal values, and the modelling of Extension work along the lines of university course offerings. In sharp contrast to Howerth, Richardson argued for education in terms of individual intellectual development and self-discipline. To describe extension's purpose, Richardson compared adults to arrows and driftwood: whereas arrows go knowingly toward their goal and reap life's rewards, driftwood 'suffer from lethargy; lack of initiative to work constructively, to plan their lives well and to carry out even what they have planned'. Extension was aimed for the arrows who would 'continually put forth efforts to increase their powers'.(52)

Lifelong learning was made the motto of the Extension Division. A strong advocate of adult education at the university level, Richardson became a leader in the dawning national movement for adult education. He was chosen by the Carnegie Commission to chair the National Organising Conference for Adult Education which launched the AAAE in 1926. Other key participants in the formation of the AAAE were James E. Russell, Charles A. Beard, Everett Dean Martin, and Eduard C. Lindeman. In 1926, Richardson was also President of the National University Extension Association (NUEA). In the expanding adult education movement, Richardson saw university extension's function as one of providing professional leadership. At the pinnacle of the emerging adult education hierarchy, universities would educate the administrators and teachers who worked in the field. Rather than pose an alternative to the formal educational hierarchy, adult education would replicate it, with university extension offering the highest level - that is, most academic - within the field of adult education.

Control of University Extension work by the regular faculty of the University has had a tremendous impact upon the development of Extension.(53) However difficult it has been to control actual practice, Extension has had constantly to answer to challenges as to its purpose in the University. It has had to demonstrate to the faculty that it is true to the University's academic values: that it is doing what the University, rather than any other educational institution, is uniquely suited to do.

Extension work has had to be translated into conventional academic terms. Courses have to be differentiated in terms of academic credit, non-credit, or professional credit. While the controls upon academic credit offerings are the most severe -

typically requiring that regular campus instructors and course syllabi be used – non-credit and professional credit courses also come under faculty scrutiny and must be justified as offerings appropriate to the university. It is this process of having to translate extension courses into an acceptable academic framework that is the significant impact of faculty controls: whether courses are approved or disapproved is of less import than the set of organisational practices set in motion which define how the work of extension gets accomplished. For example, at UCLA (University of California, Los Angeles), in response to faculty criticism, Extension has developed a set of 'Standards and Criteria' to serve as a basis to control internally the quality of Extension offerings. Criteria are that courses be of an 'appropriate academic nature', 'provide a useful community service', be 'in good taste and of high quality', and 'cover their full costs'.(54)

Extension has been in a double bind: the faculty demands that it offer university level work, and yet maintains that extension is not 'academic enough' to award academic credit that would actually count toward the fulfilment of degree requirements.(55) Extension has hoped to find its way out of this bind under the guise of continuing education. Arguing that rapid technological change requires continuing education, extension seeks academic legitimacy under the rubric of educating the university's graduates. The idea of continuing education, so much in vogue today, has been around since World War II when the universities moved actively into part-time graduate work for professionals in defence-related industries. In California, symbolising the shift in the conception of extension work away from the traditional liberal arts, Professor of Engineering, Baldwin M. Woods, a member of the U.S. National Advisory Committee on the Engineering, Science, Management Defence Training Act, was chosen to head Extension in the post-war years. In addition to engineering, extension work was oriented to other professional areas of practice, especially business, and augmented by self-development and 'recreational' offerings to local residents who could afford the high fees.

Since the 1970s, the emphasis upon continuing professional education (i.e. what is often referred to as post experience continuing education in England, discussed in Chapter 4) has been especially strong. Not only is there a more highly educated population than ever to consume education, but participation is becoming mandatory. A host of regulations mandate continuing professional education as a basis for relicensure, certification, professional membership and the receipt of public funds by institutions. In direct contradiction to liberal values about voluntarism, which have been an important part of adult education's ideology, mandatory education has been tacitly accepted as necessary by adult educators. Given that participation in continuing education has been used historically as a basis for professional advancement, informal mandatory continuing education is not new to adult education, despite the rhetoric about voluntarism. At the same time, the mass mandating of continuing education, whether formal or informal, has set up a new set of controls with which extension must reckon. There is now a host of regulations, set by licensing bodies, work places and professional associations, governing participation in continuing education. The institution of the Continuing Education Unit (CEU) and the movement toward programme accreditation are important steps in the standardisation and regulation of educational practice. A central concern has been with the control of quality. Hours of participation, the standard currently used, does nothing to stop entrepreneurs from setting up exotic cruises for those who can afford them and calling it continuing education. The trend is toward requiring some form of performance evaluation as the basis for awarding CEUs. To do so represents yet another fundamental shift in adult education practice, moving it much closer to the traditional academic model.

Ironically, the ascendance of continuing professional education poses a grave threat to the survival of extension as now known. In the economically difficult times faced by universities, the pressure is for extension to be totally self-supporting (that is, no indirect costs to be sheltered by the university). At the same time, professional schools are vying to take over extension programmes in continuing education where these are perceived to be economically lucrative. In California, schools of business, medicine and engineering have been demanding more academic control over extension work in their respective fields, as well as a share of the profits. From within the university, the pressure has been to decentralise extension to the campus, school and department level. The argument is put in terms of quality: that is, that regular campus departments are able more effectively to garner the academic resources intrinsic to quality programming than extension. But the underlying issues are economic and political: that is, who will control and reap the benefits from extension work in those areas that are economically lucrative?

Decentralisation poses a serious threat to extension's economic survival. Centralisation is more cost effective and supports a sophisticated programming staff. Extension depends upon profits from some departments to finance others that continually run deficits; for example, profits from continuing education in business are essential to maintain programmes in the less profitable liberal arts areas. Extension has learned to survive by developing a high degree of skill in marketing.

Competition for the adult continuing education market is severe. It comes not only from departments and schools within the university, but from other educational institutions, particularly the elaborate system of well-funded community colleges, as well as private entrepreneurs, professional associations, business and industry. To compete with other providers, extension has depended upon the image of quality associated with the university and the practice of marketing. Marketing strategies in this highly competitive field have reinforced extension's elitism as it seeks to establish itself as the provider in the best position to deliver the highest in quality continuing education, and to gear its offerings toward the apex of the market which can best bear the costs. An important strategy has been co-operative programming, which means co-operatio with an employer or professional association.
more and more, co-operation consists of extension acting as a vendor for programmes, supplying the university's name and non-profit status, and some programming assistance. The dimensions of the problem are illuminated in the following dialogue, taken from Power and Conflict in Continuing Professional Education:

Curran (James R., Director of Educational Research, American Bankers Association):

> In banking we use universities extensively from sophisticated graduate programs down to community colleges for entry level people. Last year we used more than 300 institutions.

Stern (Milton R., Dean of University Extension, University of California, Berkeley):

Note that word <u>used</u>.

Curran:

>That's literally it. That's our perception. But universities think of themselves as usable, if you like. Frankly, we look to universities as physical resources, located in local communities. It cuts our costs, and if the system doesn't work - and we are getting indications to that effect - we'll probably set up our own residential centers.

Berlin (Lawrence S., Director of Continuing Education, School of Social Work, University of Michigan):

>What do you want from the university that you can't get from a private entrepreneur - and don't just say, 'Quality'.

Curran:

>No, not quality. We have a more pragmatic viewpoint. It's an overwhelming task to train 300,000 people a year, with limited resources within our own association. We have a large complex curriculum. A great deal of it is in areas that can be provided much better in the academic environment.

Suliman (Anver, marketer and private practitioner of continuing professional education)

>Aren't you, in effect, franchising universities on a local basis to offer programs to audiences that you are mandating for them?

Curran:

>Probably.[56]

What is so unusual about the development of continuing professional education is that universities have not succeeded in establishing a monopoly over the delivery of education. The long-term consequences are as yet unknown, but in the short-term they have thrown extension into a crisis about the nature of its work and its future survival. What is overlooked in this crisis is a fundamental challenge to the assumed relationship between academic knowledge and professional expertise. For the most part, this relationship has been assumed by continuing educators. Few would disagree with Cyril Houle, the leading spokesman for continuing professional education when he said that professionalising occupations are distinctive 'because their leaders seek to encourage and regulate standards of practice based on a profound central mission and on <u>advanced and esoteric bodies of knowledge</u>'.(57)

Universities, of course, develop, teach and control this body of knowledge. This is the 'excellence' that universities are uniquely suited to offer. The trend away from the universities suggests that this conception of excellence may have little relevance to effective practice. As has been pointed out, the discourse, experience and accountability of the professor are very different from that of the everyday world of the practitioner. Lawrence Berlin has noted the 'distance, even dissonance, between the professional school and the world of practice', ruminating that this is 'a near insoluble problem'.(58) He may be right, unless ways are found to relate directly the theoretical to the everyday tasks and issues confronted by the professional in his or her work situation. In the critical analysis of that work situation may lie a key; another would seem to be finding ways to break through the opacity of most academic discourse.

As marketing has become the operating reality for extension, the result is a private business enterprise within a public educational institution. Marketing represents a major shift with serious consequences for the way in which extension works. No longer are there signs of genuine effort, or even of pretension, toward serving people who cannot afford the high extension fees. Elitism is now an overtly accepted part of extension policy. The emphasis is clearly upon the design of high quality offerings for a highly educated population. As one Extension Dean phrased it, 'the market wants competency-based, high-level training over a period of time'. True, elitism has always been there, but it is now firmly in control. Ironically, the elitist direction is justified in democratic liberal terms: there is a highly educated population, of unprecedented proportions, which wants our programmes - our responsibility is to meet its need; in our highly professionalised society, quality continuing education offerings are essential. With the proliferation of adult educational opportunities in other sectors, university extension argues that its uniqueness rests in the quality of its programmes: a quality that is inherent in the pool of academic resources it has access to, the maintenance of high academic standards, educational know-how, and the high status of staff and students.

With the ascendance of continuing professional education and marketing values, there is a real question as to whether or not liberal values can still be seen to underpin UAE. There was a time when content and method were seriously debated within adult education. Controversies centred upon specialisation, practicality and immediate needs as the dawning method of adult education. Upholders of the liberal tradition argued for the integrity of 'civilisation', exposing students to the wisdom of the past, using books and discussing ideas in accordance with rational standards of inquiry. The goal of education was to create 'a liberal mind'.
..... 'What do we mean by a liberal mind?', asks Lotus Coffman, President of the University of Minnesota:

> ..... We mean a mind that has broad interests, wide knowledge, cultivated tastes, appreciation, and sound perspective. We mean a mind that is open and tolerant, ready and willing to face new situations and to interpret them in terms of knowledge as it relates to social welfare. We mean a mind that recognises a standard of ethics and feels a keen sense of responsibility ..... The essence of democracy is an enlightened 'give and take'. This likewise, is the essence of a liberal education.(59)

The liberal tradition in the USA has not come to terms with its blending of elite, pragmatic and idealistic, egalitarian values. Essential to the maintenance of liberal ideals is a capacity for self-criticism, as well as social criticism, that has been lost in the pragmatic requisites of survival within a particular political, economic and educational system. The university is integral to the maintenance of the dominant economic power structures. The location of adult education in the university and the problems it poses have not been critically analysed; there appear to be no alternatives to participation in the system. The values of democracy, equality of opportunity, service and excellence, that represent the liberal tradition as manifest in adult education, have been spoken of in idealistic terms, their pragmatic and conflictual aspects largely ignored. Contradictions within the liberal tradition between the elite-pragmatic and the egalitarian-idealistic in each of the arguments for adult education, have given way in the direction of the elite-pragmatic. Like the 'double think' of Orwell's Nineteen Eighty-Four, the key to democracy becomes conformity and unity, not freedom; equality becomes advancement of those able to benefit from contact with the elite; service is to vested interests, not to the cries for change; and excellence means the survival of academe - control through the scientific, rational method as the only legitimate form of knowledge - not the capacity for critical reflection or social transformation. The elite-pragmatic tendencies in liberalism have triumphed, much to its own demise.

NOTES

A variety of sources is used in this chapter to develop a picture of how the liberal tradition has been manifest in UAE. Some of the material is drawn from a larger study by the author (Kathleen Rockhill) on the history of University Extension in California. While the California case may differ from some others in the direction of elitism, discussions over the years suggest that the inner dynamics and operating pressures are quite typical. Other major sources are journals and literature in the field of adult education, as well as university extension, especially the publications of the national professional associations. Historically, the most important of these has been the AAAE. While its purview was not limited to UAE, its leadership was drawn primarily from the ranks of universities or 'university-like' educational experiments for adults. In the formative years, this organisation, at the behest of Carnegie funds, developed the professional stock of knowledge - and ideology - that continue to frame beliefs about professional practice.

1. Charles A. Beard, What is this Democracy? in American Association for Adult Education (ed) Adult Education and Democracy. New York, 1936. p. 1.
2. John Lukacs, The American Conservatives: Where they came from and where they are going, Harpers, January 1984, Vol. 26B, No. 1604.
3. Sidney Griffith Raybould, Universities, Adult Education, and Social Criticism, Syracuse, 1970, p. 5.

4. President's Commission on Higher Education, Higher Education for American Democracy, Vol. 1, 'Establishing the Goals', Washington, 1947, p. 9.
5. Alexander Meikeljohn, The Return to the Book, in C. Hartley Grattan, American Ideas about Adult Education: 1710-1951. New York, 1959, pp. 125 - 126.
6. John W. Studebaker and C. S. Williams, Education for Democracy, Washington: U.S. Office of Education, Bulletin, 1935, No. 17, quoted by Mary L. Ely, Why Forums? New York: 1937.
7. Ibid. (Ely), pp. 211 - 212.
8. Morse Adams Cartwright, Ten Years of Adult Education. New York, 1935, p. 22.
9. Morse Adams Cartwright, A Decade of Adult Education, in American Association for Adult Education (ed) Adult Education and Democracy. New York, 1936, p. 40.
10. Ibid., p. 63.
11. Cartwright, op. cit., (Ten Years of Adult Education), p. 202.
12. Eduard C. Lindeman, The Meaning of Adult Education. Montreal: 1961, pp. 23 - 28. Originally printed in 1926.
13. James Earl Russell, The American Paradox: An American Solution, Journal of Adult Education, 1929.
14. Richard H. de Lone, Small Futures: Children, Inequality, and the Limits of Liberal Reform. New York, 1979, p. 28.
15. Edward L. Thorndike, et al., Adult Learning. New York, 1928, pp. 177 - 179.
16. President's Commission, op. cit., p. 41.
17. Ibid., Vol. I, Equalizing and Expanding Individual Opportunity, p. 3.
18. P. L. 96-374, Sec. 101(a), 94 Stat. 1373, Amended October 3, 1980.
19. Freda H. Goldman, Foreword in James B. Whipple et al., Liberal Education Reconsidered: Reflections on Continuing Education for Contemporary Man, Syracuse: 1969.
20. Nell Keddie, Adult Education: An Ideology of Individualism, in ed. Jane Thompson, Adult Education for a Change, London, 1980.
21. P. L. 96-374, op. cit.
22. U. S. C. 1001, Enacted Nov. 8, 1965 P. L. 89-329, Sec. 101, 79 Stat. 1219.
23. P. L. 96-374, op. cit.
24. Loc. cit.
25. Loc. cit.
26. Zillah R. Eisenstein, Feminism and Sexual

Equality: Crisis in Liberal America, New York, 1984, p. 74.
27. Ibid., Vol. 1, p. 10.
28. United States Statutes at Large, 503-5, excerpted in (ed.) Richard Hofstadter and Wilson Smith, American Higher Education: A Documentary History. Chicago, 1961, Vol. II, p. 568.
29. Kathleen Rockhill, Academic Excellence and Public Service: A History of University Extension in California. New Brunswick, New Jersey, 1983.
30. Alain Touraine, The Academic System in American Society, New York, 1974, p. 21.
31. Lester F., Ward, Applied Sociology: A Treatise on the Conscious Improvement of Society by Society (1906), reprinted in Grattan, op. cit., pp. 111 - 115.
32. Louis E. Reber, The Scope of University Extension and its Organization and Subdivision, in National University Extension Association, Proceedings 1915, p. 25.
33. Minutes of the Board of Regents, University of California, November 11, 1917.
34. Faculty means the regularly appointed, tenure-track faculty of the university who are members of the Academic Senate, the faculty governing body. It is important to note that extension has no regular faculty; its professional staff consists of administrators and programme developers.
35. A Description and Evaluation of the Oakland Project, University of California Extension, Berkeley, 1962 - 1967, draft report, compiled under the leadership of John Denton.
36. U. S. C. 1001 ... P. L. 89-329, op. cit.
37. Interview conducted in October 1982 by Kathleen Rockhill.
38. Magali Sarfatti Larson, The Rise of Professionalism: A Sociological Analysis, Berkeley, 1977, p. 58.
39. Interview conducted in October 1982 by Kathleen Rockhill.
40. Glen Burch to James R. Sullivan re University Public Policy: The Role of Extension, August 27, 1982 in Berkeley Extension files.
41. Everett Dean Martin, The Dangers of Democracy, Journal of Adult Education, 1929, pp. 257 - 261.
42. Larson, op. cit., p. 44.
43. Martin, op. cit.
44. Everett Dean Martin and Lyman Bryson, To Educate Everybody, Journal of Adult Education. Vol.

VI, No. 4, October, 1934, pp. 395 - 399.
    45. Harry A. Overstreet, When Words Go Forth to Battle, <u>Journal of Adult Education</u>, Vol. X, No. 1, January 1938, pp. 5 - 16.
    46. Charles Mills Gayley, <u>Idols of Education</u>. New York, 1910, pp. 62 - 65.
    47. Ira Woods Howerth, University Extension, <u>Berkeley Civic Bulletin</u>, February 15, 1913, p. 65.
    48. Rockhill, op. cit. The Californian experience in University Adult Education is more fully developed in this work.
    49. Ira W. Howerth, A Tentative Plan for the Organization of University Extension, Presidents' Files, University of California, 1912.
    50. Ira W. Howerth, A Reply to a Statement of the Regents of the University of California Regarding the Case of Ira Woods Howerth, (n.d.) in Presidents' Files, 1919:490.
    51. Ira Woods Howerth, An Ethnic View of Higher Education, <u>Educational Review</u>, XX, November, 1900, p. 352 as quoted by Laurence R. Veysey, <u>The Emergence of the American University</u>. Chicago, 1965, p. 417.
    52. Leon J. Richardson, <u>Arrows and Driftwood</u>, Berkeley, 1935, p. 13.
    53. The forms and intensity of faculty control vary from institution to institution, and are typically most rigorous at the more academically prestigious institutions. Until recently the University administration has been more supportive of Extension than the faculty. This is shifting as administrators become more concerned about balanced budgets and increasing regular campus enrolments.
    54. UCLA Extension Standards and Criteria for Non-Degree Programs. November 1, 1979, in UCLA Extension Files.
    55. Technically, Extension can offer academic credit, but the control over which credits will actually count toward degrees resides in the regular faculty; it is at this level that Extension work is discredited. One way around this dilemma has been the development of part-time degree programmes which are part of the regular University offerings.
    56. (ed.) Milton R. Stern, <u>Power and Conflict in Continuing Professional Education</u>, Belmont, California, 1983, p. 131.
    57. Cyril O. Houle, <u>Continuing Learning in the Professions</u>, San Francisco, 1980, p. 49. Emphasis added.
    58. Lawrence S. Berlin, The University and Continuing Education: A Contrary View, in Stern,

op. cit., p. 123.

59. Lotus D. Coffman, Freedom through Education, *Journal of Adult Education*, Vol. XI, No. 1, January 1939, pp. 17 - 21.

Chapter Seven

IDEOLOGICAL SOLIDIFICATION OF LIBERALISM IN UNIVERSITY ADULT EDUCATION: CONFRONTATION OVER WORKERS' EDUCATION IN THE USA

In contrast to England, in the USA the education of workers has not been central to UAE, whereas the education of professionals has always been. With few exceptions, as the ideology of university public service developed, neither working class education, nor the education of workers as workers, was seen as consistent with the university's mission, until the post World War II years when the focus shifted to industrial relations and the training of labour leaders to negotiate with management. In the earlier years, workers' education came to be seen as quite contrary to the university's interpretation of its broader responsibilities for service to the 'general public'. As has been argued in the preceding chapter, service has been interpreted pragmatically in terms of furthering the interests of the university and, through it, the state. While these interests have been seen as dependent upon maintaining a 'healthy' economic base, the education of workers has been in terms of vocational training - and this has been seen as inappropriate to the university, especially once the vocational function began to be assumed by other institutions.

THE UNIVERSITIES AND THE LABOUR MOVEMENT

A critical turning point in workers' education came in the Depression years: not in terms of posing an economic alternative to capitalism, but in the acceptance of the argument that the well-being of the workers is dependent upon the well-being of capitalism. Maintaining the strength of American democracy depends upon a strong economy, and this requires that workers see that their interests are tied to industrial expansion through the stimulation of private enterprise. Workers' education is translated to mean job training to keep abreast of technological advance. And workers' education has come to mean the training of labour leaders to bargain with management; since effective bargaining depends upon a shared perception of mutual interest, workers' education is transformed into industrial relations. As labour has become a powerful political force with vested interests in serving the state and the capitalist economy, the university has served workers through the development of industrial relations and the training of labour leaders. But, where workers' education has been concerned with the development of working class consciousness, or with the goal of social reconstruction, it has not found an acceptable home in the university.

The service ideology is not the only legitimising argument for UAE that has worked against the education of workers. Each of the themes developed in the preceding chapter - education as the key to democracy, equality of opportunity, and academic interpretations of excellence - have worked against the education of workers. Maintaining American democracy has been manifest in calls for consensus and unity in support of the state; working class education has been perceived to be a direct threat to that consensus. Education has been interpreted as the provider of equality of opportunity, not for workers as a separate interest group, but for workers as adults who, through education, would be able to advance - for in the USA, the land of opportunity, there are held to be no class boundaries. Excellence, and the elitist position of the university in the educational hierarchy, has meant that the education of workers is the proper province of other educational institutions. In the 1960s the hierarchical differentiation of adult education according to educational level was formalised in state plans for education, institutionalising an informal tradition.

Ironically, the ideals of working class education as developed in England, captivated the imaginations of many American adult educators. Albert Mansbridge was heralded in the USA; adult education leaders were eager to experiment with his ideas. As a consequence, a few universities did embark upon programmes in workers' education in the 1920s. California was the first university to do so. In 1921, Extension Director Leon Richardson visited England to meet with Mansbridge and study the Workers' Educational Association (WEA); upon his return Richardson enthusiastically announced that the 'first WEA course organised in America' was about to begin.(1)

In 1923, the American Federation of Labour (AFofL) undertook the leadership of the newly formed Workers' Education Bureau (WEB) of America. The University of California was the first university to affiliate with the AFofL, establishing a Workers' Education Bureau within Extension. A Joint Committee on Workers' Education was established in an advisory capacity to the Bureau. It consisted of an equal number of representatives from labour and the University, plus the director of the Bureau, who was also a member of labour. The programme consisted of a number of classes, the most popular of which were economics, public speaking, English, labour problems and labour history. Richardson had not become involved in a questionable undertaking:

> We have distinctly told the laboring men that we should not take part in their controversial questions. We conceive our business to be solely teaching such subjects as fall within the field of University instruction.(2)

Apparently this was true. When controversy developed over the left political leanings of Ann Sumner, an Extension programmer in the Bureau, she was fired. Despite the Joint Committee on Workers' Education, Richardson managed to maintain University control over courses. He told his colleagues in the National University Extension Association that labour must have the sense of control, but there was no need for concern:

> That is done for purely theoretical purposes, five are members of labor organisations and four of the faculty of the university. Now when these men get together, the five men belonging to the labour organisation said, 'Now you men know the business of teaching, you go ahead. All we want is to tell the world that we have five men here'. Then we laid out the whole plan. They accepted it.(3)

As Richardson saw it, a fitting motto for workers' education might be borrowed from Thomas Jefferson: 'You can trust men if you train them'. The purposes of workers' education were twofold: to provide an educational opportunity to 'those who have missed their chance' and to 'keep them within bounds, so they wouldn't do anything foolish in the way of starting rioting or things of that kind at any time'.(4) In later years, Richardson reminisced: 'We didn't favor socialism: we favored a mode of education that would bring the men to a rational view of society, and that included among other things loyalty to our government'.(5)

While the California Bureau was nationally acclaimed by the AFofL, the director of the Bureau, John Kerchen, did not feel that the programme had been successful. He argued that university standards were too high, that workers were primarily interested in 'bread and butter' offerings which they would have been willing to pay for, and that workers should be prepared for an active role in society.(6) Because of its perceived public relations value, the WEB was maintained by the University over the Depression years.(7) In World War II, it was phased out; its nominal successor, the Institute of Industrial Relations, was established in 1945.

The contrast between Kerchen's explanation for the limited success of the programme and Richardson's is illustrative of the difference in perspective between the university and labour. Rather than attribute the limitations of the programme to structural problems (for example, standards, fees, the need to take an activist stance), Richardson attributed the difficulty to the workers' attitudes: 'Men in America have not yet got to the point where workers are willing to give large blocks of time and long sustained effort as we find in countries across the Atlantic. The men among us show an uprising surge of a will to power. They seek to gain it, less by education than by organisation'.(8)

Other universities sponsored programmes in workers' education, with mixed results. Best known was the Wisconsin School for Workers, but it too met with limited success. One historian has attributed failure to the mutual mistrust of labour and the universities. When labour organised its own courses, 'this seemed to threaten community integration and welfare, and many colleges and universities volunteered to offer to workers courses designed to overcome their growing group-consciousness ..... The movement failed. Labour leaders correctly surmized the motives behind the program and refused to sanction it'.(9) Among the most effective programmes for workers were the few sponsored by women's colleges for women workers. The most famous of these was the Bryn Mawr Summer School for Women Workers in Industry. But here, too, labour's view of education clashed with the university's. Controversy between the Summer School and the College erupted in 1934: five years later the School finally withdrew from the Bryn Mawr campus on the premise that 'it is time for an independent workers' school that has real academic freedom to emerge on its own independent grounds'.(10)

Within the labour movement in the USA, there has been extensive controversy over whether workers' education should be sponsored exclusively by labour, or in collaboration with educational institutions. Labour leaders have been suspicious of universities whose vested interests are in serving business and professional classes. University Governing Boards have been dominated by corporate leaders, with no representation from labour. Where experiments have been undertaken, controversy has had to be avoided in order to survive, inevitably, a conservative influence upon workers' education in the universities.

Unions have been much more active in workers' education than universities. Left progressive unions have seen their educational mission in terms of social reconstruction, whereas universities have been liberal and pragmatic in their vision. It took the ascendance of the AFofL in the labour movement and its control of the WEB for co-operation between universities and labour to occur. Even under the more pragmatic and conservative AFofL, co-operation was charged with controversy.

Early pioneers in the development of workers' education through unions were the International Ladies' Garment Workers, the American Federation of Hosiery Workers and the Amalgamated Clothing Workers. More than twenty years later it was noted that 'the educational ideologies of the ILGWU, the ACWA and the AFHW have not greatly changed over the years. From the beginning, social reconstruction as well as effective collective bargaining has been the goal'.(11) In the formative years workers' education out of unions was also infused with the goal of social reconstruction. Brookwood Labour College was very influential in training labour leaders, as was the Rand School of Social Science. The leadership of the early labour education movement was decidedly socialist in leaning. At the first national meeting on workers' education, convened in 1921, speaker after speaker called for social reconstruction through the development of worker participation and working class consciousness. In the words of Fannia M. Cohn, one of the conference conveners and Secretary of the Educational Department

International Ladies' Garment Workers Union:

> At first, though we had no definite aim, we were certain that workers' education must have a vital connection with the Labor Movement ..... It has always been our conviction that the Labor Movement stands, consciously or unconsciously, for the reconstruction of society. It strives toward a new life. It dreams of a world where economic and social justice will prevail, where the welfare of mankind will be the aim of all activity, where society will be organised as a cooperative commonwealth ...(12)

Out of this meeting came the formation of the WEB, a co-ordinating agency of labour education which soon affiliated with the AFofL.

While affiliation with the AFofL gave workers' education the necessary link to the Labour Movement, it also contributed to a more conservative turn in workers' education. The AFofL accepted the capitalist order; its programme concentrated on gaining improved conditions for labour. Instead of arguing for social reconstruction, labour's attention turned to 'practical' goals, like higher wages and shorter working hours. It became a 'partner of business' and government 'in promoting the American system of acquisition and enjoyment'.(13) Workers' education took a practical turn. 'Business principles again dominated the trade unions'.(14) The goal of workers' education was to serve the trade unions. The programme became politically narrow. A critic observed: 'No Workers' education programme has been able to receive active aid, if criticism of the American Federation of Labour is allowed'.(15) In 1929, the WEB nullified the membership of Brookwood Labour College, labelling it as communistic. Brookwood closed its doors in 1937.

The WEB was not opposed to working with established educational institutions. The University of California effort has already been mentioned. More successful and indicative of a new direction in workers' education was the labour institute held in conjunction with Rutgers University and the State Federation of Labour under the sponsorship of the WEB, beginning in 1931. The programme involved an analysis of labour's problems 'by detached, academic minds, and by frank discussions with business and social leaders'.(16) As workers' education shifted in focus to the education of labour leaders, it took a functional approach to workers' education.

In a national study of workers' education in universities conducted in 1950 by Irvine Kerrison, head of the Labour Programme, Rutgers Institute of Management and Labor Relations, it was explained that the functional approach:

> ..... is not class education ..... It fits smoothly into the context of an evolving capitalism under which industrial relations will be as stable as is consistent with the freedom of choice and enterprise inherent in the system ..... The function of the workers' education classroom, when dealing with the employment contract, is to give labor the knowledge, skills and techniques that will enable its representative to bargain in an informed and intelligent manner.(17)

Still, labour educators were pressured by universities to conduct open classes - that is, classes for both management and labour. Kerrison was opposed to this policy, arguing that it was:

> ..... motivated by a groundless fear that classes for workers alone will promote the class struggle concept. What, apparently, they do not understand is that labor leaders and older and more thoughtful union members (who comprise the majority in organised labour) are committed to a policy of gradual adjustment - they are not flaming revolutionaries. These people want a prosperous industry so that they can share in its gains.(18)

Labour educators who opposed the concept of the open classroom saw improved industrial relations as dependent upon functioning equals, and maintained that workers' education could equalise the power differential between capital and labour.

In the post World War II period, the U.S. Congress considered establishing a National Labor Extension Service which would provide for workers a national educational programme modelled on that established for farmers at the turn of the century. The model involved a three-way partnership in which universities, state government and labour would participate. The initiative was unsuccessful, broken by controversy over the viability of labour's sharing control with universities and the state, both of which were seen to be under the control of big business. Critical to the withdrawal of the AFofL's support for the proposed legislation was the closure of the University of Michigan's Workers' Education Service in 1949. Controversy over the Michigan programme erupted over the allegation of a General Motors' economist who was attending a Workers' Education course, that the 'Marxist idea of class economics' was being taught. He further contended that pamphlets were distributed in class which were critical of General Motors. Under pressure from General Motors and the Governor of the state, the University closed the programme.(19)

The question of control has been the focus of controversy in workers' education. As labour moved more into mainstream politics, it found itself in a paradoxical position with respect to university involvement: it wanted the academic legitimacy and status conferred by the university, but at the same time did not want programmes under the control of business interests. Again and again, labour argued that it was not allowed the same autonomy as schools or business or management in the conduct of its education. In this sense, it did not ask to be treated differently, but to have the same rights as other areas of academic and professional education.

Differences in ideological perspective have been masked by the controversy over control. Even though the ideology of labour shifted to embrace the dominant liberal ideology of the institutional mainstream, its stance was more egalitarian and populist than that of the more elitist university. And, however much the tendency has been to reconcile differences between business and labour, their alliance is an uneasy one: increased wages must come out of profits.

Nevertheless, the shift in the ideology of workers' education from social reconstruction to the improvement of industrial relations through consensual collective bargaining, is a radical one, and reflects the movement of labour from the status of oppositional social movement into establishment politics, as it has gained institutional legitimacy and integration into the existing social and political system. Before, after and during World War I, critical social thought and action were severely repressed. Symbolic was the imprisonment of Eugene Debs, the head of the Socialist Party, and many others who were imprisoned or forced to leave the country under the Espionage Act. Immigrants were particularly vulnerable, and much of the left support came from the ranks of immigrant workers. In the Depression years, the voices of practicality muted dissent as job training, employment, and negotiation skills sought to keep pace with changing needs of the labour market. The New Deal of Franklin Roosevelt watered down opposition arguments for social reconstruction, and the National Labor Relations Act of 1934 committed labour to the bargaining table with management. Thus there was a significant redefinition of the problems of labour in terms of training in the skills necessary to hold a job effectively. Security was seen as staying with the same job and improving skills to keep abreast of technological change, or as moving up the hierarchy.

Against this broad national backdrop, it is easy to lose sight of controversies within adult education which contributed substantially to the failure of workers' education becoming a priority of educational institutions. Quite contrary to the experience in England, in the USA workers' education has been inimical to the liberal ideology of adult education, especially as it has been manifest in the university. Workers' education, and the issues it raised for liberal adult educators, touched off a storm of controversy during the inter-war years. Because these were the most critical years in the history of adult education - the years when the institutional and ideological foundation of the emerging field of professional practice was established - the debate over workers' education and its outcome had a very fundamental impact upon the development of adult education. Current assumptions about the way adult education must be conducted derive from this debate, which was really about the perceived threat of socialism to American democracy.

The outcome was that workers' education - as workers' education, not the industrial relations focus that in fact emerged - was deemed inappropriate to adult education. Workers' education itself was not attacked, but the premises upon which it was based were. It was argued against as separatist, divisive, propagandist, activist, conflict-oriented and revolutionary - the very antithesis of liberal educational principles as conceived within orthodox circles in the USA. In the process, liberalism was narrowly reconstructed to eliminate the progressive, left liberal position from within the framework of adult education. This meant the virtual annihilation of either a critical or a socialist perspective, silencing questions of social purpose and commitment, social action, empowerment or collectivism: and, similarly, the ascendance of professional pragmatism.

The conservative shift of liberalism in the inter-war years is critical to understanding the barrenness of the liberal tradition in the USA as a touchstone for radical perspectives of UAE in the present era, when market economics have come to dominate programme decisions. From the argument put forth against workers' education, it is possible to reconstruct the left-progressive-socialist perspective which has been silenced and delegitimised in adult education in the USA.

THE ANNIHILATION OF LEFT-PROGRESSIVE AND SOCIALIST PERSPECTIVES IN ADULT EDUCATION

'Against Separatism' is the title T. R. Adam chose for a 1939 article published in the Journal of Adult Education. As Adam correctly pointed out, the issue goes far beyond workers' education, though that is the arena in which separatism has been most extensively contested. He maintained that the cultural, social and political arguments put forward in defence of separatism are understandable but mistaken. Separatism leaves the minority isolated and, understandably, a target of the majority. Instead of isolating themselves, minorities should contribute to the formulation of a general culture and to the development of a public educational system that is truly representative, that is, committed to equality of opportunity through the advancement of the whole community. Using the example of the Jews, Adam suggested that they are the cause of the discrimination they suffer. 'The Jew is singled out as a quarry for the bestial hunt because he retains, with his ancient and mystic tradition, some trace of the alien'. Recognising American fear of the alien, Adam argued that 'if the elements of particularism and separatism could be courageously weeded out of organisations such as Jewish centers, it would be possible to visualize them as dynamic forces for the education of the whole community'.(20)

From his influential position as the link between the Carnegie Foundation and the AAAE, Executive Director Morse Cartwright observed:

> It is to be doubted whether workers' education per se will ever assume great importance in America as a separatist movement. Rather it is more likely to become more and more deeply integrated in the general adult education movement, where vocational status is no bar to continued effort to overcome ignorance. Certainly

>it is desirable that present activities in
>workers' education, all connected with the
>labor movement, should be maintained and that
>they should increase. It is only through con-
>tinued adult education of both employers and
>employees that conflict harmful to all can be
>avoided. But for most of his adult education,
>the American workingman and his wife will reach
>out in precisely the same manner as the mer-
>chant, the banker, the farmer, the clerk and
>the professional man.(21)

The great fear has been that separatism will promote conflict. When the need for separatism is accepted, it is on the premise that it will enable 'disadvantaged' groups to gain the skills necessary to participate effectively in the mainstream, thereby avoiding conflict. Note that there is no discourse of 'disadvantage' in Cartwright's time: 'ignorant' workers can learn through general adult education - the assumed goal, then as now, by educators, is that workers seek education to overcome ignorance. In contrast, when labour educators argue for separatism it is to equalise power between management and labour. However, the argument is put forth in terms of the avoidance of conflict, separatism being rationalised as essential to an effective bargaining process.

Equality of opportunity is the principle invoked in arguments over separatism. While some separatism may be necessary to develop the skills essential to participate in a representative system, the premise is that equality of opportunity is available through the system, and therefore separatism is unnecessary. It can even be harmful in not giving people the skills necessary to compete within the system. Notably missing from the liberal discussion has been the question of power, its differential distribution, and the impact of this upon the supposedly representative system. Those favouring separatism have argued that solidarity around common interests and collective effort is essential to redress their lack of political power in the system; they also maintain that separatism is essential to the development of group consciousness for the views and realities of dominated peoples are not included within the framework of the system. Liberals in the USA do not agree with this interpretation. They argue that the system is representative, comprehensive and neutral; if democracy is to be effective, neutrality is particularly important if the best interests of the 'whole' are to be realised.

Separatism continues to be a controversial issue, particularly as it pertains to the education of minorities and women. Educationally, separatism can mean lack of access to public resources, to quality (for example, technology, scientific research, expert resources), to the credentials that can further the interests of a dominated group. At the same time, integration has tended to mean the loss of group identity and cohesion. Through the failure to recognise that there are differing interpretations of reality - of truth - one risks identification with a particular view of legitimate knowledge and values that can deny one's history, sense of self and community. Not only is the potential of an alternative voice, a critical perspective, lost, but the reality in which such a perspective could be grounded has been 'nihilated': (22) what is presented as true is assumed to be true. Instead of recognising multiple realities, liberalism, as practised in the USA, posits one 'truth'. The essential argument against separatism is that all people should have the opportunity to be exposed to the 'truth' as ascertained through rational inquiry. Differences are not inherent in different historical situations, or in the structure of social relationships, they are rooted in the individual whose variations from the ideal standard can be studied and sometimes mediated. Through participation in 'the system' each will have the best opportunity to realise his or her full potential.

Ironically, of course, separatism goes on all the time; it is not called separatism, but serving the varying needs of particular groups. The most common forms of separatism are separation according to educational background, age, personal interests and occupation. Individual differences and the training priorities of business, industry and the professions are readily accepted as the basis for separate education. Nowhere is this more pronounced than in UAE, where programming is based upon meeting the specific needs of different groups. However, as has been argued in Chapter 6, the concept of need is bound by an ideological set of assumptions as to what is appropriate to UAE. Education which responds to different sets of needs is not conceived as separatist, for its goal is to enable various groups to participate more fully in the mainstream. Thus special programmes for the elderly or for women re-entering the workforce are highly acceptable. What is conceived of as 'separatist' is any programme that challenges the dominant ideology. For example, feminist courses, limited to women, for the purposes of raising their consciousness as an oppressed class, are highly controversial, and frequently sabotaged as biased, activist, separatist, or a violation of the rights of men who would like to participate. Thus, it is necessary to differentiate between separatism as a politically motivated counter-force to the dominant forms of education, and separate education as legitimised in terms of need differential.

Challenges to adult education institutions and practices from politically aware groups are rare. Typically, programmes are designed from the top down - that is, from the perspective of those in the more influential positions for the less influential - which means that separatism is not apt to emerge as a political, or educational issue. 'Needs' legitimise separate approaches and are defined in terms of preconceptions as to what is appropriate to various groups and what is apt to be lucrative economically. To use an anecdote as illustration, a director of continuing education in a community with a large elderly population was very proud of the special programme they had developed, which was run largely by and with the talents of the retired elderly in the area. Asked about whether he had ever considered doing something similar for the very large latin immigrant population in the community, he responded 'Oh, we're taking care of their needs too. We've just purchased a mobile unit to go around the community offering them the chance to take courses for high school completion'. So, for the elderly a degree of programme control and a range of exciting courses that they have input into designing: for the immigrants, high school completion, if they are so motivated.

Class divisions are held not to be applicable to the USA. This has been a crucial argument in the battle against a separate working class education. In this argument, one sees the systematic denial of class in the USA, to the point that its wholesale, persistent and ideological disavowal has become a self-fulfilling prophecy: people, even generations of poor and workers, do not think in terms of class. Class consciousness has been obliterated by the internalisation of the liberal belief that there is, in the USA, complete equality of opportunity, an absolute social mobility dependent exclusively upon natural ability and individual effort.

'An organised class system is alien to the theory and practice of American society', T. R. Adam began his study of workers' education. Unlike most, Adam noted that:

> In the educational world we have never looked very steadily or frankly at the hierarchy of social status. (23)

> ..... Fortunately, class divisions in America have not yet reached the stage where most wage earners are organised firmly under political and economic leaders reflecting their occupational interests. The ordinary worker looks to a trade union or any political party for representation along strictly limited lines. In matters of general culture, citizenship takes precedence over partisan division. Equality of opportunity is still considered a working doctrine, with the state striving to provide a common fund of learning open to all in accordance with their talents and abilities. (24)

So Adam characteristically expressed the enlightened liberal point of view - some recognition that there is a problem, relief that it has not resulted in separatism, and faith in equality of opportunity - in accordance, of course, with individual talents and abilities. Morse Cartwright does not even allow that class differences may be real. Observing that 'the United States does not possess a well-knit, class-conscious workers' education movement', he explained it as due to equality of educational opportunity and:

> Easy money - both easy come and easy go - has tended to prevent class crystallisation. One's ditch digger of today might be one's landlord tomorrow. Hence there was little necessity for a workers' education movement similar to those of Europe but, on the other hand, a more general participation in education by workingmen and their families. (25)

Ignoring pressure from class conscious workers, and marginalising it as misguided, has been made easier by the apparent fluidity of American society. Stories of mobility are part of the popular folklore. That these pertain to a few white males is not noticed unless one has a degree of political consciousness and/or has listened to the blistering wisdom of those who know what it is to be outside the pale, so successful has been the obliteration of the idea of class by the dominant ideology of equality and mobility.

In 1938, The Journal of Adult Education published 'a fireside chat about adult education', entitled 'A Middle-Class Movement?' Not only does the 'chat' reveal the accepted bias of liberal adult educators against Marxism and the concept of class, it goes, paradoxically, a step further and reveals the liberal assumption that the middle class is the hope of democracy. Principal participants in the 'chat' are Jim, 'who is very far to the left', Hugh, 'a newspaper reporter without illusions', and the 'Professor, an undismayed liberal'. Rather than a dialogue, the 'chat' provides a stage for the liberal Professor to make mincemeat of Jim's left views and expound upon his theory of the middle class's pivotal role in democracy and, therefore, the legitimacy of its serving as the focus for adult education. To paraphrase, Jim sets off the controversy by asserting .....

> That's the whole trouble with adult education in this country - it's a middle-class movement.
>
> Hugh: Do we have to drag in the class struggle? .....
>
> Prof: (reacting to Jim's charge that adult education does not teach what would be of value to those not of the middle class) A little extreme, my son, but we'll let it stand. What is worth learning?
>
> Jim: What makes the world tick - the structure of the capitalist system and how it functions - the -
>
> Hugh: The gospel according to Marx?.....
>
> Prof: Let's not go barking up the tree of doctrine. Jim raises a question that has nothing to do with one's specific political affiliation. Jim indicts the adult education movement in this country as 'a middle-class movement'. The rest of you seem eager to defend it against this charge. If I were a spokesman for adult education in the United States, I should plead guilty at once. That is, if one can talk

> in terms of 'class' in this country ..... By 'middle class' in this country I mean that huge, flexible group that is not wholly absorbed in the problem of subsistence, nor wholly preoccupied in protecting its special privileges. Isn't that the body of citizens on whom democracy must depend for progress - for curbing greed, for securing a more equitable distribution of wealth, for developing public agencies to provide security for such defenseless groups as the aged, the blind, the unemployed? ..... I believe in adult education as a middle class movement ..... because I believe in democracy, and in its dependence on a great informed middle class ..... that seems to me the only reliable antidote for the propaganda of dictatorships ..... it's a middle-of-the-road faith, Jim - not dramatic or exciting. But isn't that the surest road away from both revolution and suppression, toward the fulfilment of our democracy?(26)

The 'chat' vividly demonstrates the subtle but deadly ways in which nihilism operates. Note the delegitimation of Jim's position, and of Jim in the patronising stance of the Professor, and the negative symbolism in Hugh's language as indirectly he attacks Jim's ideas as 'the gospel according to Marx'. Interesting, too, is the Professor's appropriation of the concept 'class' in such a way that it becomes the opposite of the socialist critique, symbolically legitimised as the great hope of democracy. The working class are made invisible in the Professor's restatement of Jim's position - while, paradoxically, their 'invisible presence' is subtly tied to propaganda, dictatorship, revolution and suppression. Though its form may vary, again and again the very idea of class - and its connection with socialism or Marxism - has been nihilated through processes of denial, radical reinterpretation, the use of negative symbolic associations, the invocation of fear, and the symbolic legitimation of the opposing view. The result is that the word is appropriated by the dominant ideology, but becomes meaningless. These processes operate not just with respect to class, but in relation to all aspects of a socialist perspective in adult education in the USA.

The idea of class is especially threatening as it challenges the liberal's faith in the possibility of equality. Educationally, the acceptance of structural inequality means that real equality, liberatory education, requires a radically different method. Education for social transformation is linked to the ideas of solidarity, separatism, the development of a collective consciousness that would be antithetical to capitalism, and the idea of collective social action to offset power differentials and upset the class basis of society. Nothing could be more threatening to established interests: American democracy, as wed to capitalism, is dependent upon class differentiation. The cheap labour of women, immigrants, and today the deplorable conditions of 'illegal aliens', facilitates the promise of equal opportunity. Racism, sexism and illegal civil status are used to maintain an under class of people whose 'natural' condition makes them ineligible to compete in the mobility contest.

Education oriented to the idea of class carries with it the potential of the development of class consciousness. Not only is there the linking of class to the ideas of collectivity, collective action and social transformation with which to contend, but also the very threatening ideas of 'committed' education and alternative 'truths' or versions of reality. To accept these ideas, as discussed in Chapter 3, is to challenge the fundamental liberal premises of objectivity and neutrality. Within the liberal view, to speak of educational commitment to a particular set of beliefs is unavoidably propagandistic. In the USA especially, liberals have not critically evaluated the ways in which their commitment to American democracy and capitalism affect even allegedly neutral scientific investigation. Arguing neutrality and democracy in the same breath, liberals have failed to see that these are not neutral truths, but particular views of reality.

One consequence of the obliteration of class structure as a way of understanding social inequality is that the problems which adult education must address are defined in terms of need, distribution, provision, and remediation rather than social reconstruction. The absence of class as a category of analysis has meant that the problem of social inequality is located in individuals, or categories of individuals, rather than in the social, economic and political context in which the individual is located. The structural inequalities inherent in patriarchy and capitalism remain intact. In the USA, instead of even acknowledging the concept of social class, adult education's social priorities are defined in terms of needs of the 'disadvantaged' or 'culturally deprived', and targeted in terms of specific, bureaucratically defined categories of people. The reintroduction of class structure as a basis for programming seems critical and yet, as Jane Thompson has noted, it would be very difficult to implement in mainstream adult education.(27) To express concern for illiterates, the elderly, single parents, working mothers, the handicapped, the unemployed, etc., sits very well within the liberal tradition - but to raise questions of class consciousness, economic or patriarchal structure and collective action is a boundary to be transgressed with great caution, especially in the USA. '<u>No propaganda. Democracy</u>. No particular theory of social organisation. This I puzzled over'.(28)

The labelling and marginalisation of all left liberal, socialist, Marxist and communist ideas as propaganda may have been the most effective tool used by adult educators to silence the development of a critical social perspective within the field. A key theme in adult education literature has been that education should not be propaganda. The argument against propaganda has been voiced consistently in terms of liberal values: the presentation of all views, objectivity, neutrality, deliberation, tolerance and scepticism. Perhaps there has been nothing closer to the liberal's heart, whether in England or the USA, than the idea that education must not be propaganda: quite the opposite, it must serve as the antidote to propaganda.

This creed was ardently proclaimed in connection with workers' education in the USA. Greatly feared were the propagandistic or socialistic ideas with which workers would be 'bombarded' if their education were under the control of workers. The fear was of the potential revolutionary power in the socialist idea of class consciousness, but, of course, this was not often explicitly stated. Instead, it was argued that workers, being less well educated, were more apt to be prey to propaganda. According to Morse Cartwright:

> propaganda, good and bad, never has endangered a truly educated person. But propaganda, good and bad, always will endanger poorly or partially educated persons who have not yet learned to think for themselves, who have not yet developed a selective technique. The world consists of the latter group in amazingly large majorities.(29)

A recurring theme is that education must be

non-partisan, non-political. At the same time, it must serve democracy. Mary Ely has noted the irony of this position, quoting Harold Lasswell's definition that 'the spread of controversial attitudes is propaganda; the spread of accepted attitudes and skills is education'.(30)

Lasswell's definition was also quoted in a probing panel discussion on adult education and propaganda, published on the occasion of the tenth anniversary of the AAAE.(31) This time, Roger Baldwin, Director, American Civil Liberties Union, countered: 'I don't entirely agree ..... the spread of accepted ideas may be propaganda. As a matter of fact, we meet propaganda of that sort on every side toay. Propaganda for well-established institutions and long-accepted traditions - in economics, in government, in sex relations'.

Lyman Bryson, Professor of Adult Education and chair of the panel discussion, began by asserting that 'adult education and propaganda are incompatible'. Furthermore, 'we adult educators have no more important task than that of cultivating in every man and woman who comes under our influence an attitude of stubborn resistance to all propaganda'.

Most apparent is the confusion about the difference between education and propaganda. Bryson admitted that:

> 'Propaganda' ..... is not clearly defined in my own mind. Vaguely I apprehend it as something that the other fellow is trying to do or to put across. With equal vagueness I sense that education is something that I and all the rest of the adult educationists are trying to do in order to counteract the other fellow's propaganda. I myself am a propagandist; I am well aware of that fact. I am putting forth the most effective propaganda I can against propaganda itself. I am a propagandist for a reluctant and deliberative attitude toward all new ideas until they have been halted and challenged at the threshold of reason.

Despite his own questions about the distinction between education and propaganda, Bryson rests firm in his sense that one is morally just and the other is not. Essential to his conviction are his faith in the power of deliberation and reason, in objective judgement. Leading the challenge to Bryson's position, Baldwin questions his assumption that human choices are made on the basis of reason:

'I have come to the clear conviction that what people care about, what their emotions are gripped by, is vastly more important in determining their attitudes and their actions than all the ideas arrived at by the deliberative processes you educators advocate'. Challenged are the assumptions that objective facts and judgements are possible or desirable. Even if it were possible educationally, Baldwin asked,'..... how, by means of education that presents all sides of every question and that puts a premium upon suspended judgment, are you ever going to develop men and women who have profound social convictions, who really care about anything beyond their own personal concerns?'

Challenging the liberal values of objectivity, reason and neutrality, Baldwin raised another, that of conviction. He made the important observation that adult educators do not deal with the fundamental questions of power, social structure or critical analysis:

> The point I am trying to make is that your adult education does not take account of the real fundamentals. Do you ever, for instance, in any of your classes, examine the institution of law as a social force? Do you ever ask: Whose law? Why law? Why government? Why the state? These fundamental questions are never raised in any of your schools or classes or any of your magazines and books.

Bryson concludes that the purpose of education is to promote as much objectivity, as much deliberation, to present as many views as possible before the person acts. To the view put forth by Michael Flaherty, of the Painters' Union, that 'the disinterested, liberal approach to education is not the right approach for us', Bryson responded: '..... I have a suspicion that if there is a heaven there are many roads to it and that my friends' road may be as good as mine, or better'.

The issue of commitment has been concealed by cries of 'propaganda'. Implicit in the argument against 'propagandist' education is the idea that any education which is committed to a particular set of values is, by its very nature, propagandistic. Advocates of social reconstruction, in their commitment to an ethic of social justice that differs from the liberal's capitalist and bourgeois democratic conception, believe that education should be committed to a particular set of values in order to bring

about a more egalitarian and free society. As Mary
Ely ironically noted, adult educators did not see
that their advocacy of 'education for democracy'
also carried a propagandistic intention. Because
the liberal view is in keeping with the dominant
economic and political structure, it can hide behind
the shield of neutrality, objectivity and truth.
The relation of power to the definition of legitimate knowledge or education is not taken into account. Commitment is equated with propaganda. Con-
sequently, the possibility of 'committed' education
is not considered.

The left liberal critique was evolving during
the inter-war years, but its implications for adult
education have scarcely been developed since then.
Charles Beard questioned whether education should or
could be value free. Eduard Lindeman worked extensively on questions of the relationship of education to
propaganda. As president of the Institute for Propaganda Analysis, Lindeman pointed to the pervasive-
ness of propaganda throughout American society and
the importance for educators of developing skills in
propaganda analysis. 'If we do not learn how to de-
tect and to counteract propaganda, much of our education will come to be a net loss ..... We cannot shut
ourselves off from propaganda, nor can we forbid pro-
pagandists to function. But we can protect ourselves'.(32) The principal distinctions between propaganda and education, according to Lindeman, are that
the propagandist attempts to put over a particular
view without concern for the means, whereas the educator 'insists that the ends of life come about as a
result of shared experience', and used 'educational'
means. Whether or not one agrees with Lindeman's
analysis, it is important to note that Lindeman,
an advocate of social reconstruction, was not an advocate, as he saw it, of propaganda, but of education.

The differentiation of education from propaganda is not as easy as the arguments of some liberals often make it appear. The very conception of
propaganda is embedded in liberal assumptions about
the nature of truth as based in science and reason,
as distinct from belief, faith, superstition or
politics. Education is about developing the capacity for discerning the truth, for scientifically
grounding and reasoning out one's position. Propaganda is seen to be the deliberate distortion of
reality in the effort to gain or maintain power or
ideological domination. The dichotomisation of
education and propaganda denies the extent to which

propaganda is a pervasive aspect of all education. Liberals have ignored the extent to which ideas about what constitutes knowledge, and the processes by which knowledge is constituted, is a political process. If this process were critically examined and, as Lindeman has suggested, skills in propaganda analysis developed, education would not be set in opposition to propaganda but dialectically related to it.

One might argue that, like ideology, there are positive and negative aspects to propaganda; that propaganda is integral to making sense of reality from the perspective of a social vision of the ideal. Operationally, however, the labelling of an activity or view as propagandistic has served to delegitimise perspectives that run counter to the generally agreed upon stock of knowledge as defined by the dominant ideology. The opposition of propaganda to education has been one of the most powerful weapons in ascribing negative ontological status to oppositional stances. It is currently targeted against feminists, for example, as they seek to render the invisible visible, name the pervasive violence of misogyny and patriarchy, pose alternative interpretations and perceptions of reality, and fight for the right to develop research and education which are grounded in the commitment to women's liberation.

From the perspective of committed educators working for the liberation of dominated peoples, social action is integral to the educational process. An alternative social view cannot be identified, articulated or realised without collective reflection and action. The collective is critical, for it is crucial to providing the basis necessary to realise a 'shared experience' - that is, to the development of critical consciousness when the dominant consciousness makes the experience of marginal peoples invisible, or objectifies it as inferior. Also integral is the necessity of organisation to bring together the collective, to disseminate an alternative vision, and to balance the lack of access to the major reality defining channels of society.

<u>Social Action</u> has also been delegitimised as appropriate to education. Invoking the values of the liberal perspective, adult educators have maintained that deliberation, scepticism and tolerance are to be advanced; action is defined as contrary to openness and reason, rooted in propaganda. The

marginalisation of the social action protagonists is exemplified by Morse Cartwright's defence of 'Tolerance in a Democracy':

> There has been a deal of talk in years gone by of what a certain small group of leaders has felt to be the necessity for educating adults for 'social action'. Public opinion among adult educators has shown itself to be overwhelmingly in favor of educating in preparation for 'social action', but of stopping with the process of preparation and wisely leaving the 'action' to the adult individual in some other of his capacities than that of adult student. Certain of these enthusiasts for 'pointed education' still persist, however, and to them might well be revealed the one type of immediate social action with which adult education can concern itself, namely, increased tolerance. True education, education that is something more than mere training in manipulative skills, whether of the hand, eye, or ear, can result only in a tolerant desire to see not one but all sides of any given issue. True education does not turn out one-sided partisans, possessed of the unreasoning zeal, or the deadly regularity of purpose necessary to achieve 'social action' in the merely destructive, 'reform' sense apparently considered desirable by our friends, the social action protagonists.(33)

The liberal values of reason, deliberation, tolerance and open-mindedness have been interpreted to mean that the educator must not take a stand, and, most certainly, must not advocate or engage in social action. This interpretation may be a mistaken one, but it has become a way of thinking, much to the chagrin of critics. In a revealing story, Harry Overstreet noted that his students used the word 'liberal' 'as a term of opprobrium'. Disturbed, he engaged his class in an examination of their biases about the concept. Finally, they agreed that 'a Liberal is one who seeks to apply scientific method to the solution of social problems'. Happily, he observed that 'this definition ruled out all the bitterness about sitting forever on the fence, being innocently open to all ideas, thinking and never acting. We decided that ..... the essential thing about a liberal is his persistent use of intelligence - rather than force or emotion or subterfuge - to advance human affairs'.(34)

Bitterness over the liberal's commitment to non-commitment is avoided by taking a stance in favour of the scientific method and intelligence as the means of resolving social problems. Intelligence is redefined as reason, and then more narrowly yet equated with the scientific method. Challenges to the idea that the 'scientific' interpretation of intelligence and its application to the solution of social problems, are untenable within the liberal perspective. The staunch and articulate spokesman for traditional liberal values in adult education, Everett Dean Martin, links social action to propaganda and authoritarianism, inevitably opposed to intellect: 'the theory of education for social action leads logically to Fascism and hence to the authoritarian state. Political democracy, it is said, has failed. Intellect is not enough ... The basic philosophy of the evolution of civilisation on which such degradation is justified is a Hegelian-Marxist, materialistic dialectic which conceives of struggle and a class of will as the moving force of life and history. So ideas become mere ideology and intellect but a servant of the mass will'.(35)

The very structure of organized education in the USA systematically separates thought from action. While university extension provides for the possibility of varying structures, in reality the classroom and course provide the basic structural units in which education occurs. And, as argued in Chapter 6, academic conceptions of legitimate university work and controls over extension, preclude the possibility of education having an action component. Hence, for example, community development has come to mean the training of trainers and community workers in theories of community development which they can then, ideally, integrate into their practice.

The idea that education should be divorced from action is a fundamental tenet of the liberal tradition in the USA. Like the concept of propaganda, this poses for adult educators a false dichotomy which ascribes a negative ontological status to action as oppositional to education. If, as Paulo Freire maintains, action and reflection are critical to praxis, and it is through praxis that critical consciousness occurs, the possibility of education for social transformation is eclipsed by the liberal resistance to an action component in education. And if, as many learning theorists pose, real learning depends upon action as well as thought, action may have to be reconsidered as integral to the educational process. Without a doubt, action poses considerable difficulty for the course and class boundaries of UAE - not to mention a potential upset to the <u>status quo</u> - yet, until the <u>status quo</u> is pushed, its taken for granted rules and inherent biases are difficult to reveal or to know with the depth of praxis. At stake here also is whether knowledge can safely be assumed to be limited to the intellectual realm; contrary to the practices of the liberal tradition,at least as practised in the USA, emotion, intuition, sensation and social confrontation may also be critical.

<u>Social Reconstruction</u> is the goal of those who advocate social action. Those adult educators who have identified with the interests of the working and poor classes have maintained that change in the class structure of society is the prerequisite to social justice, and that this cannot be attained by reason alone: commitment and organisation are essential. As discussed, social reconstruction was the initial goal of workers' education in the USA. Educators favouring social reconstruction and social action have been delegitimated as propagandists and revolutionaries. To quote the eloquent Everett Dean Martin again: 'all right-thinking people share their enthusiasm for social justice. But it is one thing to be socially minded and it is quite a different matter to accept uncritically popular delusions of reconstruction and to confuse the hope of social betterment with a philosophy of mass will and revolutionary conflict'.(36)

False dichotomies between education and propaganda, education and social action, reason and emotion, unity and conflict, have left, in practice, no room for the searching critique essential to open up the possibility of vitality in the liberal perspective. Facts and information are perceived to be neutral, the building blocks of reasoned deliberation, and not of concern to social reconstructionists. Action is linked, it is argued, to violent revolution, not organisation to bring about a more gradual social revolution. The need for organisation as a basis for social action is not understood as a central consideration for those without power. In a symposium on social action in adult education in 1938, the one participant who appeared to understnad the idea, argued that the line between action and education 'is not all that neat':

> ..... I think that adult education should present facts and information, but I do not think that it should seem detached or sterile to people who are living and suffering and struggling in a dynamic and not too happy society .... a great many organizations represented at this meeting are dealing with the middle class. In my educational work I deal with the lower classes, relatively speaking. It is important that they have education on all sides of a question; but because they are busy with a struggle to exist, it is also important that they have effective education for social action - not to prove that the trade unions are the most effective means of organization or that the American labor party is the most effective weapon, but to prove at least that to be inactive is to be dead.(37)

Today's issues mount: to poverty can be added environmental, personal, and indeed total, nuclear destruction. Alarmists about present day alienation and feelings of powerlessness may be advised to turn attention to a reconsideration of the liberal prohibition against social action, social commitment and social reconstruction. Perhaps 'to be inactive is to be dead'.

For some, the upheavals of the war years and Depression brought a search for direction, a questioning of the assumption that the USA was necessarily on the right path. Poverty and high unemployment were seen as evidence that capitalism was not working; repression of civil liberties, suppression of opposition movements on the left, the rising tide of racism and class hostilities, the consolidation of power in the hands of an economic elite, the silencing of social and political criticism, were all seen as evidence that democracy had failed. The <u>ideal</u> of democracy was not challenged; at issue was its <u>laissez-faire</u> economic and individualistic basis. In reaction to the conservative trend of the liberal democratic conception, a new concept - social democracy - began to appear, and with it, the emergence of a more egalitarian social vision, the call for social reconstruction and a redefinition of the purpose of education to promote radical social change.

In adult education, the primary challenge came

from supporters of workers' education. It was not only their appeal for social reconstruction that challenged the status quo; their social and political stance was rooted in an epistemology and ideology that posed a direct threat to the liberal tradition. The recognition of a class hierarchy challenged the ideology of equal opportunity; class consciousness required separatism, not unity; the idea of false consciousness threatened the assumed neutrality of education, knowledge and science; the focus on power as capital and influence was antithetical to the faith in knowledge as power; the emphasis on change through organisation required collective action, not 'enlightened' individualism or individual advancement. The focus of education made a radical shift from the individual to the collective, from assumed neutrality to the recognition of inherent bias, from consensus to the acceptance of conflict, from impartial deliberation to informed moral choice within a particular value framework, from the individual as an isolated entity acquiring skills and knowledge, to the collective analysis of the social, political and economic situation in which the group was embedded.

Most adult educators could not and/or would not consider so radical a reconstruction of their liberal values, even though such a reconstruction may have been essential to the realisation of their liberal ideal. When the contradictions and limitations of the traditional liberal perspective were exposed, adherents did not engage in the process of critical reflection so essential to the tradition itself, but rather branded critics as heretics - as revolutionaries, communists or socialists, all lumped together as one of a kind, and definitely not to be trusted.

To be realistic, adult educators in the USA continue to face insurmountable problems in advocating the kind of shift called for: the institutions for which they work are part of the status quo. Most have no autonomy. The control of the university over UAE has been discussed in Chapter 6. Because of its marginality and its being so much in the public eye, extension workers do not have the freedom of the university's academic faculty: they have no tenure, teachers are all part-time, and there are no guarantees of academic freedom. As John Studebaker noted (without dismay!) 'to the extent that we are tied to particular vested interests, the learning process must of necessity go forward within the limits of those vested interests'.(38) With lament, Alvin Johnson suggested that 'the fault with adult education (is that) we are mostly schoolmen, or ex schoolmen ..... new ideas, new movements seldom originate in the schools ..... the adult educator needs to stop regarding himself as a mere auxiliary in our grand army of education'.(39)

The major advocates of the social reconstruction stance in adult education were not practitioners of UAE, nor were they employed primarily as adult educators. Charles Beard and Eduard Lindeman were the principal articulators of left liberal or progressive thought in adult education during the inter-war years. While Beard's fame is as an historian, and Lindeman's as a social philosopher, both men were very active during the formative years of the adult education movement.

Affiliated with the New School for Social Research, Beard's contribution to adult education was primarily in the area of workers' education. Beard is best known for his economic interpretation of history: the economic basis for the liberal idealism of the USA's founding fathers. Beard was a staunch advocate of adult education for democracy: 'the supreme issue (is) - Can the ownership and use of property be so controlled as to provide that wide distribution of wealth and security which ..... forms the true basis of popular government? Can this control be brought about through the democratic processes of proposal, discussion, and decision'.(40) Calling for an integration of the real and the ideal, Beard stressed that in addition to teaching about democratic ideals and institutions, the economic ways and means essential to security must be explored. He saw serious limitations in the way capitalism was working in the USA, and called for substantive economic revision if democracy were to work.

In 1933, Beard's 'The Need for Direction' was published as the lead article in the Journal of Adult Education. The article had profound implications for the liberal tradition in adult education, but, as indicated, they were not pursued, at least not in the published literature on adult education, and there is no indication that they were pursued informally. Beard challenged the assumption that science can neutrally provide the basis for choice. The supreme command of the scientific spirit, 'get the relevant data and draw conclusions', is inappropriate, Beard argued, to the social sciences, where science cannot be divorced from ethics, the art of living. Science cannot explain, it can only describe conceptually. The accumulation of data

in the social sciences has not begun to produce laws
of the social world. The assumption that one must
wait until all the data and findings are collected
before making decisions may not be valid: indeed,
it may even be ludicrous:

> Amid such circumstances the only command that
> a social scientist who proceeds on the hypoth-
> esis of the natural scientist can issue is
> this: Make no choices until we have found the
> laws of social action and evolution. With re-
> spect to human affairs, it is the command of
> paralysis, which only students without respon-
> sibilities can obey. Adults confronting the
> exigencies of life cannot, for they must make
> choices continually.

Challenging the possibility of neutrality,
Beard uses the examples of economics:

> ..... (Economics) is not a collection of ax-
> ioms independent of human choices and opinions
> - axioms on which the whole body of economic
> writers can agree as accurately descriptive of
> economic occurrences. It is shot through with
> group and class opinions, with conceptions
> about the nature of social evolution in gener-
> al, with choices of things deemed desirable
> ..... All great works of social science .....
> have been written by men of experience bent on
> attaining ends which they held desirable .....
> all had before them some framework of an ideal
> future with reference to which choices of dir-
> ection were to be made ..... Adult education
> ..... needs something besides a carefully bal-
> anced program of data without indications of
> direction ..... (41)

In 1926, Eduard C. Lindeman's classic work,
The Meaning of Adult Education, was published. In
the foreword, he warned: ..... 'we have become hab-
ituated to a method of achievement which is in
essence antithetical to intelligence. We measure
results quantitatively ..... The chief danger which
confronts adult education lies in the possibility
that we may 'Americanize' it before we understand
its meaning'.(42) Lindeman argued that adult education must use a situational approach, helping
people to understand how their experience is rooted
in a specific socio-historical situation, and fac-
ilitating their quest for life's meaning, for

coming to terms with how they are 'caught within a social milieu'. Freedom is conscious conduct, intelligence must be critical, reflective, as well as informed, and it must be democratised. Collectivity is a fact of life: 'collectivism is the road to power, the predominant reality of modern life'.(43) Education must orient itself not to the individual, but to the social and collective reality in which the person is located. It can do this by 'revealing the nature of social process; transforming the battle of interests from warfare into creative conflict and ..... making the collective life an educational experience'. Lindeman maintained that the credo of individualism was inappropriate to the times. 'Mere self-improvement is a delusion ..... Adult Education will become an agency of progress if its short-time goal of self-improvement can be made compatible with a long-time, experimental but resolute policy of changing the social order'.(44)

Critical of the tie of education into capitalism and profit production, Lindeman warned:

> If this system, both on its economic and educational sides, becomes too rigid and too oppressive and incapable of sincere self-criticism, nothing short of violent revolution will suffice to change its direction. But if adults approach education with the end-in-view that their new knowledge is to be the instrument of a probable future revolution, they will almost certainly defeat the very purposes of learning. Revolutions are essential only when the true learning process has broken down, failed. We revolt when we can no longer think or when we are assured that thinking has lost its efficacy. Revolution is the last resort of a society which has lost faith in intelligence.(45)

For Lindeman, intelligence was not equated with the scientific method. Like Beard, he questioned the idea that intelligence can be neutral, stressing the personal factor in all human intelligence:

> An intelligent person sees facts, not merely in relation to each other but in relation to himself. Indeed, one of the first marks of intelligence is to recognise that mental views of the real are aspects of reality. Intelligence then becomes a way of appropriating facts - a way of integrating facts with the

total aspects of the personality. Only the
educated specialist naively sees facts as discrete, objective and external units of experience. He speaks of the 'laws of nature' as
if man's mind were not somehow mixed with the
formulation of those laws. (46)

Adult education is an essential '<u>tool for social
movements</u> which are central to the democratic struggle: every social action group should at the same
time be an adult education group, and I go even so
far as to believe that all successful adult education groups sooner or later become social action
groups'. (47)

The view that adult education is an 'essential
tool for social movements' has been overlooked in
the history or current experience of the field. It
is a very important key to the socialist and left
progressive perspectives. In this context - that is,
adult education as an integral component of social
movement - one can readily see the importance of
collective consciousness, critical thought, committed
education and social action. Given the goal of social reconstruction, the integration of adult education into social movement is crucial. Significantly, in the USA, adult education - that is, the
professionally recognised field of adult education
- has been integrated into established institutions,
not social movements, and its goal has not been that
of social reconstruction. While the work that has
taken place in connection with social movements has
at times been appropriated by the adult education
profession (noteworthy examples are Highlander Folk
School and Women's Consciousness Raising Groups), in
actuality these have had virtually no connection
with the mainstream of adult education in theory,
practice or sense of purpose. While they serve to
present an important vision of a radically different
way of practising adult education - a vision highly
valued by progressive adult educators - there is
scarcely a hint of that vision in the grinding institutional reality of the mainstream field.

<u>Socialism</u> and socialist theory have been totally silenced as a perspective with adult education
in the USA. The workers' education movement was
marginalised until it overcame its socialist leanings. True, there have been occasional courses on
Marxism, typically at more independent institutions
such as the New School for Social Research. When
mentioned in the literature of adult education,
which is uncommon, socialism is lumped together with

communism, Marxism and fascism and treated as a propagandist doctrine of revolution and totalitarianism, a definite threat to democracy. In the understated words of L. J. Richardson, quoted earlier, '..... we didn't favor socialism ..... we favored a mode of education that would bring men to a rational view of society and included among other things loyalty to our government'.

Adult educators viciously attacked socialism in the name of liberalism and democracy: dogmatically, they held that it was antithetical to both because of its dogmatic stance. Those who spoke earnestly from a left liberal, possibly socialist perspective, like Lindeman and Beard, did not mention the word 'socialism' in their adult education writings.
There appear to be no self-identified socialists in the adult education mainstream, at least not in leadership positions. Socialism has not been publicly explored as a political, economic, social or educational ideology, or philosophy. For that matter, neither has liberalism; although it has been extensively alluded to, it has been <u>assumed</u>, its tenets accepted as givens. Threats to its vitality have been feared, and have brought adult educators to its defence, but the liberal tradition never has been subjected to critical examination.

In 1946, Lindeman alluded to the irony inherent in the unexamined liberal tradition:

> The terms 'left', 'right', 'liberal', 'reactionary', et cetera, no longer carry adequately clear meanings. They are not functional terms. The first two are ideological in origin and are used to distinguish Marxists from non-Marxists. The two latter terms are residues of nineteenth century political thought. Our age stands in need of a new terminology to express political and economic ideas. Since the new words have not yet been coined, we are obliged to wrestle with these emotionally-laden symbols which belong more to the realm of propaganda than to serious and reasonable discourse.(48)

Lindeman differentiated the left liberal from the right reactionary perspective. Contrasts are in terms of orientation toward change, commitment to the welfare of the masses and the extension of democratic principles, social versus individual responsibility, and the role of government. Lindeman observed that he would prefer to refer to the left liberal as liberal for '..... in this country, more so than in Europe, everybody labeled as a <u>left-liberal</u> is presumed to be either a Communist or a fellow traveller'. He felt that he could not use the term 'liberal' to signify the left liberal perspective. It is argued here that a significant transformation in the everyday use of the word 'liberal' had taken place: liberalism had become identified with the <u>status quo</u>, the elite, <u>laissez-faire</u> capitalism, the champion of bourgeois individualism.

In thinking about the liberal tradition in adult education in the USA it is critical to realise that socialism has essentially been eradicated as a viable category of social thought in education, mirroring the more general eradication of socialism as a viable political or economic philosophy. It simply is not discussed in the mainstream: it has been rendered invisible. It has been argued here that, rather than championing the right to free speech, free thought, alternative conceptions or egalitarian ideals of human liberation, the liberal tradition in adult education has contributed above all else to the silencing of socialism. One does not have to be an active proponent of socialism to be subject to attack. For example, Lindeman was frequently attacked as a communist, atheist and socialist; though a popular speaker, it was not uncommon for public appearances and the projects he supported to be cancelled or the subject of extensive controversy. Even in the last year of his life, his teaching summer session at Lewis & Clark College in Oregon touched off a controversy. 'I had trouble before I arrived', he wrote to Max Otto. 'Some crackpot tried to stop me from coming, same old charges: socialism, atheism, and progressive education. The president of the College got cold feet but the faculty didn't, and so we went ahead and nothing happened. It wasn't pleasant, however'.(49)

INSTITUTIONAL HEGEMONY

The period between World Wars I and II was critical in the development of adult education as a field of educational practice. Not only was it the period when the professional and institutional bases of adult education were carved out of the educational landscape, but, most significantly, the ideology of the dawning 'profession' was solidified. The professional, the institutional and the ideological premises of the new movement reinforced one another, ultimately divorcing adult educaton from its birth place - in social movements - and moving it into the realm of established educational systems. True, informal adult education continues to be an aspect of social movements, but this strain is not of the more formally recognised field of practice.

Workers' education is a paramount case in the severance of adult education from social movement and its transformation into an institutionally legitimised field of practice. The obvious explanation for the transition from workers' education into the more functional approach of labour education lies in the institutionalisation of labour as a bargaining unit with management. An important part of the drama also took place within adult education. Not all workers are in unions, not all union members are involved in collective bargaining, and collective bargaining is not the only concern of workers: why did adult educators turn their attention away from working class education?

Working class education was delegitimated by the newly emergent profession of adult education. Liberal educational values as they came to be institutionalised in UAE, provided the basis for the annihilation of working class education as an approach to the education of workers. The attack was not launched against working class education _per se_, but rather the tenets upon which it was based were delegitimised. In the process, the ideological premises of adult education were solidified; liberalism moved from an unformulated and sometimes contradictory set of assumptions into the articulated conception of practice. Once solidified, the liberal tradition again receded into the background: vigilance was no longer necessary as the institutional structures, educational form and premises upon which adult education operated, were set firmly in place. The rival conception had been eradicated.

The ramifications went far beyond working class education. The education of all marginal groups, and the potential of adult education in the process of social movement - its potential as a vehicle for social transformation - have been fundamentally affected by the hegemony of the liberal tradition and its ideological solidification during the interwar years.

To summarise, the liberal tradition has provided the symbolic legitimation of adult education: in the name of democracy, equality, service and excellence, adult education has been promoted. With ideological rigidification, each of these premises - in their ambiguous mixture of liberalism and pragmatism, egalitarianism and elitism - have been defined in a conservative direction. The interests of the state and its established social hierarchies were reinforced: democracy became the U.S. Government; equality became equality of opportunity for each person who had the desire and ability to participate in education for individual economic advancement; service shifted its focus from social reform to serving the interests of sponsoring institutions, employers, professional and other elites, and the state; excellence became the means of establishing institutional controls over adult education under the guise of enforcing academic standards.

Along with the symbolic legitimation of adult education went the symbolic delegitimation of potentially rival conceptions. Essentially, liberalism became solidified as the unifying professional ideology, nihilating a socialistic or left progressive perspective. While a socialistic and/or social reconstruction perspective has not been articulated as such within adult education, it is implicit in the tenets of working class education which stress 'separate' education to develop critical consciousness, 'committed' education, collective identification and action to bring about social reconstruction. Education directed towards a specific group has been deemed separatist, the very idea of class is deemed to be inappropriate in the USA where each has the opportunity to advance. 'Committed' education is declared propagandistic, social action is declared anti-educational, and socialism is consistently linked with communism, fascism and totalitarianism. In the nihilation of this potentially rival conception, the values of the liberal tradition have been invoked: equality, individual advancement, neutrality, deliberation, unity, tolerance, consensus, rationality and the use of science as an instrument of social progress.

The process of delegitimising the left progressive perspective within adult education is a significant chapter in the social construction of reality: certainly it was a critical stage in the initial consolidation of adult education as a professional area of practice. The inter_war years in the history of adult education exemplify the process of symbolic legitimation critical to institutionalisation. According to Berger and Luckmann 'if the institutional order is to be taken for granted in its totality as a meaningful whole, it must be legitimated by "placement" in a symbolic universe. ..... Specific procedures of universe-maintenance become necessary when the symbolic universe becomes <u>a problem</u> .....'(50) Nihilation is a process of universe maintenance whereby everything outside the ideological universe is conceptually liquidated by ascribing to it a negative ontological status and by translating the deviant conception into the dominant conception: i.e. there are no classes in the USA, but adult education is a middle class movement ..... socialism is revolution ..... commitment is propaganda ....., etc. With nihilation, the rival conception is either distorted or silenced: ultimately a whole sector of human experience is made invisible. Such has been the case of a left progressive perspective in adult education. The ideas of socialism and class are not only alien to professional adult educators, they are generally not even <u>acknowledged</u> as legitimate. Ironically, one encounters opposition to the idea of 'non-neutral' and 'separatist' education despite a history dominated by continuing professional education. The phrases 'social action' and 'social change' are ever present in the rhetoric, but in actuality, practice is dominated by the 'new' ideologies of marketing and the standardisation of performance criteria.

It is important to note that, while the forces of nihilation have been very effective, they have not succeeded totally. The alternative vision continues to survive: noteworthy are the Highlander Folk School, indigenous programmes among marginal groups (workers, immigrants, Indians, women, poor, blacks, etc.), the valiant voices of a handful of professionally identified but progressive adult educators, the publication, 'Second Thoughts', and the inspirational work of the International Council for Adult Education. For the most part, these progressive programmes are not identified with the institutionally defined 'field' of adult education.

Recently a noteworthy effort to reach workers has been made through a number of Colleges for Working Adults, funded by the Postsecondary Education Commission and modelled on the Wayne State Weekend College. These provide the opportunity for workers to earn college degrees, typically as a group, in collaboration with their unions. Included in the interdisciplinary programme of study is the critical analysis of the worker in society. To quote

Eric Fenster, who has worked closely with the Wayne State Project:

> ..... the additional value of education is not only the personal satisfaction it brings to its possessor; education can also provide the tools for groups of people to reflect upon their social reality and how it may be improved. The curriculum is socially oriented ..... the emphasis on teaching requiring personal contact and discussion and the accent on relationships with organizations in which people have already found common purpose post a challenge to examine the risks of excessive individualism in a complex and interdependent world and suggest the spirit of collective advancement in its place.(51)

Grounded in the principles of separate education, critical reflection and group solidarity, these colleges may exemplify a way in which critical consciousness can be built into a more traditional conception of the degree-granting function of the university, if established images of what the regular university offers and conservative control under the guise of university standards can be overcome. The ways in which this may have been accomplished merits further study. The Colleges for Working Adults are a major outcome of labour's participation in post secondary education, as institutionalised in the 1980 Amendment to the Higher Education Act, discussed in Chapter 6. There are other exceptions in UAE, but typically these have been marginalised and, in the current period of fiscal conservatism, forced out of the market place.

UAE has been very much a leader in the controversies outlined in this chapter. As the bastion of the liberal tradition in adult education, UAE has also been the seat of tension between the pragmatic and the idealistic, the egalitarian and the elite strains within the liberal tradition as manifest in higher education in the USA. As adult educators employ sophisticated marketing techniques in their missionary endeavour to reach the widest possible adult audience with the highest quality offerings they can produce, the university faculty and administration look on with hesitation and often scorn, wondering by what right adult education is promoted under university sponsorship, acceding finally to its public relations value so long as it does not mar the university's academic image or mission.

Continuing professional education provides the meeting ground between the internal university and the adult education specialist; it is the hope of each for survival if they do not give in to the temptation to compete with one another for the rich market. While continuing professional education has always been the mainstay of UAE, the current situation is unusual in the unparalleled social legitimacy and high level demand.

During the last decade, the commodification of UAE has been rampant. This process of commodification, of breaking down education into saleable units, is integral to the marketing process. Wexler and Grabiner describe how the process of commodification, marketisation and corporatisation are fundamental to the reorganisation of the educational system.(52) Clearly UAE is far ahead, with corporatisation dating back to co-operative programmes with the defence industry during World War II. What is new in the 1970s and 1980s is the wholesale domination of UAE by this process which has become absolutely fundamental to its survival financially. As pointed out in Chapter 6, marketing and co-operative programmes define practice. Needs assessment has become a marketing, not an educational, strategy. Programme design in UAE is really about marketing.

All this is a far cry from the original conception of workers' education. The accountability movement and the concomitant proletarianisation of the professions, as manifest in the development of performance standards and demand for competency based education, provide fertile ground for the commodification of continuing professional education. Even more fertile is the commodity orientation of the new class of 'Young Urban Professionals' (dubbed the YUPPIES by an astute observer of the Los Angeles scene). This class of affluent, highly educated, typically single or childless professionals lives through consumption of gourmet foods, designer clothes, adventure and personal growth. UAE appeals to this market, selling personal growth, career change, professional advancement and providing an 'alternative to the bar' as a meeting ground for singles.

The ideology of personal growth is the current manifestation of need fulfilment for the affluent. In adult education, the liberal tradition has taken a curiously anti-intellectual turn as it stresses process and scorns content. It is professionally legitimised by the theory of andragogy which puts the adult learner at the centre, and the teacher in the role of facilitator. The theory assumes that adults are mature, have a rich background of experience, know what they want to know, and learn best when they are in charge of their own learning. Self-directed learning and group discussion are the methodologies of adult education, grounded in the more romantic liberal humanism of innate potential and personal freedom.

Not only does andragogy raise serious questions for the liberal intellectual tradition, but the methodologies of adult education are becoming very inappropriate for work with people who are not already highly educated, for work oriented toward the development of critical skills or social transformation, or for work oriented to people who do not want to learn a given subject matter. It has also meant that, despite all the talk about methodology, adult education has avoided raising serious methodological issues as it ignores the structure implicit in the chosen method. Commodification brings the necessity of the customer being pleased - having a pleasant time - as UAE becomes an important arena for leisure activity, whether by choice or mandate. Today's 'Yuppies' want to enjoy themselves and are prepared to pay the price to do so.

The issues raised in this chapter suggest that the liberal tradition in UAE in the USA has been so distorted by the need to survive economically in an elite educational institution and a conservative political climate that it no longer has any viable meaning except for its power as a tool of ideological justification. Education for critical thought, social transformation, egalitarian ideals, or human liberation will not take place through UAE. Its very structure, methodology and ideology militate against this possibility. True, there are isolated instances that are exceptions to this generalisation, but their rarity and invisibility, hidden behind closed classroom doors, testifies to the validity of the generalisation.

If an alternative conception of adult education is to have a chance, some of the issues raised in this chapter need attention. How can we work toward social transformation if we stay divorced from social movements, remaining accountable to institutions rather than ideas? There has been much talk about education for critical consciousness, mouthing the words of Paulo Freire without considering the severe institutional and ideological limitations placed upon its possibility. Instead, in true liberal fashion, the idea of critical consciousness has become trivialised as personal development and growth.

If we are to take seriously the idea that our work is to educate for critical consciousness and social transformation, we must be prepared to address some of the serious challenges that this raises for the liberal tradition as it has been manifest in UAE in the USA. It means that education must sometimes be separate and separatist, that it must be committed to an ideal, that it must stress critical interpretation including, among others, a Marxist analysis of class and commodification, as well as a feminist analysis of patriarchy, and that it must consider collective action as part of the educational process. To the idea of the 'objective attitude' as developed in Chapter 3, is added the idea of objectivity as a critical perspective, through which the person can come to understand how the personal is constructed by the objectifying, generalising processes in society; that is, how our commonsense understanding of the personal is a product of the political and economic as we internalise the dominant ideology as our personal truth. Along with the development of critical consciousness we need to find ways to render the invisible visible, to move beyond the constraints of ideology, and to find ways of directly contributing to the educational work of progressive social movements. If we can develop a clearer perception of the possibilities, some of this work might even be possible within the conservative framework of UAE.

The liberal tradition is at its darkest moment in the history of the USA. Conservatism now provides a new basis of symbolic legitimation and, as it consolidates its hold, it is working to nihilate liberalism. The seeds of its destruction were planted more than fifty years ago as liberalism moved to the right, delegitimising its left liberal voice. It is critical that the voice be reconstructed if the liberal tradition is to be revivified in the USA. If liberals had heeded their own tradition, if they had been able to be truly open, to incorporate rather than annihilate, to reflect critically rather than reject, the history of adult education may have been different. Challenges to the gospel of social reform according to scientific expertise cannot go unheeded. The hegemony of the scientific method and rationalism as the basis of all truth, is open to question, with vast implications for the liberal epistemological premises that underlie education. The ties of the liberal tradition to the dominant political and economic structures require critical reflection and fundamental change. Is it possible to adhere to even the finest values of the liberal tradition within the current framework of state, capitalistic and institutional support of adult education?

LIBERALISM AND LIBERATION

> I hold it, that a little rebellion, now and then is a good thing, and as necessary in the political world as storms in the physical.
>
> Thomas Jefferson.(53)

The tragedy of the liberal tradition is that it has lost sight of the ideals which originally fired it. The American Revolution was fought in the name of those ideals: liberty, equality, and justice for all. The incompatibility of those ideals with a hierarchically organised society has been the constant contradiction with which liberalism has had to contend. It has done so through reform and compromise, shunning conflict, protecting power in the name of democracy. In doing so, it has failed to confront the structures and practices that harbour and perpetuate inequality. If liberalism is to survive in any meaningful way, it must confront those structures: it must reclaim the banner of social reconstruction, recapturing its original revolutionary fervour. Once the voice of revolution, liberalism has become a tradition, a buttress to the <u>status quo</u>, fearful for its continued survival in a world turned materialistic, and out of control.

If liberalism is to be on the side of life, of humanity, the awesome tide of today's world must be confronted. Issues of power and structure can no longer be ignored. In adult education idealistic fervour has given way to the glory of institution building - or to the harsh realities of survival in times of economic recession. The institutional location of adult education in organisations whose primary purpose is something other than the education of adults, has resulted in a dependency which has contributed to the distortion of liberal ideals. The location of UAE in the university is particularly problematic. While it allows a certain amount of intellectual freedom and protection, it brings adult education full square into the hierarchical structure of society, and of education, mandating its subservience to the university's elitism and conservatism. As long as the university defines legitimate practice, adult education's potential as a vehicle for social reconstruction will be severely limited.

There are, however, two fronts on which UAE might make some progress: one is the front of equality, the other that of critical theory. If UAE were to fight for equality - real equality - the revolutionary potential of the liberal tradition might be realised. This means that all would have the right to an education that is liberatory - one that encourages critical analysis, group consciousness and determination, as well as personal self-confrontation and expansion. The appeal is not only to each individual, but to people as members of groups with distinctive histories, cultures, and class locations. An important goal would be to work toward understanding how the personal is politically and socially constructed. Herein lies the essence of critical theory. Challenging the epistemological base of liberalism, such an approach would necessitate the recognition of multiple realities, distorted truths, inevitable bias, the politics of knowledge production, different ways of knowing, and, most important, the significance of commitment to an ideal. As feminism is beginning to show, the struggle for real equality - not only in terms of access, but also in terms of the production and legitimation or delegitimation of knowledge - has revolutionary potential. Unfortunately, feminists also know only too well what it is to be marginalised by their paternalistic liberal co-workers.

If the liberal tradition is to fight once again for its ideals, UAE cannot be its only front. Direct links with social movements and disempowered groups are critical if liberal adult education is to play a viable part in social transformation. The peace movement, the green movement, the women's movement, liberation movements for all peoples, require education for information, reflection, and action. In Latin America, popular education has emerged as a vital educational approach to social transformation. It offers a method that blends critical theory, content and process worthy of attention.

The battle over working class education in the USA provides some clues as to what is essential if education is to be oriented toward social transformation. Central is the importance of education for the development of critical consciousness. This means that education must sometimes be separatist, collective and critical if a group is to render the invisible visible, building its history, cutting through myths and systematic scientific distortion, using collective and personal experiences as the starting point from which to engage in a critical dialogue with establishment truth. Class and gender consciousness are central to this process, for critical awareness depends upon experiencing the personal as collective, as well as political.

And action cannot be sharply severed from education. It is time that the liberal tradition learned from experience and recognised that votes alone do not make change. In the face of overwhelming alienation and feelings of powerlessness, as one observer notes, 'to be inactive is to be dead'. Integral to liberal education should be study, action, and critical reflection upon action alternatives. For example, with respect to nuclear disarmament, it is doubtful that people need more information on the effects of nuclear war, but they do need to know how to stop its inevitable march. Can the liberal tradition open its doors to action considerations?

Finally, a word about ideology and propaganda. These weapons have been too effective in silencing critical thought to be taken lightly. Knowledge production and dissemination unavoidably include elements of ideology and propaganda. The task is to be discerning with respect to their presence and the subtle ways in which they work, rather than to delegitimise them. So precarious is the balance, so easy to label, so quick to silence. The risk is too grave - all perspectives must be heard, and their rights protected at all costs - even if an eye must be closed to what one considers to be propaganda. One person's propaganda is another's education. If the method and power of the critical perspective are to be realised, all theories, ideas and ideals have to be accessible, within the boundaries of basic human rights.

To forge a new path, it is essential that those who identify with the ideals of liberalism submit the liberal tradition to rigorous scrutiny. Significant critiques of science, education and ideological practices are mounting: to continue to ignore them would be a mistake. To reclaim its ideals, the tradition must bend before its paternalistic elitism, learn from its critics, move beyond the fortress of academe, walk the streets of darkness and hunger, face how little it has to offer beyond the hallowed walls of the classroom, and learn to fight - through a revitalised conception of education – for the ideal of human liberation.

NOTES

1. Leon J. Richardson to F. C. Stephens, August 31, 1923, in President's Files, 1923:23.
2. Leon J. Richardson to William W. Campbell, June 13, 1924, in President's Files, 1924:248.
3. L. J. Richardson, Proceedings, National University Extension Association, 1928, p. 202.
4. L. J. Richardson, Annual Report, University Extension Division, 1921-22.
5. L. J. Richardson, Berkeley, Culture, University of California and University Extension, 1892 - 1960, transcript, tape-recorded interview. Regional Cultural History Project (Berkeley, 1962), p. 146.
6. J. L. Kerchen, Report for the Department of Workers' Education, in President's Files, 1931: 149 and Annual Reports of the Extension Division, 1921-41.
7. T. R. Adam, The Worker's Road to Learning, New York: American Association for Adult Education, 1940, p. 53.
8. M. E. Deutsch to R. G. Sproul, March 31 and June 2, 1933, in President's Files, 1933:201.
9. F. M. Rosenteter, The Boundaries of the Campus: A History of the University of Wisconsin Extension Division, 1884-1945, Madison, 1957, p. 103.
10. F. H. Schneider, Patterns of Workers' Education: The Story of Bryn Mawr Summer School, Washington: American Council on Public Affairs, 1941, p. 72.
11. Ibid., p. 28.
12. Fannia M. Cohn, Educational Department of the International Ladies' Garment Workers Union, in Workers Education in the United States, New York: Workers Education Bureau of America, 1921, p. 47.
13. C. A. Beard, The Rise of American Civilization, New York: 1930, p. 225.
14. Schneider, op. cit., p. 17.
15. Ibid., p. 51.
16. Adam, op. cit., p. 57.
17. J. Kerrison, Workers' Education at the University Level, New Brunswick, New Jersey, 1951, p. 119.
18. Ibid., p. 122.
19. Ibid., pp. 20 - 43.
20. T. R. Adam, Against Separatism, Journal of Adult Education, 1939, p. 121.

21. M. A. Cartwright, Ten Years of Adult Education, New York, 1935, pp. 201 - 202.
22. Nihilation is the term used by Berger and Luckmann to name the liquidation processes used to delegitimise rival conceptions of reality, i.e. those posing a threat to the dominant conceptions. The process includes giving deviant conceptions a negative ontological status and incorporating alternative conceptions by radically redefining them to fit one's own universe. See P. L. Berger and T. Luckmann, The Social Construction of Reality, Garden City, New York, 1967, p. 114.
23. Adam, op. cit., p. 1.
24. Ibid., p. 144.
25. Cartwright, op. cit., p. 200.
26. A Middle Class Movement? Journal of Adult Education, 1938.
27. Jane Thompson, Adult education and the disadvantaged, in (ed.) Thompson, Adult Education for a Change, London: 1980.
28. M. L. Ely, Why Forums?, New York: 1937, p. 212.
29. Cartwright, op. cit., p. 55.
30. Ely, op. cit.
31. American Association for Adult Education, Adult Education and Propaganda: A Panel Discussion, in Adult Education and Democracy, New York, 1936, pp. 20 - 38.
32. Eduard C. Lindeman, The Democratic Man, Boston: 1956, pp. 144 - 149.
33. Morse A. Cartwright, Tolerance in a Democracy, Journal of Adult Education, pp. 235 - 241.
34. Harry A. Overstreet, When Words Go Forth to Battle, Journal of Adult Education, January 1938, Vol. 10, No. 1, pp. 5 - 9.
35. Everett Dean Martin, The Revolt Against Reason, Journal of Adult Education, January 1938, Vol. 10, No. 1, pp. 17 - 22.
36. Ibid.
37. To What Extent Do We Educate for Social Action?, a colloquy in Journal of Adult Education, Vol. 10, No. 3, June 1938, pp. 271 - 276, Miss Leslie quoted.
38. Loc. cit.
39. Alvin Johnson, A Reaffirmation, Journal of Adult Education, June 1935, p. 258.
40. Charles A. Beard, What is This Democracy?, in American Association for Adult Education, Adult Education and Democracy, New York: 1936, p. 4.
41. Charles A. Beard, The Need for Direction, Journal of Adult Education, January 1933, Vol. 5,

No. 1, pp. 5 - 10.
  42. Eduard C. Lindeman, The Meaning of Adult Education, Montreal: 1961, p. xxx. Original published in 1926 in New York.
  43. Ibid., p. 97.
  44. Ibid., p. 405.
  45. Ibid., p. 49.
  46. Ibid., p. 15.
  47. Lindeman, The Democratic Man, op. cit. p. 168.
  48. Ibid., p. 230.
  49. Ibid., p. 34.
  50. Berger and Luckmann, op. cit., pp. 104 - 105.
  51. Eric Fenster, Adult Higher Education: an American Model, Focus, U.S. Embassy, Paris, January 1982.
  52. Philip Wexler and Gene Grabiner, The Education Question and America During the Crisis, 1984, unpublished.
  53. Thomas Jefferson to James Madison, January 30, 1787.

Chapter Eight

THE FUTURE OF UNIVERSITY ADULT EDUCATION

INTRODUCTION

The central theme of our analysis of UAE in both England and the USA has been the historical prominence and importance of the liberal tradition, in all its forms, and its problematic and varied relationships with both conservative and radical perspectives and practices within UAE. It remains, in this final chapter, to consider the future of UAE in the context of this debate.

Whilst both the context and the practice of UAE differ widely in the two countries, there is no doubt that UAE is undergoing rapid change in both England and the USA, and that the liberal tradition in particular is under attack from varied quarters. In both countries there are immediate and pressing financial and structural problems, as governments of monetarist persuasions attempt to cut back on 'subsidised' education and force UAE into the market place.

These immediate pressures, however, are buttressed by the longer term tendencies that were noted in earlier chapters.

The overall balance and structure of UAE has been changing over recent decades, irrespective of immediate government constraints. The details of these changes, the reasons underlying them, and the likely long term consequences have already been discussed and there is no need to reiterate the arguments. But it is in this context that the future of UAE must be analysed.

CRITIQUES OF THE LIBERAL TRADITION

There are many who dismiss the liberal tradition as either irrelevant or undesirable (or both) for UAE both now and in the future. These critics fall broadly into two categories: those who advocate a reorientation of UAE towards a more professional and post experience structure of provision; and those who espouse a radical/socialist stance. 'The case against' the liberal tradition, and the consequent alternative futures proposed, can be assessed from within these two contrasting perspectives.

In the USA, those advocating the former perspective have been very much in the ascendant for the past two decades. Not only is the liberal tradition used as a rhetorical justification for essentially conservative and establishment orthodoxies (as discussed in Chapters 6 and 7, and as analysed further below), it is now under direct attack from the predominating conservatism of the USA of the 1980s. Moreover, the current climate within universities in the USA has given unparalleled legitimacy to the concept of UAE being construed as essentially continuing professional education. As was argued in Chapter 7, the need to survive economically has become so dominant that it has all but eclipsed what was anyway a gravely weakened adherence within UAE to the educational values of the liberal tradition.

In England the situation has been somewhat more complex. The more post experience oriented critics of the liberal tradition[1] have drawn attention to the outmoded, irrelevant, elitist and expensive traditional tutorial class format. Moreover, it is argued, such provision, although still forming the ideological basis of UAE in England (and in other countries where the English tradition is predominant), is in sharp decline and now comprises only a small percentage of UAE provision. The traditional liberal adult education approach is held to be now wholly invalid. It is claimed that it attracts a very small number of predominantly middle class adults to classes, which are increasingly out of touch with the contemporary world - especially in their neglect of science and technology. The exclusively liberal approach neither responds to nor caters for the educational needs and demands of modern society.

However, the root of the problem, according to these critics, lies deeper than such practical considerations, important though these undoubtedly are. The liberal tradition, it is argued, is based upon an empiricist epistemology, which has resulted, in education, in a hierarchy of knowledge, structured within formal subject disciplines, and subject to a strong implicit belief that rational, scientific enquiry is the highest form of educational attainment. (Similar criticisms of the 'rationalism' of the liberal tradition as practised in UAE in the USA were made in Chapter 6).

All education is thus construed as either the imparting of this knowledge by experts to the uninitiated, or the process of extending further our knowledge of the world (the quest for truth through discipline-based research). The resultant structure is thus necessarily elitist: the expert teacher mediating between the complex, sophisticated and large body of knowledge with which s/he is familiar, and the learners, who can have no direct access to such knowledge. In UAE the liberal tradition is regarded as both the pedagogic structure and the ideology through which this mainstream epistemology, with all its social and political connotations, has been articulated.

If this epistemological framework is to be rejected, what is to be put in its place, and what are the practical policy implications of such a change for UAE? According to one recent critic, a 'contextualist' epistemology is emerging to replace the outmoded liberal tradition:

> The major strands of this transformation are coming from ecological psychology, from developments in the philosophy of science and the sociology of knowledge, from experience in the human awareness movement and with eastern religion and philosophies ..... (and) in the 'new physics' of quantum mechanics.[2]

This 'contextualist' epistemology denies the Cartesian distinction between the individual observer and the external world. Thus, any notion of a body of objective knowledge is untenable: 'it is the world, reality, which has primacy in the educational process, rather than formal knowledge'.[3] The role of the teacher becomes thus that of facilitator, and the central educational task is transformed into the 'creating and managing (of) learning settings'.[4] The didactic and pedagogic role in UAE thus needs to be replaced by the 'resource, or catalyst orientation'.[5]

The policy implications are dramatic - and would lead to a UAE structure in England both more similar to that which predominates in the USA, and more congruent with current government policies towards UAE. In terms of provision, such critics have argued that UAE should concentrate upon part-time degrees and diplomas, and, above all else, continuing professional education. Only in this way can UAE become a centrally important and university-wide function. It is argued that the crucial change must be from a structure in which UAE is undertaken by a single, separate and quasi-autonomous department, to one in which UAE is 'a generalised function of the University as a whole'.(6) If this were to be the practice, then the resources and expertise of the whole university could be put to the service of the community. The role of the UAE specialist department would thus be to act primarily as a catalyst, a resource and an agency for establishing 'learning settings', rather than as a direct provider of classes, courses and adult tutors.

This, then, is a proposal (which is typical of much contemporary thinking about UAE both in England and the USA) for a very fundamental restructuring and reorienting of UAE, and, crucially, a rejection, or at the least a drastic downgrading, of the liberal tradition.

The critique from the Left is, not unnaturally, very different. Again, although the contexts are rather different, there are fundamental similarities between the position adopted by radical and socialist critics in England and the USA. In the USA, as was argued in Chapters 6 and 7, radicals see the liberal tradition as a purely rhetorical smokescreen to justify and rationalise what is essentially an important part of the process of buttressing pro-capitalist ideology. At every level, the pattern of liberal democracy, and the beliefs about society in the USA which inhere within it, have become wholly dominant. Any views or analyses falling outside these parameters are either disregarded or seen as subversive. In as much as there has continued to be a 'social purpose' element within the liberal tradition of UAE in the USA, it has been seen as expanding the access to higher education, and enabling mature students to obtain degrees by part-time study: it has not been concerned with social transformation of any sort. Nor has it even been concerned seriously with exploring alternative analyses of the USA's social, economic and political problems. UAE's adherence in the USA, therefore, has been to the monolithic culture. Paradoxically, in a country where there are the most obvious manifestations of diverse cultural influences and lifestyles, the political ideology and political culture is almost wholly unilinear and conformist. Within this framework UAE has come to serve, and to service, orthodoxy.

Such a stance, it is argued from the Left, has led UAE in the USA to jettison much that was of value in the early articulations of social purpose adult education. There can, for example, be no real consideration of structural inequality in the USA: liberalism holds to the view that the USA is the land of opportunity, and, hence, that individuals who fail to 'get on' have only themselves to blame. Similarly, since liberalism denies the existence of social classes in the USA, there can be no such thing as working class education, let alone positive discrimination.

There are many other examples of the effects of this monolithic culture on the ideology and practice of UAE: but these have been discussed in some detail in Chapters 6 and 7 and need not be re-entered into here. The net effect of this whole process has been to incorporate UAE within the established orthodoxy of the predominant culture of the USA. Whilst operating in the name of democracy, equality service et al, UAE is, in reality, buttressing the hegemonic culture. It is thus fulfilling a role not dissimilar from that of which social democratic parties in western societies were accused by Cecil Wright Mills: in effect, such organisations act as 'managers of discontent' - as safety valves for siphoning off potential radicalism. Thus UAE's major role has become that of providing ideological justification for the practices and values of contemporary capitalist society in the USA.

As was argued at the end of Chapter 7, if this is the view taken, then, unless there are very radical changes in the liberal tradition, UAE cannot be regarded as a viable vehicle for progressive educational ideas. Moreover, UAE as at present constituted, bears little or no relation to the rhetorical claims made by the liberal tradition regarding its practice and its objectives. In effect, therefore, the liberal tradition is held to obscure the need for urgent and radical changes in methods, practices and objectives within UAE.

In England, although the criticisms are not dissimilar, the situation is rather more complex because of the greater diversity of perspectives both within UAE and within the wider society.

At the heart of the modern critics' perspective is the disillusion that has resulted from the general educational (and social and political) experiences since the 1950s. At the outset, after the war and the 1945 Labour election victory, optimistic idealism was in the ascendancy, in adult education as elsewhere. Keith Jackson has summarised the mood succinctly:

> A liberal progressive movement for educational change thrived from 1945 to the early 1970s. It was a major project of social engineering whose main platform was that education could be a primary factor in reshaping the world for the better. Education could both promote equality and enable every person to develop to their full potential ..... It seemed that reformed, Keynesian, mixed-economy capitalism would work if only people were able to break through their ignorance and prejudice. Expand education, give us the resources, and we would give people the opportunity they required.(7)

These expectations did not materialise in education any more than in other spheres of social and political life. In this context, the wide-ranging debate about <u>why</u> this occurred cannot be entered into. The salient point here is that, for most socialists in education as elsewhere, there was a need for a fundamental reappraisal by the 1970s. A harder, more political view of adult education, including UAE, has since prevailed. Education is no longer seen as the means by which capitalist society might be transformed.

From this position, it is political struggle <u>per se</u>, and especially class struggle in both its economic and political forms, which is of central importance. The inequalities of the educational system, and the bourgeois nature of the ideology which is promulgated through that system, can only be rectified by <u>political</u>, not autonomously educational, activity. There can be no separation, ultimately, it is argued, between education and politics. Both the content and the form of education, including adult education, are either inherently bourgeois or inherently socialist: education either buttresses or subverts the existing ideology and socio-economic structure. Adult educators thus have to decide how their part of the structure will operate. From the radical viewpoint, then, adult education should provide the means of collective understanding through educational experience of the nature of existing society (at all levels - personal and psychological, as well as collective and political) with the primary aim of building oppositional consciousness. The radical thus sees educational criteria as wholly political: 'the task of the educator should be to change society: its success or failure should be measured accordingly'.(8) Within this process, there are several <u>educational</u> changes to adult education that need to be made: the breaking down of distinctions between 'teachers and taught' along Freirean lines; the democratisation of the educational experience to move away from the empiricist model; and the restructuring of programmes, approaches and course locations to make provision more relevant to the needs of working class people.(9) All these reforms, however, are not to be seen within the liberal context of critical, open-ended education, but rather as part of an overall radicalisation of the working class and ultimately of the whole of society. And the nature of this radicalisation, as well as its justification, is wholly political.

As with the American context, therefore, such critics tend to dismiss the liberal tradition as at best an irrelevance, and at worst a part of the cultural false consciousness which plays such a large part in maintaining the hegemony of capitalism.

DEFENDING THE LIBERAL TRADITION

For both 'dynamic conservatives' and 'radical socialists', in England and the USA, UAE can have a viable future only if the liberal tradition is jettisoned. The scenarios of these critics for future development differ sharply, of course, but they are agreed upon the need to rid UAE of the outdated, and indeed dangerous mythology of the liberal tradition.

How valid are such criticisms? Should the liberal tradition be abandoned as an outdated and irrelevant basis from which to approach UAE development for the future?

There are aspects of both critiques which are wholly tenable. 'Conservative' critics are surely correct in asserting that there is an urgent need to increase greatly access to the university and its expertise for a far larger proportion of the community. In this context, an expansion in part-time degree and other qualifications oriented provision for mature students who have been denied conventional access to tertiary education, must be a major priority. Moreover, UAE has a crucial role to play in devising appropriate curricula and teaching methods for those mature students who have had little previous post school educational experience. Similarly, there <u>is</u> a strong case for the general involvement of the <u>whole</u> university in UAE, with the UAE department acting as a central resource of UAE skill, experience and organisational and professional contact with the regional community.

To the extent that, in England, the liberal tradition represents a blinkered commitment to the still dominant pattern of course provision for a small minority of predominantly middle class adults in conventional academic subjects, then it must be reviewed and reformed with some vigour. Scarce resources cannot justifiably be expended almost exclusively on such work.

There is also considerable merit in much of the argument put forward by radical socialist critics. The liberal tradition, particularly in the USA but also in England, <u>has</u> acted as a legitimating vehicle for the promulgation of establishment orthodoxies and bourgeois ideology. While UAE has had a minority element in England that has emphasised social purpose education, this element has become weaker and more marginalised, particularly in recent years, in response to both governmental and wider societal pressures. In the USA, such a perspective has been all but eliminated, as was argued in Chapters 6 and 7. This has led, in both countries, to a divorce in much of UAE between theory and practice: between abstract knowledge and lived experience. And the dominance of the liberal tradition has meant that both educational objectives and the modes of academic analysis have been seen in predominantly individualistic terms.

All this, and much more, <u>has</u> led to the <u>incorporation</u>, partial in England but almost total in the USA, of the liberal tradition of UAE into the established order, with the resultant effects on programmes, priorities and policies in UAE which have been described in previous chapters.

Nevertheless, neither of these critiques is acceptable <u>in toto</u>. Both have fundamental weaknesses and flaws. Moreover, the liberal tradition of UAE - articulated in a radically revised form (as is argued below) - has a central role to play within the future development of UAE. Indeed, that role, given the hostile climate for adult education generally in both England and the USA, can be argued to be more vital than ever before.

The fundamental criticism of the 'conservative' critique as outlined is that it misrepresents the liberal tradition. In England, that tradition represents a <u>continuum</u>, including the individualistic and conservative dimension, but also including, as was illustrated in some detail in Chapter 5 in relation to contemporary developments, a very real and important element of commitment to social purpose, collectivist and working class UAE. In the USA, such a continuum does not exist (or not to any significant extent: see Chapter 7); but the failure of the practice of the liberal tradition in UAE to live up to its theoretical (and rhetorical) claims does not mean necessarily that those claims should be jettisoned. Rather, it entails a rigorous analysis of whether the practice could or should be reformed in such a way that the objectives inherent in the liberal tradition of UAE might in reality be achieved.

Why is it claimed that the liberal tradition is still so important? First, the drift away from <u>education</u> and towards <u>training</u> must be resisted; and the reassertion of the centrality of the liberal approach is crucial in this process. The distinctive, and valuable, characteristic of UAE is its unique ability to combine the liberal, university teaching and research approach, with the pedagogic and organisational expertise necessary to construct and provide an educational programme for adults. To destroy the liberal tradition would be to destroy this symbiotic relationship and to remove the rationale of UAE altogether. In this context it should also be noted that this liberal approach is much more likely to be preserved by a body of full-time specialist UAE academic staff than it would be by a small administrative unit whose function was solely to organise and publicise an extramural programme taught by academic staff from internal departments, and other part-time tutors.

The second reason underlying the advocacy of the liberal tradition relates to wider social and political issues. Those who advocate a reorientation of UAE towards post experience continuing education are urging in effect that an even greater proportion of scarce educational resources should be devoted to that small minority which has already benefited from tertiary education. In the USA this process has been virtually accomplished; and in England it shows signs of gathering momentum. To counteract this process the reassertion and the practice of the radical objectives of the social purpose aspects of the liberal tradition are essential.

One of the major justifications for UAE is to make some contribution to the mitigation of the grossly unequal educational structures in both England and the USA, and to make available to the community at large, and the working class in particular, the expertise and knowledge of the university.

This is an essentially <u>democratic</u> view of UAE. In part, the motivation is to make available to as large a proportion of the community as possible the human and material resources of the university. The university should be a 'community resource', in practice as well as in principle. It is also the case, in our view, that the liberal tradition at its best upholds and extends democratic practice in that it provides students with as wide a range of information, competing analyses and varying perspectives as is possible, <u>and</u> imparts the critical skills which enable them to make their own choices and decisions (over subject matter studied, and interpretations to be accepted or dismissed). This is in sharp contrast to the prevailing utilitarian model in which some external authority (the government, industry, or whatever) determines the appropriate educational needs, and curricula are designed accordingly. Not only does such a system exclude effectively student participation in shaping the educational experience, it also entails an essentially authoritarian view of the educational process.

This position is taken on the basis of a political value judgement, of course. And this value judgement inheres within an educational philosophy which is democratic, egalitarian and essentially liberal in nature. In this context it should be asserted <u>a priori</u> that such a stance is not only viable but necessary in societies so beset by inequalities and class tensions. This position can be rejected on equally <u>a priori</u> grounds: but such a rejection can be based only upon a series of essentially elitist and/or clearly vocational assertions, none of which conservative critics seem prepared to make explicitly. On the contrary, they tend to retreat into rather vaguely defined 'university roles' for UAE.

The third objection to the conservative critics' view of the liberal tradition relates to the notion of the avowedly inextricable link between the liberal tradition and an empiricist ideology. As was emphasised in Chapter 2, and detailed in the contemporary context in Chapters 4 and 5, the liberal tradition of UAE in England covers a <u>continuum</u> of epistemological and ideological perspectives, including the social democratic and Marxist, as well as the liberal, ideologies. In the USA, such a continuum no longer exists in reality: the liberal tradition, as has been argued above and in Chapters 6 and 7, has become a legitimating, rhetorical device for the promulgation of a monolithic orthodoxy. Nevertheless, the liberal tradition framework has the <u>potential</u>, if it were to be subjected to radical reappraisal and return genuinely to its original objectives, to provide the basis for the development of such a continuum. This is the implication of the final section ('Liberalism and Liberation') of Chapter 7, with its plea for a fresh start and approach in UAE in the USA.

Thus, in a 'contextualist' epistemology such as that advocated by conservative critics, the open-ended critical, liberal tradition has a crucial role to play. If experience and 'reality' are to be brought more within the educational universe and considered to be of at least equal status to 'received knowledge', then, surely, there is a greater need than ever for an ideological pluralism: for a rigorous examination of all analyses of issues, relationships and subject areas, however multi-disciplinary. And it is this pluralism and methodological rigour which, it has been argued, lies at the heart of the theory of the liberal tradition, even if this has not always been the practice.

For all these reasons, therefore, the case for the liberal tradition emerges from such criticisms as these, stronger rather than weaker.

But what of the radical socialist critique: is there perhaps more validity in this?

Whilst there is considerable merit, in the authors' opinion, in this socialist critique there are, so it is argued here, substantial problems with a position that rejects in its entirety the liberal tradition.

At the outset it must be pointed out that such a perspective denies the whole rationale of universities <u>per se</u>. It is not only that universities are held to be representative of the gross inequalities in society in terms of the class composition of their student bodies, and also to represent the predominantly bourgeois ideology of the society of which they are a part; it is also that the very <u>raison d'etre</u> of universities - to further knowledge through research and scholarship, and to communicate this knowledge through teaching, untrammelled by governmental or other interests - is denied. On this radical model, universities would necessarily be recast - not 'merely' to make them more democratic, increase the number of working class students, radicalise curricula, and so forth - but reconstituted in their fundamental role. They would become, essentially, the educational arm of a socialist political movement: undoubtedly, they would be far more sophisticated, large scale, intellectually powerful, and wide-ranging than the old NCLC, but they would be expected to fulfil the same sort of functions.(10)

If this *is* the contention of radical critics - and nowhere is the argument followed through to these stark conclusions - it must be resisted. Whilst education and politics are indeed inextricably connected, the educational and political task is not to foreclose options and push people 'inevitably' towards a particular set of conclusions and perspectives, but rather to democratise the educational process and to expose students to the full range of analyses and arguments within the subject or issue under discussion.

This does not, of course, preclude positive discrimination to counter the gross distortions of the existing system. Such discrimination could, and should, take the form both of priorities for particular groups (women, the unemployed, ethnic minorities, etc), *and* discrimination in terms of emphasising the importance, and taking time to analyse and discuss, ideological perspectives which are deviant from those which predominate. There should be more emphasis, for example, upon Marxism, feminism, ecological ideas, non-Western philosophical and religious systems, and so on. And there should be more scope for 'separatist' adult education for particular groups, as was argued in Chapter 7. Such a stance does preclude, however, the essentially propagandist approach: '*we* have the real (socialist) truth, *you* are suffering from false consciousness because of the class oppression of capitalism; *our* task is therefore to liberate *you* by replacing your false ideology with our true one'. This may be a caricature, but it represents the underlying approach often held by such advocates. This is a position and an approach which must be rejected absolutely, as being both educationally and politically unacceptable - and, indeed, fundamentally unsocialist because of its authoritarian, repressive and closed stance, and, ironically, its essentially *elitist* implications.

There are, of course, problems with this position. Universities, in both England and the USA, whilst not monolithic institutions and whilst having an unusual degree of autonomy, are still essentially a part of the existing order. Universities as a whole, including UAE departments, do not operate on the radical liberal model just outlined. The state, in its various guises, intervenes if 'subversion' is suspected. Furthermore, the large majority of those responsible for university policy and practice in both England and the USA are not themselves anxious to challenge orthodoxy. 'Radicals' in universities, as elsewhere, are in a minority, especially in the higher reaches of university management.

Given all this, radical socialists argue, if radicalism in UAE became a serious threat to the hegemony of the state, then the rhetorical adherence to liberal freedoms would be jettisoned unceremoniously and UAE programmes dismantled. The price of liberal freedom in UAE, it is thus argued, is liberal failure.

There are two major objections to this line of argument. First, that it regards bourgeois society at large, and universities in particular, as monolithic and omnipotent, whereas, in reality, both are riven with contradictory ideologies and political structures. Thus, universities do have a genuine adherence to liberal notions of academic freedom, scholarly independence and so on, at the same time as they are part of the state system. The very process of changing our society - including our universities - entails encouraging and extending those areas of democratic freedoms. Social, and educational, emancipation comes not through monolithic confrontation, but through building upon those tendencies, traditions and structures conducive to democratic practice, and engaging in conflict with authority over particular issues which threaten to curtail the extension of that democratic practice.

Second, and even more simply, to argue that all social institutions, including universities, are wholly incorporated into the bourgeois, capitalist system and that radicals should therefore have nothing to do with them, is tantamount to inaction. It is perfectly possible to withdraw from the world, with radical purity intact, to await the new society, but such withdrawal does little to bring that change nearer. And to clamour from the outside is a thankless, not to say pointless, activity, as the sectarian Left has found to its cost.

What is needed, therefore, is a realisation that whilst those of radical persuasions in UAE in both England and USA will be working in an institutional context which is fundamentally opposed to their stance and objectives, there are several quite legitimate and well-established tendencies within the university system which will enable substantial advances to be made in UAE as in other sectors. Moreover, there are no alternatives - except withdrawal or capitulation - to continuing to press for advances <u>within</u> the university structure.

In relation to UAE, then, we should return to the original contention: that the liberal tradition <u>is</u> in need of radical revision, but, equally, that it provides the basic framework within which UAE must continue to work. The pressures against this continuance are very great. Not only is the liberal tradition under attack from the Left and the Right within its own institutional structure, as we have been discussing in this chapter, but it is also threatened by both the universities themselves and the government, and by wider pressures within society towards trivialisation and unthinking dependence upon the slick and seemingly omniscient media.

If UAE is to maintain a liberal tradition as the basis of its approach, it is clear, then, that it is facing powerful and deep-rooted opposition from a number of quarters. There must therefore be a clear conception of how, in practical terms, that revised tradition can best be implemented and integrated into the overall framework of UAE in the future.

REVITALISING THE LIBERAL TRADITION

The starting point must be to emphasise, as has been done in this chapter and throughout the book, the importance of free, open and democratic analysis and discussion of all issues, however sensitive and controversial. In terms of the democratic element, UAE must strive to achieve that complementary unity between education and experience, which enables academic knowledge to interact with life experience, in a context where the group as a group - rather than the tutor/lecturer - decides upon the syllabus. This is linked closely to the importance of the <u>methodology</u> underlying the liberal tradition. As was argued in Chapters 2 and 3, the standard claim within the liberal tradition of objectivity is at best simplistic and at worst devious and dishonest. But what <u>is</u> essential for the promulgation of a genuinely liberal education is the methodology, which stresses the acquisition of techniques enabling students to analyse sources critically, and assess the competing arguments over the issues under discussion. The detailed discussion of this methodological stance has been undertaken in Chapter 3. What needs emphasis here is that this methodology, combined with the democratic impulse, forms the basis of a revised and revitalised liberal tradition within UAE.

If these aspects of the framework are given priority, taken seriously, and put into practice, then - in conjunction with an emphasis upon the social purpose orientation - the basis for a revitalised UAE can be created. Of course, the dangers of incorporation (or, alternatively, intervention and/or restrictive action by the state) are present continuously. Awareness of these dangers on the part of those working in UAE, and a determination to take flexible but responsible ad hoc policy decisions which protect the core values of UAE but show political sensitivity, will give as much protection as is possible against such dangers.

Such a 'practice' may not be entirely satisfactory: it lacks the purity and precision of more tightly defined theoretical positions. But if UAE of a radical liberal type is to survive and develop, political realities must be confronted. The temptations, for radicals and socialists, of a wholly propagandist and proselitysing approach to UAE, must be resisted, for the reasons outlined earlier. This is not only because, if it were successful (which is highly unlikely), no bourgeois government could countenance subsidised subversion; more importantly, such an approach negates the whole purpose of education per se.

A revised, radical liberal tradition is thus an essential core component of UAE. This is particularly so in societies where both the tendencies towards state authoritarianism, and the increasing alienation and atomisation of the individual, are evident trends. To move away from liberal, social purpose adult education would be to exacerbate such trends, and to endanger the potential for advance, through UAE, towards genuinely democratic and participatory structures and procedures within the contemporary societies of England and the USA.

None of this should be taken to imply a rejection of the validity or viability of either professional continuing education or more traditional UAE provision. The former field is one of great importance and obvious relevance for both universities in general and UAE in particular. And its deep-rooted and prominent position within UAE in the USA will doubtless be replicated in England (and elsewhere) in the near future. Nor should the claims of the more traditional UAE be neglected. There must still be a place within a democratically controlled UAE, for the serious, committed UAE group which wants to study medieval archaeology, seventeenth century French poetry, or whatever. Any subject students wish to study should be included in the programme, provided it is suitable for rigorous and critical analysis.

The key point, however, is that neither of these legitimate areas of UAE must be developed at the expense of social purpose liberal adult education. Moreover, for the reasons already given, the highest priority must in future be given to the development of this work within UAE.

The specific ways in which a radicalised and revitalised liberal tradition might inform future UAE provision of course differs considerably in the two countries because of the very different contexts. And there is no need here to reiterate the areas of work recommended for development within such a scheme: these have been described and analysed in some detail in earlier chapters.

What does need emphasis here, however, is the stress that should be laid overall upon a pluralistic UAE structure, within which a revised liberal tradition has the central role to play. It is a model carrying with it wider political and social motivations, not in the sense of 'socialist subversion', but because it is based essentially upon democratic and egalitarian conceptions of the nature of the educational process.

CONCLUSION

One of the most fundamental dissimilarities between UAE in the two countries is thus the extent to which the liberal tradition is perceived as the basis for a more progressive and pluralistic UAE in the future. It has been argued here that there is the possibility of socially purposive UAE in England, within the existing structures and within the ideological parameters of the liberal tradition. In the USA no such possibility apparently exists. Fundamentally, this results from the nature of contemporary society in the USA, where both the socio-economic structure and the ideological parameters of the established order are more rigid, unilinear, and exclusive than is the case in England. The absence, in the USA, of any significant socialist sub-culture, and of any politically conscious Labour Movement, has interacted with a fundamentally conservative university system to produce a highly conformist university structure overall. UAE, anyway a highly marginalised university activity, has been integrated into this wider structure, and has largely absorbed its values and priorities. Whatever tendencies towards radical, open-ended education the liberal tradition in the USA might have had, have been all but eradicated by these combined pressures.

In both countries, the necessary location of UAE within the university creates fundamental problems for those who advocate a radical realignment of UAE priorities and perspectives. Whilst its location in the university provides a degree of genuine intellectual freedom and protection, it brings UAE fully within both the superstructure and the cultural and ultimately political control of the established order. As long as the <u>status quo</u> persists in both societies, and as long as universities remain a generally conservative force within that <u>status quo</u>, UAE's potential for radical realignment will be severely limited.

Nevertheless, there <u>are</u> possibilities for a revised, radical liberal tradition to play a major role in a future movement towards a more progressive UAE in both England and the USA. Neither universities nor the wider societies of which they are an integral, and integrated, part, are monolithic. Different traditions, pressures and values inhere within universities, as has been argued above. And some of these are congruent with the values embodied in the original liberal tradition: a commitment to liberty, equality, justice; an overriding belief in the need to democratise education, and a belief that priority must be given to education for social purpose. Moreover, the aim of a radicalised UAE, far from being totalitarian and propagandist, as the ideologues of the Right argue, is to create a genuinely <u>pluralistic</u> structure, within which all issues, subjects, perspectives and analyses would be given rigorous consideration. These are objectives to which universities continue to pay lip-service, however far their practice departs from this ideal concept. The task for UAE, therefore, as for other sectors of the higher educational system, is, to some extent, to ensure that the wayward practice returns to the theoretical concepts upon which it is based, and to play a part in rescuing universities from their increasingly illiberal tendencies.

To achieve this objective, two important claims must be emphasised: that a return to the egalitarian and democratic principles of the original liberal tradition is essential; and that the aim is to create a pluralistic (not a rival unilinear) system, in which there will be a place, for example, for post experience continuing professional education.

Such a radicalised UAE, which could form the basis of a revitalised structure of provision in both England and the USA, would require a fundamental, but possible, transformation of UAE. First, as has been argued throughout this book, UAE must put at the centre of its activities a concern, in the educational sphere, with issues, themes and subjects which are of central social, economic and political importance. This entails the acceptance, not of a revolutionary stance, but of <u>social purpose</u> as a legitimate and central aim of UAE activity. Indeed, equipping students with the intellectual tools to confront the structures and practices that underlie and perpetuate inequality must become, once again, an essential aspect of UAE

Second, and implicit in the commitment to social purpose, there must be equality of access to UAE (and an attempt to move towards a far greater degree of access for working class and disadvantaged groups into higher education as a whole). In practice this implies positive discrimination in favour of those social groups that have been denied this equal access, and those social movements and disempowered groups which are centrally concerned with the egalitarian transformation of society. Thus, UAE should pay special attention not only to workers' education, but also to such movements as the peace movement, the green movement, the women's movement, and liberation movements for all peoples.

Third, and again closely related, UAE must accept the notion of praxis. If it is to be socially purposive, committed to equality of access, and to a more egalitarian society, then that part of its provision related to social, political and economic issues must be seen to be of value to social action. This has long been a contentious issue, and all too often UAE has appeared to be a deterrent to action, by encouraging its students to sit forever on the fence, considering the pros and cons, never deciding upon, and putting into practice, a course of <u>action</u>. It is an old argument, but the solution is clear. Liberal UAE must embody sustained study, critical reflection upon alternative

courses of action, leading on occasion to group
and/or individual decisions on the appropriate
course(s) of action. The resultant action will
take place outside the educational context, but will
result in part from the educational experience.

But this does depend upon a fourth essential
strand of the liberal tradition: a genuinely free,
open and democratic analysis and discussion of all
the issues. Of course it is, or should be, recognised that a completely objective presentation of
all aspects of a subject or issue can never be
achieved. Knowledge production and dissemination
unavoidably include elements of ideology and propaganda. Part of the task of UAE must be to help
students to acquire the techniques to enable them
to analyse and assess competing arguments for themselves, so that they can discern the subtle effects
of ideology and propaganda (and, in particular, of
the dominant ideology of their own society which
masquerades as 'common sense'). Within this framework, all perspectives must be discussed and analysed, and all theories, ideas and ideals must be
accessible. As was said long ago, 'the basis of
discrimination between education and propaganda is
not the particular opinions held by the teacher
or the students, but the intellectual competence and
quality of the former and the seriousness and con-
tinuity of study by the latter'.(11)

It is this intellectual quality and seriousness
of study, rather than notions of objective truth,
that are the real guarantors of a free and open
forum of discussion. Indeed, it has been argued
in this book that the liberal tradition should require discrimination in favour of perspectives
which are deviant from those which predominate.

Ultimately, however, in accord with the fundamental tenets of the liberal tradition, adult students must be allowed to find their own way to
their own conclusions and beliefs. UAE is uniquely
equipped, potentially, to provide the context in
which this process and the resultant action can
best be pursued. Within a reformed UAE, students
would arrive at their _own_ conclusions, not through
propagandist or selective education, but through
exposure to the widest possible range of values,
perspectives and ideological interpretations.

To radicalise UAE successfully and significantly, it is essential that the liberal tradition be
submitted, by its advocates as well as its critics,
to rigorous scrutiny. If it is to recapture its
initial ideological radicalism, and to translate

this into effective practice, the liberal tradition must jettison its elitism, and its conservatism, and learn from the critiques of established liberal methodological assumptions in science and education. UAE must again move out into the community, adapt its curriculum and its perspectives to evolve provision that is relevant to the needs of the whole population, not merely the tertiary educated elite.

This revitalised conception of UAE - within which a radical reorientation of the liberal tradition has a central role - thus carries with it implications for larger changes in the social, economic and political system. UAE of the sort delineated is based upon essentially democratic, libertarian and egalitarian premises. Such a system would be in part cause and in part effect of general movements having these objectives within the wider society.

Attitudes to educational philosophy are thus indicative of more fundamental political perspectives. UAE may be a minor part of the overall educational structure, but UAE's future development, and the place within it of a revised liberal tradition, are contributory elements to processes which will determine the sort of society that emerges in the closing years of the twentieth century.

NOTES

1. For interesting articulations of this position see Alastair Crombie and Gwyn Harries-Jenkins, The Demise of the Liberal Tradition, Leeds Studies in Adult and Continuing Education, Department of Adult and Continuing Education, University of Leeds, 1983.
2. Alastair Crombie, Does University adult education in Britain have a future?, in ibid., p. 69.
3. Ibid., p. 71.
4. Ibid., p. 73.
5. Ibid., p. 75.
6. Ibid., p. 89.
7. Keith Jackson, Foreword to (ed.) Jane Thompson, Adult Education for a Change, 1980. pp. 9-10.
8. J. E. Thomas, Radical Adult Education: Theory and Practice, Nottingham Studies in the Theory and Practice of the Education of Adults, Department of Adult Education, University of Nottingham, 1982, p. 21.
9. For a discussion of some of these issues,

see Nell Keddie, Adult Education: an ideology of individualism, in (ed.) Thompson, op. cit.

10. As Roy Shaw wrote, in a highly critical review of (ed.) Jane Thompson, op. cit., '..... the NCLC was more consistent: it refused to have anything to do with universities, and fiercely denounced the WEA for collaborating with those "organs of class rule". Now, the Trojan horse has been pulled inside the citadel, and many of our latter-day Marxists denounce the institutions that employ them'. <u>Times Higher Educational Supplement</u>, 5 December, 1980.

11. Ministry of Reconstruction Adult Education Committee, Final Report, 1919, p. 118.

INDEX

(action, see social action)
Adam, T R 184, 188
Adams, H B 8
Adult Education Committee, Ministry of Reconstruction, Final Report (1919) 33
Alger, H 136
Allaway, A J 46
Amalgamated Clothing Workers 179
American Association for Adult Education 13, 123, 132, 133, 134, 139, 163, 184, 193
American Civil Liberties Union 193
American Federation of Hosiery Workers 179
American Federation of Labour 177-181
American Society for the Extension of University Teaching 8
andragogy 212-213
Andreski, S 55
applied social studies 75-76
archaeology 68
art 16
Ashcroft, R 90, 101
Association of Tutors in Adult Education 42, 43
Aston, University of 60

Baldwin, R 193, 194
Batten, E 93

Beard, C 5, 123, 158, 163, 195, 202-204, 206
Berdahl, R O 52, 53
Berger, P L 209-210
Berlin, L S 167, 168
Birmingham, University of 64
black liberation movement 144
Bradford, University of 60
Bristol, University of 70
Brookwood Labour College 179, 180
Brown, G F 100
Bryn Mawr Summer School for women workers in industry 178-179
Bryson, L 139, 158, 193-194
Burch, G 155
'Butler Act' 1944 63
'Butskellism' 65

California, University of 139, 151, 152, 154, 155, 159-170, 176-178, 180
Cambridge, University of 4, 56, 63, 70
Cartwright, M 132, 133, 135, 139, 184, 185, 188, 192, 197
Carnegie Foundation 13

242

Carnegie Foundation (cont'd)
   130, 131, 132, 133, 135,
   139, 163, 184
Centre for the Study of the
   Liberal Education of
   Adults 13, 141, 145
Central Joint Advisory
   Committee on Tutorial
   Classes 6
Cherwell, Lord 59
Coffman, L 169
Cohn, F M 179
Cole, G D H 42, 47
Colleges of Advanced Tech-
   nology 58-59
Colleges for Working
   Adults 210-211
Collins, H 45
Columbia, University of
   139
commodification 212-214
community adult education/
   community education 22,
   44, 77, 85, 86, 90-113,
   116
community development
   projects 91, 92
community work 90, 92, 198
Conservative governments
   1951-1964, 65;
   1979-1983, 74;
   1983 -   , 74
Continuing Education Unit
   165
Cotgrove, S 92
Council of Europe 95
critical theory 216
Crossman, R H S 41
Curran, J R 166-167

Debs, E 182
democracy, in relation to
   UAE in USA 127, 128-135,
   159, 176, 183, 208
Department of Education
   and Science 60, 72-74,
   100, 105, 108, 109
Duff, A 92
Dyson, R F 68

Eames, J 29

East Anglia, University
   of 58
(Education Act 1944,
   see 'Butler Act')
Educational Advice
   Service for Adults
   106
Eisenstein, Z 144
(elderly, educational
   provision for, see
   retired)
Ely, M 131, 193, 195
Engineering Science
   Management War Train-
   ing Act 13
Epictetus 130
equality 127, 135-145,
   147, 159, 185, 208,
   209, 216, 237-238
Equal Rights Amendment
   144
Espionage and Sedition
   Acts 11, 182
Essex, University of
   58
ethnic minorities 90,
   104, 106-107, 187,
   232
excellence 127, 156-170,
   176, 209
Exeter, University of
   58

feminism 144, 214, 216,
   232
Flaherty, M 194
Ford Foundation Fund
   for Adult Education
   13, 141, 152
Fordham, P 75-76
Freire, P 90, 113, 198,
   213, 227

Gayley, C M 160
G.I. Bill 13, 140, 143
Gosden, P A J 61
Gramsci, A 94
green movement 216, 238
Groombridge, B 69

Halstead, R 29

243

Harehills Housing Aid 105
Harper, W R 8
Hatch Act 12
health and safety courses 87-88
Higher Education Act 1954 141
Higher Education Act 1965 10, 142, 153
Higher Education Amendment Acts 1980 142-143, 211
'Higher Education for Democracy' (President's Commission Report, 1948) 13, 126
Highlander Folk High School 205, 210
'The Highway' 35, 45, 46, 48
Hobhouse, L T 30
Hobson, J A 30
Hodges, H A 30, 41
Hodgkin, T 31, 45-48
Hoggart, R 57
Houle, C 168
Howerth, I 152, 160-163
Hull, University of 58, 88, 115

Illich, I 90, 113
Imperial College, University of London 59
(industrial education, see trade union education)
Institute of Industrial Relations 178
Institute for Propaganda Analysis 195
International Council for Adult Education 210
International Ladies Garment Workers 179-180

Jackson, K 90, 93, 101-102, 226
Jacksonian Democrats 11
Jefferson, T 177, 215
Johnson, A 201
Joint Committees 5, 72
'Journal of Adult Education' 131, 184, 189, 202

Keddie, N 141
Keele, University of 58, 70, 100
Kent, University of 58, 115
Kerchen, J 178
Kerrison, I 181
'Keynesianism' 65

Labour government of 1945 63, 65, 225
Lancaster, University of 58, 115
Larson, M 153, 157
Lasswell, H 193
Lawson, K H 98
Leeds, University of (Department of Adult and Continuing Education) 31, 64, 70, 72, 75, 88, 98, 100, 103-115
Leicester, University of 58, 70
Lenin V I 94
Lewis and Clark College, Oregon 207
Lindeman, E 134, 150, 163, 195, 196, 202-204, 206, 208
Lindsay, A D 33, 36
Liverpool, University of 75, 98, 100-103, 104, 110, 113
Local Education Authorities 75, 98, 103, 105, 109
London, University of 63, 69
de Lone, R 136
Lovett, T 90-91, 94, 95, 100, 102
Loughborough, University of 70
Luckmann, T 209-210

MacArthur, B 60
McCarthyism 11

244

MacRae, D 55
Manchester, University of 40, 42, 76
Mansbridge, A 18, 176
marketing 156-170
Martin, E D 158, 163, 198-199
Marx, Marxism 5, 21-23, 30, 33, 45-48, 89-90, 94, 96-97, 102, 182, 189-190, 192, 198, 205-206, 214, 230
Mechanics' Institutes 4
Meikeljohn, A 129
Michigan, University of (Workers Education Service) 182
Miliband, R 92
Minogue, K 53-54
MIND 105
Morrill Federal Land Grant Act 12, 146-148
Moulton, R G 8

NACRO 105
National Advisory Committee on the Engineering, Science, Management Defence Training Act 164
National Council of Labour Colleges 5, 22, 89, 232
National Institute of Adult and Continuing Education 105
National Labour Extension Service 181
National Labour Relations Act 183
National Organizing Conference for Adult Education 163
National University Extension Association 9, 163, 177
Nelson and Colne College 115
('new opportunities' courses, see 'second chance to learn')

New School for Social Research 202, 205
nihilation 186, 209-210
'Nineteen Eighty-Four' 32, 170
Northern College, Yorkshire 102
Nottingham, University of 58, 70, 88, 100

Oakland project 152
objectivity 23, Chapter 3 passim, 88-89, 191, 214, 239
Open College 115
Open University 7, 58, 68, 93, 115
Otto, M 207
Overstreet, H 159, 197
'Oxford and Working Class Education' Report 1908 5
Oxford, University of, and Delegacy 4, 5, 34, 41, 47, 56, 63

part-time degrees, 7, 86, 114, 224
Paterson, R W K 99-100
peace movement 216, 238
'Pioneer Work' (at University of Leeds) 7, 103-112
Plebs League 5
Polanyi, K 34, 41
Polytechnics 60, 115-116
post experience vocational education 7, 65, 69-74, 76-77, 97-98, 116, 164, 212, 222, 224
Post Secondary Education Commission 210
Probation Service 105
professional adult education 70, 75-76, 116, 212
(professional continuing education, see applied social studies and post experience

245

vocational education)

Rand School of Social Science 179
Raybould, S G 31, 35, 43, 64, 75, 125-126
Reading, University of 58
Reagan, R, and 'Reaganite' 19, 142
Responsible Bodies 6, 40, 72-73, 89, 96, 98, 107-108
Reber, L 150
retired people, educational provision for 104, 106, 186-187
Richardson, L 162-163, 176-178, 206
Robbins Report 61
Rockefeller, J D 8
Roderick, G 56, 98
Roosevelt, F D 183
Ruskin College, Oxford 5
Russell, J E 134-135, 163
Russell Report 7, 100
Rutgers University 180-181

Salford, University of 60
'second chance to learn' courses 86, 102, 106, 114-116
'Second Thoughts' 210
separatism 184-188, 210, 214, 232
service 24-26, 127, 145-155, 159, 176, 208-209
Sheats, P 24, 152
Sheffield, University of 88, 100
Skeffington Report 91
social action 25, 183, 191, 196-199, 209-210
social reconstruction 199-205
Southampton, University of 58, 75, 100, 115

State Federation of Labour 180
Steering Committee on Adult Unemployed Projects 105
Stephens, M 56, 98-99
Stern, M R 166
Stocks, M 42
Studebaker, J 131-132, 201
Suliman, A 167
Sumner, A 177
Surrey, University of 76

Tawney, R H 38, 40
Thatcher, M, and 'Thatcherite' 19, 61, 74
Thomas, J E 96, 97, 99
Thompson, E P 31, 34-35, 44
Thompson, J 90, 97, 192
Thorndike, E 138-139, 150
Tivey, J 93
Touraine, A 149
trade union and industrial education 22, 68, 75, 77, 85-90, 98, 112, 116
Trades Union Congress 40, 86-89, 112
Tress, R 54
Truman Commission 139

Ulster, University of 70
unemployed, centres for 105; educational provision for 104-106, 232
Universities Council for Adult Education 6
Universities Council for Adult and Continuing Education 65, 68-71
University Grants Council 53, 55, 57, 59-62, 100
University of the Third Age 106
U.S. Office of Education

246

Vincent, J 8
Vrooman, W 5

Wales, University of 58
'War on Poverty' programme 13
Ward, L F 149-150
Warwick, University of 58
Wayne State Weekend College 210-211
Weir, D 56
Wilson, H 56
Wisconsin School for Workers 178
Wisconsin, University of 9, 150, 152
women's consciousness raising groups 205
women, educational provision for 106, 114-115, 186, 232
women's movement 216, 238
Woods, B M 164
Woolton, Lord 59
Workers' Educational Association 4-6, 21, 40, 42, 44, 47, 63, 72, 86-89, 94, 98, 101, 109, 176-177
Workers' Education Bureau 177-180
Workers' Educational Trade Union Committee 6, 86-87
Wright Mills, C 225

York, University of 58
'Yuppies' 212-213

For Product Safety Concerns and Information please contact our EU representative GPSR@taylorandfrancis.com
Taylor & Francis Verlag GmbH, Kaufingerstraße 24, 80331 München, Germany

www.ingramcontent.com/pod-product-compliance
Lightning Source LLC
Chambersburg PA
CBHW060559230426
43670CB00011B/1890